Sweden in the Seventeenth Century

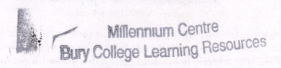

European History in Perspective
General Editor: Jeremy Black

Benjamin Arnold *Medieval Germany, 500–1300*
Ronald Asch *The Thirty Years' War*
Christopher Bartlett *Peace, War and the European Powers, 1814–1914*
Robert Bireley *The Refashioning of Catholicism, 1450–1700*
Donna Bohanan *Crown and Nobility in Early Modern France*
Arden Bucholz *Moltke and the German Wars, 1864–1871*
Patricia Clavin *The Great Depression, 1929–1939*
Paula Sutter Fichtner *The Habsburg Monarchy, 1490–1848*
Mark Galeotti *Gorbachev and his Revolution*
David Gates *Warfare in the Nineteenth Century*
Alexander Grab *Napoleon and the Transformation of Europe*
Martin P. Johnson *The Dreyfus Affair*
Paul Douglas Lockhart *Sweden is the Seventeenth Century*
Peter Musgrave *The Early Modern European Economy*
J.L. Price *The Dutch Republic in the Seventeenth Century*
A.W. Purdue *The Second World War*
Christopher Read *The Making and Breaking of the Soviet System*
Francisco J. Romero-Salvado *Twentieth-Century Spain*
Matthew S. Seligmann and Roderick R. McLean
Germany from Reich to Republic, 1871–1918
Brendan Simms *The Struggle for Mastery in Germany, 1779–1850*
David Sturdy *Louis XIV*
David J. Sturdy *Richelieu and Mazarin*
Hunt Tooley *The Western Front*
Peter Waldron *The End of Imperial Russia, 1855–1917*
Peter G. Wallace *The Long European Reformation*
James D. White *Lenin*
Patrick Williams *Philip II*

European History in Perspective
Series Standing Order
ISBN 0–333–71694–9 hardcover
ISBN 0–333–69336–1 paperback
(*outside North America only*)

You can receive future titles in this series as they are published by placing a standing order. Please contact your bookseller or, in the case of difficulty, write to us at the address below with your name and address, the title of the series and the ISBN quoted above.

Customer Services Department, Palgrave Ltd
Houndmills, Basingstoke, Hampshire RG21 6XS, England

Sweden in the Seventeenth Century

PAUL DOUGLAS LOCKHART

palgrave
macmillan

First published 2004 by
PALGRAVE MACMILLAN
Houndmills, Basingstoke, Hampshire RG21 6XS and
175 Fifth Avenue, New York, N.Y. 10010
Companies and representatives throughout the world

PALGRAVE MACMILLAN is the global academic imprint of the Palgrave Macmillan division of St. Martin's Press, LLC and of Palgrave Macmillan Ltd. Macmillan® is a registered trademark in the United States, United Kingdom and other countries. Palgrave is a registered trademark in the European Union and other countries.

ISBN 0–333–73156–5 hardback
ISBN 0–333–73157–3 paperback

This book is printed on paper suitable for recycling and made from fully managed and sustained forest sources.

A catalogue record for this book is available from the British Library.

A catalog record for this book is available from the Library of Congress.

10   9   8   7   6   5   4   3   2   1
13 12 11 10 09 08 07 06 05 04

Printed in China

To my *Schwiegermutter*, Maria,
and
to my parents,
Newton and Marilyn,
with love

Contents

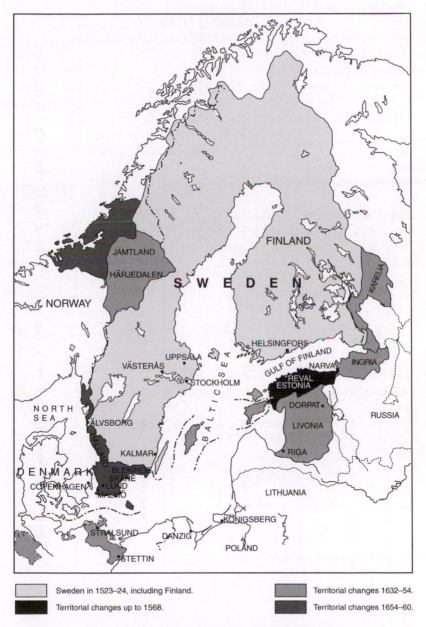

JÄMTLAND

HÄRJEDALEN

S W E D E N

FINLAND

NORWAY

KARELIA

HELSINGFORS

UPPSALA

GULF OF FINLAND

VÄSTERÅS

NARVA

INGRIA

BALTIC SEA

STOCKHOLM

REVAL
ESTONIA

NORTH
SEA

DORPAT

RUSSIA

ÄLVSBORG

LIVONIA

KALMAR

RIGA

DENMARK

BLEKINGE
SKÅNE

COPENHAGEN

LUND

MALMÖ

LITHUANIA

KÖNIGSBERG

STRALSUND

DANZIG

POLAND

STETTIN

Sweden in 1523–24, including Finland.

Territorial changes 1632–54.

Territorial changes up to 1568.

Territorial changes 1654–60.

Map of the Swedish Empire in the Seventeenth Century

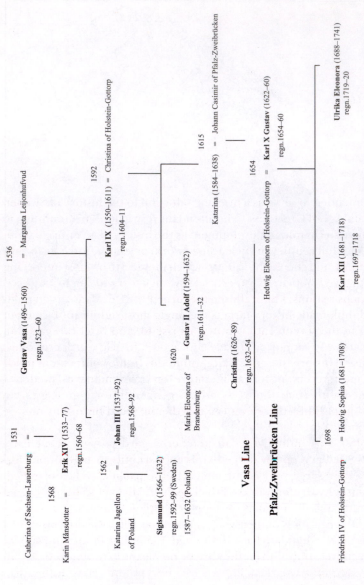

Rulers of Sweden: The Vasa and Pfalz-Zweibrücken Dynasties

Preface

This is intended to serve as a brief introduction to the history of Sweden during its 'Age of Greatness'. The attendant restrictions in attempting to summarize so complex a development as the history of an entire nation-state over a full century in such a short work, of course, force historians to either pick and choose those topics which they feel to be most important, or else to give a hopelessly superficial coverage to a wide array of topics. For obvious reasons, I have chosen the former course. My focus on political and diplomatic history targets the single most significant fact about Sweden in the seventeenth century: its rise to, and brief career as, an empire and a 'great power'. I have endeavored to give social, economic, and cultural history their due place within this framework; but, as much of the most recent historical literature on early modern Sweden – concerned with such things as crime, gender history, and agrarian history – is not directly relevant to this theme, social historians may be disappointed.

The task was intimidating in another regard as well. That early modern Sweden is not an altogether unknown entity to anglophone historians can in large part be attributed to the prolific, well-researched, and beautifully written works of the late Prof. Michael Roberts, a name that is undoubtedly familiar to the past couple of generations of early modernists regardless of their geographical specialty. Roberts' published writings on Sweden date back to the mid-1950s, but though now quite old and entirely out-of-print they are by no means to be ignored. As Jan Glete has recently remarked, Roberts' *opus* has become 'classic' rather than 'dated'; his work is as well-respected in Scandinavia as it is in Britain and North America. His shoes will be difficult ones to fill, and that is not my intention here. What I have set out to do from the very beginning,

rather, is to bring together the results of the latest research in Swedish
history into a cohesive whole. For these reasons, and for considerations
of space, my notes and my bibliography are accordingly limited in scope.
In the notes, I have restricted myself to citing – whenever possible –
books and articles published within the past two to three decades; the
bibliography is more of a list of suggested readings in English than a true
compendium of sources cited. This, I believe, will probably be of greater
utility to those who read this book. I should point out, however, that
most Swedish-language monographs and many journal articles appearing
over the past thirty years are accompanied by abstracts written in English,
or on occasion in German.

A couple of conventions ought to be mentioned from the start.
Recently, Scandinavian historians have on occasion taken to the practice
of using the term 'Sweden–Finland' when referring to the Swedish–
Finnish core of the Swedish empire, and for similar reasons using
'Denmark–Norway' when discussing the Oldenburg monarchy. Since
Finland was a mere province of Sweden, as was Norway of Denmark,
such usage is technically incorrect; in this text, 'Sweden' should be taken to
mean Sweden and Finland, just as 'Denmark' embraces Denmark, Norway,
and (before 1660) the Scanian provinces. With regard to monetary
units, I have rendered all of these in Swedish *riksdaler* (sometimes spelled
as *rixdaler* or *rixdollar* in older literature). Throughout the seventeenth
century, the *riksdaler* was roughly the equivalent in value of the Danish
rigsdaler and the German *Reichsthaler*; about four *riksdaler* made up one
English pound.

In writing this book, as in all of my research, I owe considerable
scholarly debts to at least a score of individual scholars and colleagues.
I dare not attempt to name them all, for fear of excluding some, but
I would like to extend my particular thanks to my friend and colleague
Ed Melton of Wright State University, who read and commented on the
typescript in its nearly final form. I should also like to express my grati-
tude to the head of interlibrary loan at Wright State, Ms Diana Kaylor,
and her staff, who patiently filled scores of requests for me, thereby allowing me to undertake much of the research involved in this book without
having to spend extended periods of time outside Ohio. The editorial
staff at Palgrave Macmillan, including series editor Prof. Jeremy Black,
were most forgiving and kind in allowing me to extend deadlines when
ill health forced me to slow the pace of my work; for that I am most
grateful. It should almost go without saying that my greatest debt is
to my wife, Jo Anna, who put her own professional career on hold

for the past two years while I pursued this and other research projects, and who spent countless hours on this book as my research assistant, patiently listening to me trying to explain my views on early modern Scandinavian history.

PDL
Kettering, Ohio

A Brief Chronology

1513–23   Reign of Christian II of Denmark
  1520   Stockholm Bloodbath: execution of leading Swedish nobles
  1521   Gustav Vasa elected as 'Protector' (*riksföreståndare*) of Sweden
  1523   Diet at Strängnäs: Gustav Vasa elected as king

The Vasa Dynasty

1523–60   Reign of Gustav Vasa
  1527   Diet of Västerås: break with Rome, confiscation of Church
         property
  1540   Noble meeting at Örebro: recognition of Gustav Vasa's heirs
  1542–43   Uprising of Niels Dacke (*Dackefejde*)
  1544   Diet of Västerås: monarchy declared to be hereditary
  1554   Publication of Johannes Magnus' *Historia Gothorum Sveonumque*
  1560   Gustav Vasa's 'Testament'; creation of royal duchies
         Death of Gustav Vasa; succession of Erik XIV

1560–68   Reign of Erik XIV
  1561   Reval appeals to Sweden for protection
  1563–70   Seven Years' War of the North (against Denmark)
    1565   Battle of Axtorna; Swedish defeat
    1567–68   Erik XIV's mental illness; Dukes Johan and Karl revolt
    1569   Erik deposed; Duke Johan crowned as King Johan III

xiv

1569–92   Reign of Johan III
  1570   Peace of Stettin ends war with Denmark, with foreign mediation
  1576   Introduction of Catholic-like liturgy in the 'Red Book'
  1581–92   Fighting with Russia over Estonia
  1587   Prince Sigismund, Johan III's son, becomes king of Poland
  1592   Death of Johan III; succession of Sigismund

1592–99   Reign of Sigismund
  1593   Uppsala Assembly: formal introduction of Lutheranism University at Uppsala reopened
  1594   *Riksdag* at Uppsala: limitations on Sigismund's powers; Duke Karl becomes Protector
  1595   Peace of Teusina with Russia; confirms Swedish possession of Estonia
  1596–97   'Club War' uprising in Finland
  1598   Battle of Stångebro; Duke Karl defeats Sigismund
  1599   *Riksdag* at Linköping; Sigismund deposed
  1600   'Linköping Bloodbath'; Karl executes aristocratic opposition
  1604   Duke Karl crowned as Karl IX

1604–11   Reign of Karl IX
  1605   Treason trials of aristocratic opposition
    Battle of Kirkholm; Swedes defeated by Poles
  1607   Town of Göteborg founded by Karl IX
  1611–13   Kalmar War with Denmark
  1611   Death of Karl IX; succession of Gustav II Adolf

1611–32   Reign of Gustav II Adolf
  1611–12   *Riksdag* at Nyköping. Charter of 1612 limits royal prerogative
  1612   Axel Oxenstierna becomes chancellor
    Fall of Älvsborg to Danish forces
  1613   Peace of Knäröd ends Kalmar War; Älvsborg held for 'ransom' by Denmark
    Alliance with the Netherlands
  1614–15   Creation of *Svea Hovrätt* and high court system
  1614–17   War with Russia over Kexholm and Ingria; Swedish conquests confirmed by Peace of Stolbova 1617
  1617   Reform of *Riksdag*
    Örebro decrees against Catholics

1643–48 Peace negotiations at Osnabrück

1643–45 Torstensson War; Swedish invasion of Denmark

1644 Christina reaches age of majority; regency ends

1645 Peace of Brömsebro; ends Torstensson War in Sweden's favor

1648 Battle of Zusmarshausen; final Swedish victory over Bavaria
      Peace of Osnabrück ratified; Sweden a guarantor of peace

1650 Protests against 'oven tax' in Stockholm
      Riksdag: protest against taxation and conscription; first discussion of *reduktion*, crown reclamation of alienated lands
      Death of Réné Descartes in Stockholm

1654 *Riksdag* in Uppsala; Christina, converted to Catholicism, announces abdication; succession of Karl Gustav, Count Palatine

The Pfalz-Zweibrücken Dynasty

1654–60 Reign of Karl X Gustav

1654 Death of Axel Oxenstierna
      Withdrawal of Swedish forces from Germany

1655 New Sweden colony falls to the Dutch
      Founding of Swedish colony of Cabo Corso in Africa
      Karl X Gustav invades Poland
      Riksdag: discussion of *reduktion* issue

1656 Truce of Marienburg with Elector of Brandenburg

1656–58 War with Russia over Livonia

1657 Danish troops attack Sweden and Swedish possessions in Germany
      Karl X Gustav invades Denmark; takes Danish fortress of Frederiksodde

1658 Swedish forces occupy most of Denmark
      Peace of Roskilde with Denmark; Danes make huge territorial concessions to Sweden. Karl X Gustav renews war with Denmark shortly thereafter

1660 Death of Karl X Gustav; succession of Karl XI as a minor

1660–97 Reign of Karl XI

1660–72 Regency of Magnus De la Gardie

1660–61 Peace treaties at Copenhagen, Oliva, and Kardis end wars with Denmark, Poland, Brandenburg, and Russia

1661   Gustav Bonde introduces proposal for balanced budget
1663   Fall of Cabo Corso colony to the Dutch
1668   'Blue Book' report on corruption and malfeasance in the regency
       government
       University at Lund founded
       Sweden joins Triple Alliance with England and the Netherlands
1672   Subsidy treaty with Louis XIV of France
       Karl XI reaches age of majority
1674–79 Scanian War
   1675   Battle of Fehrbellin; Swedish army defeated by Brandenburg
          Danish invasion of Skåne
   1676   Battle of Lund; Swedish victory over Danish invaders
   1677   Battle of Køge Bugt; Danish naval victory over Sweden
   1679   Treaties of St. Germain, Fontainebleau, and Lund end the
          Scanian War; Swedish territorial losses restored with French
          assistance
1680   *Riksdag* at Stockholm; creation of the Great Commission
       to investigate conduct of the Regency; limited *reduktion* imple-
       mented
1681   Guarantee Treaty with the Netherlands
1682   *Riksdag*: full implementation of *reduktion*; reform of conscription
       and introduction of new system, the *indelningsverk*
1685   Swedish naval headquarters established at Karlskrona, in
       formerly Danish Blekinge
1686   New Church ordinance standardizes liturgy throughout the
       Swedish empire
1687   Creation of Law Commission to rewrite Swedish national law
1689   *Riksdag* approves *Kassationsakt*; king cannot be questioned or
       contradicted
       Altona Settlement with Denmark curbs Danish ambitions in
       northern Germany
1697   Death of Karl XI; succession of Karl XII

1697–1718 Reign of Karl XII
   1700–21   The Great Northern War pits Sweden against Denmark,
             Russia, and Poland-Saxony
       1700   Swedish invasion of Denmark forces Denmark out of the war
              Battle of Narva; Swedish victory over Russia temporarily
              ends Russian onslaught in Ingria

1701–06   Swedish invasion of Poland
1709   Karl XII invades Russia
           Swedish army destroyed at Poltava by army of Peter the
           Great
1709–14   Karl XII in exile in Ottoman Empire
1718   Karl XII killed in action before Fredriksten, Norway
1720–21   Treaties of Stockholm, Frederiksborg, and Nystad end
           the war

Chapter 1: The Sixteenth-Century Inheritance

In 1523, Sweden was a newly autonomous kingdom, poor and devoid of a bureaucratic structure; existing only in the shadow of its more powerful neighbors, its future status as an independent state seemed very unlikely. A century and a quarter later, Sweden was the predominant power in the Baltic and a guarantor of the Peace of Westphalia alongside its ally France. To be sure, it could be argued that the application of the label 'great power' to seventeenth-century Sweden is of questionable validity. Certainly Sweden never dominated European politics in the manner of Philip II's Spain. Yet for nearly three decades it came very close. Its actions in the last half of the Thirty Years' War, and for twelve years after the war's close, determined the fate of other nations, and its diplomatic and military reach extended some distance beyond the horizons of its Baltic environs. Any academic distinction between what constitutes a 'major power' and what makes a major power 'great' is necessarily subjective, but given the weight of Sweden's international influence between 1632 and 1660 it seems fair to rank Sweden among the great powers of Europe.

That status, however, would not last for long. Within thirty years of Westphalia, Sweden's career as a major power would decline visibly; in another forty, its empire disintegrated. Sweden's precipitous rise to, and fall from, great power status in the seventeenth century was an astonishing development to contemporary statesmen, and remains so to more recent scholars. During its brief career as a European state of the first rank – a period that Swedish historians have labeled the

1

stormaktstid, or 'great power era' – Sweden would never achieve the heights of literary, artistic, scholarly, or commercial sophistication of states like England, France, Spain, or the Netherlands. But it excelled at something absolutely necessary for success in seventeenth-century Europe: the ability to make war for prolonged periods with limited resources. Indeed, this was the entire *raison d'être* of the Swedish state. Far more so than in any other European state of the early modern period, all of the institutions of Swedish life were geared towards building up and sustaining Sweden's military capacity. Sweden was the archetype of what Otto Hintze and later historians would call the 'military' or 'power state'.

From all appearances, Sweden was ill-equipped to be a 'great power' at the dawn of the seventeenth century. Compared with the other territorial states along the Baltic rim – Denmark, Poland, and Russia – Sweden was poor, primitive, and dangerously underpopulated. Moreover, Sweden was Europe's newest monarchy, and as such had been compelled to create *ex nihilo* its own bureaucratic and administrative machinery. Sweden's very existence as an autonomous state threatened the territorial interests of its Baltic neighbors, and hence from its beginnings as an independent polity Sweden had powerful enemies. To the larger kingdoms of western Europe, Sweden was as yet a distant non-entity beyond the periphery of mainstream European political intercourse, but within the Baltic region the first two centuries of Sweden's independent statehood were – at least as seen from Stockholm – nothing short of a struggle for survival.

These two factors – the search for both economic and political security in a hostile environment – shaped the rise of this most unlikely great power of the seventeenth century. Whether its belligerence stemmed from a quest for steady revenues, or from a desire to break free from perceived territorial encirclement, the Vasa state was either at war or preparing for war during the period 1563–1721. More than anything else, war conditioned both the nature and extent of Swedish expansion, and in no other European state was political and social development so closely linked to military institutions and policies. Five different monarchs would rule Sweden during its so-called *stormaktstid* ('great power period' or 'age of greatness'): four of them actively sought the expansion of Sweden's Baltic empire through conquest; all of them became involved in large-scale wars on the Continent.

Resources, Demographics, and the Structure of Society

Sixteenth-century Sweden was poor. Like all of the major Baltic states of the early modern period, it comprised a significant expanse of territory, including most of contemporary Sweden and Finland. Nonetheless, its size could be deceiving, for the realm was sparsely populated. The aggregate population of the Vasa territories in 1560 was about 1 million, perhaps growing to 1.25 million by 1620. In comparison with more densely populated states, like England (ca. 4 million inhabitants in 1600) or France (ca. 20 million), this was insignificant. Sweden was roughly equal to Denmark in population, but had no more than one-sixth the population of Poland–Lithuania and perhaps one-tenth of Russia's population. Most Swedes dwelt within the southern and south-central portions of Sweden and Finland while the northern extremes of the kingdom, on either side of the Arctic Circle, were a deserted wasteland. Even much of central Sweden was heavily forested, uncultivated, and barely inhabited. Throughout this vast expanse of land, there were no towns worthy of mention except the administrative capital at Stockholm. And even Stockholm, with around 6000 inhabitants, would hardly merit a comparison with the major commercial centers of England, France, the Netherlands, or the Hanseatic League.[1]

Nor were there, prior to the last quarter of the sixteenth century, significant natural resources that had been exploited to any degree. Sweden did possess significant deposits of iron and copper ore, concentrated in southern Dalarna, northeastern Västmanland and southern Närke. Already in the sixteenth century, trade in these metals was lucrative. The early Vasa kings encouraged modernization, and imported foreign entrepreneurs, experts, and capital to help develop the industry; by the early seventeenth century, Sweden was the leading exporter of these metals to northern Europe. In 1637, copper and iron would constitute nearly 63 percent of total national exports, and in 1685 the aggregate would be over 80 percent.[2] The vast forests of Finland and central Sweden were also a significant commercial asset, for they provided charcoal and coveted naval stores – primarily mast timbers and pine pitch – that helped make the Baltic trade so attractive to the maritime states of northern Europe. But Sweden's commercial potential was hampered by its geopolitical position. Through its possession of the three provinces at the southernmost tip of the Scandinavian peninsula – Blekinge, Halland, and Skåne, collectively called the Scanian provinces – Denmark dominated the Sound, the major navigable passageway between the North and the Baltic Seas. Only a single port, that of Älvsborg, gave Sweden direct access to the North Sea, and Älvsborg would remain Sweden's sole window on the world outside the Baltic. Sweden was especially poor in agricultural production. Poland, north-eastern Germany, and Denmark dominated the Baltic grain trade; Sweden's position on the northern periphery of arable Europe ensured marginal yields of cereal grains and other staple crops.[3]

Although Sweden did experience an economic upswing late in the sixteenth century, its share in the overall prosperity of post-Reformation Europe was comparatively trivial. Before Sweden's entrance onto the European stage in 1630, those few foreigners who traveled there described the Vasa state in terms that were hardly glowing. There were no magnificent noble country houses that could compare to those which dominated the French and English landscapes, nor even to the spartan manor houses of the Danish aristocracy. The Swedish nobility, on the contrary, lived but meanly, though its poverty should not be exaggerated, since it was due as much to cultural distance and parochialism as to economic hardship. Still, the lifestyle of the Swedish nobility was bereft of splendor or ostentatious display. Throughout the sixteenth century, the nobility was quite small; it accounted for 0.5 percent of the total population, similar in proportion to the Danish nobility but tiny in comparison to the nobilities of continental Europe. Altogether, the noble estate numbered around 400 adult males in 1600, and collectively owned 16 percent of all farmsteads in the kingdom, and about 50 percent in Finland. It was hardly a homogeneous estate. A small aristocracy of eleven to fifteen elite families possessed around 60 percent of seignorial land; many of these aristocrats held title to several hundred peasant farms. By contrast, the remainder of the nobility enjoyed much more modest wealth. Some 40 percent of all noble landowners did not own more than one or two peasant farms. All noblemen were exempt from ordinary taxation, in return for their obligation to provide heavy cavalry (*rusttjänst*, or 'knight service') to the crown. The Swedish noble estate was remarkably open. The early Vasa kings granted noble status to deserving commoners only infrequently, but it was not unheard-of for members of the lesser or middling nobility to intermarry with prosperous commoners.[4]

The lack of towns meant that there was as yet no significant mercantile class. The few merchant families that did live in Sweden in 1600 were concentrated in Stockholm and in lesser trade centers, like Söderköping and Kalmar, where they acted as middlemen to Hanseatic and Dutch merchants.[5] The vast majority of the population was, as elsewhere in

Europe, rural, but in political status and in the distribution of land the Swedish peasantry was unusual. Serfdom as such did not exist in sixteenth-century Sweden; all male peasants, regardless of the nature of their tenancies, were considered freemen. Most peasants were free-holders, called 'tax peasants' (*skattebönder*), who collectively owned nearly 63 percent of the more than 100,000 farmsteads (*gårdar*) accounted for in 1560. Peasants residing on noble land (*frälsebönder*) worked another 16 percent of these farmsteads, and the remaining farms (21 percent) were owned by the crown. *Frälsebönder* had the advantage of partial exemption from ordinary taxes, but on the whole paid higher rents than those residing on crown lands (*kronobönder*). Economic conditions varied greatly from region to region. Peasants living near forests or in mining districts had considerable opportunities to supplement their incomes. In Närke, a center of iron production and weapons manufacturing near Örebro, peasants who accepted government contracts for weapons were exempt from taxes and conscription, and not infrequently accumulated enough wealth to send their sons to university.[6] The 'average' Swedish peasant, however, was not so well-off, especially in the last decades of the sixteenth century. Annual mean temperatures and crop yields declined in tandem between 1570 and 1650. There were rare 'good' harvests – perhaps one in every eight – but more often there were periods of crushing want, like the great famines of 1570 and 1597. In a way, how-ever, the abject poverty of the ordinary Swedish peasant constituted an advantage. Inured to hardship, the Swedish peasant was unusually tough. In the words of Georg Friedrich von Waldeck, 'The Swedes are a hungry people, and hence they are dangerous and hard-hearted.'[7]

The Creation of the Vasa State

Sweden had been a kingdom for some time when the Vasa dynasty took control of the state in 1523, but at the dawn of the early modern period it had been under foreign domination for well over a century. The Kalmar Union of 1397 brought together the Nordic lands – Denmark, Sweden-Finland, and Norway with its fiefdom of Iceland – under a single elective monarchy. It was not a union of equals; Denmark, the most highly developed and centralized of the three kingdoms, dominated the Kalmar Union, though Norway and Sweden maintained some rights of election. Separatist tendencies and a kind of proto-nationalism in Norway and Sweden further compromised the effectiveness of the Union. While it would not be accurate to claim that the population of fifteenth- and sixteenth-century Sweden subscribed to the same species of national consciousness as did their descendants in the nineteenth and twentieth centuries, nonetheless there existed a pervasive feeling that their land was not a mere part of Denmark. The Danish kings, by relying primarily on Danish administrators to rule Sweden, exacerbated this sense of separation. The collective Swedish reaction to foreign rule was the occasional election of popular anti-kings and a sporadic series of uprisings, such as that led by Engelbrekt Engelbrektsson in the 1430s. By the early sixteenth century, noble and popular discontent with Denmark centered around the humbly born Sture family from the rough and fiercely independent province of Dalarna. The brutal centralizing policies of Denmark's King Christian II (1513–23), which culminated in the summary execution of 82 leading Swedish noblemen in the 'Stockholm Bloodbath' of November 1520, broke the leadership of the Sture clan and nearly neutralized the resistance of the nobility as a whole. Leadership of the opposition after the Bloodbath devolved by default to a young nobleman from Dalarna: Gustav Eriksson Vasa.[8]

Gustav Vasa was a natural leader. He was tied to the Sture clan by blood and marriage; his earlier imprisonment at Kalø Castle in Denmark, in addition to the gruesome fate suffered by several of his family members in the Bloodbath, gave him a personal animus against the Danes. He also possessed considerable skills as an orator and a demagogue. Within a year he had supplanted the Stures. In 1521, the remnants of the native aristocracy hailed him as 'Protector of the Realm' (*riksföreståndare*), a title traditionally held by the Stures. Military assistance from the Hanseatic city of Lübeck enabled Gustav Vasa and his rebel forces to take Stockholm in 1523. Shortly thereafter, on 6 June 1523, a convocation of the Estates at Strängnäs elected Gustav Vasa as king of Sweden.

In part, sheer luck allowed Gustav Vasa to succeed where other would-be Swedish kings had failed. Denmark was in no condition to respond; early in 1523, the Danish nobility had deposed Christian II, and the newly elected King Frederik I (1523–33) evinced little interest in keeping the Union together by force. Gustav's success in establishing a viable monarchy within Sweden, however, was due primarily to his political acumen. His position as king did not go unchallenged within Sweden. Before 1523, Gustav Vasa had posed as the successor to the Stures, capitalizing on traditional resistance to central authority. Now, however, Gustav Vasa *was* that central authority, and there were those among his subjects who perceived the king as having betrayed the Sture legacy, especially since the financial burdens of revolt required heavy and regular taxation. Gustav faced the prospect of violent opposition to his rule: no fewer than three peasant uprisings in Dalarna between 1524 and 1531, the formidable revolt led by the Småland peasant Niels Dacke in 1542–43, and a noble insurrection in Västergötland in 1529. Still, Gustav Vasa triumphed. He enjoyed the support of most of the nobility, burghers, and peasants, and managed to suppress – brutally – all of the insurrections of his reign. Employing his skills as a populist and an orator, Gustav made frequent use of the national Diet to carry out royal policies. As a result, the period between 1527 and the king's death in 1560 witnessed remarkable growth in the efficacy and reach of the central authority. Already harboring Lutheran sympathies, in 1527 the king convinced the Diet at Västerås to agree to royal seizure of church properties and revenues. The king generously remanded much of the property gained at Västerås to the care of his nobility, but the monarchy profitted dramatically: the proportion of farms in Sweden and Finland owned by the crown grew from 3.5 percent to 21.3 percent.

The creation of a primitive but effective bureaucracy accompanied this explosive growth of crown holdings and revenues. Aided by career bureaucrats of German birth, Gustav Vasa built up both a Chancery (*Kansliet*) and a Treasury (*Kammaren*). In local administration, crown officers (*fogdar*) and prominent noblemen who administered royal fiefs (*län*) represented the interests of the crown. Noble fiefholders enjoyed extensive powers over the tenants on their fiefs, but the crown kept a watchful eye on their activities.[9] The constitutional pillars of Vasa kingship, however, were to be found in the traditional organs of medieval governance: the Council (*Riksråd*) and the Diet.

Sweden and Denmark shared a common political tradition that Scandinavian historians have labeled 'council-constitutionalism', and in superficial ways the relationship between king, nobility, and commons was much the same in both monarchies. In Denmark, the Council was the primary governing institution, and through it the aristocracy was able to restrict the royal prerogative; the estates had faded into obscurity by the sixteenth century and would not reappear until the late 1620s. A similar arrangement was established in Sweden's law code and tacit constitution, the Land Law of Magnus Eriksson (1353). The Land Law stipulated that monarchy in Sweden would be elective, that the king would have to rule by law and not by force, and that the native nobility would work with the king towards this end. From the beginning of the Vasa dynasty, however, it had become clear that the Council's role was to advise and not to dictate or restrict. Real power rested with the meetings of the Diet, after 1561 called the *Riksdag* (plural *Riksdagar*). The Land Law did not provide for a Diet *per se*, but during the fifteenth century, Sweden's kings and regents had found in the estates a useful counter to the Council. The *Riksdag* recognized four distinct estates: the clergy, the nobility, the towns, and the peasants. The clergy, little more than civil servants in a constitutional sense after the Västerås diet in 1527, could be expected to support the king. So long as the king was able to sway the opinion of the lower orders, then the *Riksdag* would not constitute a hurdle to royal authority. On the contrary: the *Riksdag* would serve as an invaluable tool for the Vasa kings. It allowed the king to sample public opinion, and gave all classes an opportunity to air their grievances directly to the sovereign; most important, it allowed the kings to legitimize their policies with the stamp of popular approval.[10]

Gustav Vasa had, within two decades of his election at Strängnäs, created a reasonably secure and well-ordered monarchy. The Västerås diet broke the power of the clergy; generous distribution of confiscated church properties ensured noble support for the king; clever use of the *Riksdag* earned the loyalty of the lower orders, and merciless repression of insurrection cowed those who would not conform. Two voluntary acts signified the constitutional success of the regime: in 1540, an assembly of noblemen at Örebro recognized the king's sons Erik and Johan as his heirs; four years later, a *Riksdag* at Västerås proclaimed that Sweden was, and always would be, a hereditary monarchy (*arvrike*). Gustav Vasa had achieved by 1544 what the Danish kings would not be able to do until 1660 – the destruction of the elective principle, and the liberation of kingship from most constitutional restrictions.

Gustav's offspring would not be so successful or fortunate. The king's two marriages had produced four sons, three of whom would succeed their father as sovereign. Gustav's eldest son, Erik, was the heir apparent; each of the other three sons, according to the terms of the king's 'Testament' of 1560, would be invested with a large duchy of his own, to enable them to live in princely fashion and thereby – hopefully – obviating the possibility of political intrigue within the dynasty. Unfortunately, the Testament accomplished just the opposite, for it provided the jealous and ambitious younger sons with their own power-bases some distance from the capital. The Testament of 1560 would prove to be the bane of the monarchy for the next half century. The heir apparent succeeded Gustav Vasa in 1560 as Erik XIV (1560–68). Erik, unlike his father, was erudite and cultured, but mentally unstable and suspicious to the point of paranoia. The nobility had few qualms about Erik's decision to go to war with Denmark in 1563, or about his interest in the eastern Baltic, but the king's open contempt for the landed aristocracy soon alienated the noble estate. Instead of bestowing large royal fiefs upon the great noble houses, Erik preferred to grant much smaller properties (*förläningar*) with minimal rights of jurisdiction.[11] The king's preference for 'rule by secretaries' – the employment of foreign- or basely born bureaucrats in the central administration – was particularly repugnant to the nobility. Erik, whose mental state worsened noticeably in the last years of his reign, grew suspicious of disloyalty amongst his nobility; as the nobility saw its privileges eroding, that suspicion became a self-fulfilling prophecy. The greatest blow to noble pride was the creation of the hated High Court, designed by Erik and his unpopular favorite Jöran Persson to ferret out potential traitors within the nobility. To add insult to injury, Erik married a woman of peasant origins, Karin Månsdotter, had her crowned as queen, and elevated the hated Persson to noble status.[12]

The opposition to Erik XIV was formidable. Two of his younger half-brothers, Duke Johan of Finland and Duke Karl of Södermanland, had no reason to love their king, and the ducal courts became the focal points of resistance to the king. In the Articles of Arboga of 1561, Erik had sought to place the Vasa duchies firmly under royal control, and in 1563 the king had even imprisoned Johan for his attempts to create a personal alliance with the Jagiellon dynasty in Poland. Erik's descent into madness in 1567, culminating in delusional outbursts before the *Riksdag* and his random massacre of noblemen held prisoner at Uppsala, gave the opposition the opportunity it needed. Johan and Karl led the rebellion against Erik in 1568, seizing Stockholm the following year, and together the two dukes convinced the *Riksdag* to depose Erik and hail the eldest duke as King Johan III (1569–92).

Johan's career as king was only marginally more successful than Erik's except in the acquisition of new territories and in longevity. Johan had indeed seized the throne by force, but it was the acclamation of the *Riksdag* that made him sovereign. The king owed his elevation to the cooperation of the nobility, and the nobility did not let him forget it. Initially, Johan was sufficiently astute to manifest some magnanimity towards the nobility, through generous grants of *förläningar*. The unity of king and nobility, however, was soon over. The new king, a brilliant theologian and something of an aesthete, was indolent and indifferent to administrative affairs. He brought the war with Denmark to an end in 1570, and was largely responsible for Sweden's first real military successes in his war against Russia over possession of Livonia. But Johan's reign also witnessed an explosive growth in the size of the central bureaucracy, unaccompanied by a corresponding increase in efficiency; the vast expenses of the crown, accruing not only from constant warfare but also from the king's prodigal spending-habits as he indulged his tastes in architecture and art, were not offset by any increase in revenues. Paperwork piled up, the finances of the crown fell into disarray, and the king reverted to Erik's habit of relying on common- or foreign-born secretaries. Worse still were Johan's confessional inclinations. Although not a Catholic himself, the king was drawn to the grandeur of the Roman rite and was married to a Jagiellon princess. His leanings were noted in Rome and encouraged by the papacy. Johan tolerated the presence of Jesuit missionaries in Stockholm and briefly toyed with the idea of alliances with France and Spain, largely as a means of bolstering his own position in Baltic affairs. The king's negotiations with the papacy fell through; Johan's vision of a *via media* Swedish church, one that allowed clerical marriage and mass in the vernacular, did not meet with papal approval. Yet the flirtation with Catholicism did much to damage Johan politically. There was a considerable number of Catholic sympathisers within Sweden, but the clergy as a body was aghast at Johan's introduction of a Romanist liturgy, the 'Red Book' of 1576. Moreover, the Catholic experiment exacerbated the growing split between Johan and his brother Karl of Södermanland. Karl, who ruled his duchy as an autonomous enclave rather than as a royal fief, could barely conceal his hostility towards his older brother.[13] The Catholic experiment allowed Karl to pose as the defender of the Lutheran faith.

Johan III managed to suppress Karl's ambitions, and before the end of the reign the two brothers had reconciled, at least formally. But by the late 1580s, as Johan drew closer to death, the likelihood of a smooth dynastic succession did not appear promising. Johan's eldest son and designated heir, Prince Sigismund, had converted to Catholicism as a boy, and refused to give up his faith when Johan ceased his efforts to return Sweden to papal obedience. In 1587, following the death of King Stefan Bathory of Poland, the Poles elected Sigismund as their king. Within two years, both Johan and Sigismund would have reason to regret this, even though it had been a matter of priority in Johan's foreign policy for some time, but neither the Poles nor the Swedish nobility would allow Sigismund to abdicate. Johan felt that his nobility, and his aristocratic Council in particular, had demonstrated disloyalty. Accusing them collectively of treason, he purged his Council of its most prominent members and reduced the rest to silent obedience. The king's death in November 1592 left the Swedish nobility subdued and humiliated, but resentful of royal authority and as yet unbroken.[14]

Johan's son Sigismund inherited an impossible task when he succeeded to the Vasa throne in 1592. He had to govern a realm where the nobility had been opposed to his father, and where the populace as a whole was hostile towards Sigismund's religion. Moreover, he had to exercise his authority from distant Cracow, where his Polish subjects intended to keep him, and where the no-less-difficult task of governing Poland–Lithuania absorbed much of his time and energy. Sigismund would visit Sweden only twice during his brief reign – in 1593–94 and again in 1598 – and his absence allowed his uncle, Duke Karl, to realize his own political ambitions.[15] Fear of Catholicism brought Karl, the Council, the clergy, and the *Riksdag* together; in 1594, they forced Sigismund to accept a royal prerogative that was tightly circumscribed and far more limited in scope than that exercised by the earlier Vasa kings. Karl's thirst for power was by no means slaked. Breaking with the Council, who would not countenance open rebellion against their legitimate sovereign, Karl turned to the lower orders for support. The duke was motivated both by political ambition and a very real fear of Romanism. As a demagogue and a populist, Karl was very much his father's son, though he was less principled than Gustav had been. His angry and inflated rhetoric, given freely at meetings of the *Riksdag*, on streetcorners and in marketplaces – Michael Roberts styled him a 'stump orator' – earned Karl the undying support of the peasantry and the burghers. In Finland, Karl's calls for action against the heavy-handed governance of Klas Fleming, Sigismund's governor (*ståthållare*) there, led directly to the bloody peasant uprising known as the 'Club War' of 1596–97.[16] Leading members of the Council, fearful of Karl, turned in desperation to Sigismund, but the rightful king could not help them. Karl's forces ousted all of the provincial governors appointed by Sigismund, and though Sigismund's invading army took Stockholm, Karl still managed to hand his nephew a stinging defeat at Stångebro (September 1598). Karl's victory was complete: Sigismund conceded defeat and even expelled those members of the Council who had sought sanctuary at his court; the *Riksdag* at Linköping declared Sigismund deposed in 1599. Directing his wrath towards those who had opposed him, Karl dragged dozens of noblemen to stand trial for treason before the *Riksdag*. In the end, five leading councillors, including the outspoken constitutionalist Erik Sparre, went to the block at Linköping in March 1600.

Sigismund and his heirs would not give up their claim to the Swedish throne until 1660, and Karl made no claim on the throne himself, but the duke was nonetheless the real ruler of Sweden after 1600. After initially refusing the crown offered by the *Riksdag* in 1599, Karl finally accepted the title in 1604 and was crowned as Karl IX (1604–11) three years later. Abject fear of their new king kept the nobility in line during Karl's brief reign. Karl did not deliberately cultivate terror as a political instrument, but terror prevailed just the same. The upper ranks of the nobility had much reason to hate Karl. He had confiscated much of their property in the aftermath of the Linköping *Riksdag*, and had humiliated and decimated the Council through the judicial murders of 1600. There was hardly a single family in the conciliar aristocracy that could not count a member among those martyred on the scaffold at Linköping or exiled in Poland. Karl's attempts at reconciliation with his aristocracy were fruitless, but then so were the aristocracy's attempts at resistance. Efforts to overthrow the usurper were suppressed with the same cruel excess that Karl had demonstrated at Linköping. A massive treason trial held before the *Riksdag* at Stockholm in 1605 ended in a spate of quasi-legal searches, seizures, arrests, tortures, and executions. The aristocracy suffered more heavily under Karl IX than at any time since the Stockholm Bloodbath of 1520. The Council could no longer function as a body, and Karl relied in the main on his professional bureaucrats, army officers, and the support of the *Riksdag* to assist him in governing the realm.[17]

The reign of Karl IX firmly established Lutheranism as the state religion and cemented Sweden's reputation as an unswervingly Protestant state. Prior to 1593, Sweden's confessional identity, though favoring Lutheranism, was ambiguous. Neither Gustav Vasa nor Erik XIV succeeded in defining an official theology or doctrine, and it was not until 1571 that an official Church Ordinance set standards for religious education and the hierarchy of the clergy. Lutheranism was nonetheless pervasive throughout the clergy and population; Johan III's 'Red Book' of 1576 met with a cold reception from clergy and laity alike. Immediately following Johan's death in late 1592, Karl – with the willing participation of the clergy – summoned a general synod to meet at Uppsala in February 1593. The Uppsala Assembly scrapped Johan's 'popish' liturgy, reinstated the 1571 Ordinance, and affirmed their adherence to the *confessio augustana*. The spirit of unity prevailing at Uppsala, however, was deceptive. For the remainder of Karl's life, he and the clergy sparred over doctrinal and liturgical issues: Karl, who was personally

inclined towards Calvinism in some matters of doctrine, aspired to royal
supremacy in all matters of religion; the more orthodox clergy, who as
a group subscribed unofficially to the 1577 Formula of Concord, fought
their regent tenaciously. But any realistic hope of a Catholic revival in
Sweden evaporated when Sigismund was deposed in 1599, and the
Riksdag stipulated that all Swedish kings must henceforth be Protestant.[18]

Geopolitics and War

Over the past decade or so, Swedish scholars have eschewed research in
the history of foreign and military policy in favor of studies concentrat-
ing on topics in social and economic history. Even so, the debate over the
motivations and factors behind Swedish expansionism between 1561
and 1721 has not abated. Historians of early modern Sweden fall into
one of three categories. Traditionalists, like Niels Ahnlund, tend to view
Swedish empire-building as a response to fear of territorial encirclement. These historians of the 'old school', as Michael Roberts labeled
them, argue that Sweden's wars against its Baltic neighbors arose from
a quest for security, as Swedish kings and statesmen sought to break free
from the isolation that was imposed on them by Denmark, Poland, and
Russia. Wars of aggression were primarily preemptive strikes, designed
to keep Sweden's enemies at bay before they could attack Sweden
themselves.[19] The so-called 'new school' historians have countered that
economic benefits, and not security concerns, were the primary motivating
force behind Swedish foreign policy in the *stormaktstid*. For Artur Attman,
this meant a Swedish bid to control Baltic markets. For more recent
scholars heavily influenced by Marxism, this meant something far more
insidious. Jan Peters has argued that the economic self-interest of the
nobility drove Swedish expansionism. To Jan Lindegren, it seems that
conscription and wartime taxation were not merely means of fueling the
state at war, but rather the opposite – war *justified* conscription and the
levying of taxes. War was a way of legitimizing the expansion of central
authority and the compulsory redistribution of the 'social surplus' of the
peasantry to the aristocratic elite.[20]

   None of these single-cause explanations can be applied universally to
a full century and a half of Swedish expansionism. For reasons that
we will examine later, the 'warfare as a means of social and economic
control' thesis proposed by Lindegren is most difficult to substantiate.
The 'encirclement' theory has its merits, but cannot fully explain the

actions of Karl X Gustav (1654–60) and the Regency that followed his death, when Swedish armies went to war on the Continent in part because Sweden could not afford to sustain sizable military forces on home soil. And other, less tangible considerations enter into the picture at various points throughout the *stormaktstid*; Gustav Adolf's intervention in the Thirty Years' War, for example, could also be partially attributed to confessional motivations and a desire to prove Sweden's military might to the world. Disparate as these interpretations seem on the surface, they actually add up to a cogent foreign and military policy. In short, Sweden was a state whose governing elite felt themselves surrounded by hostile forces, be they Danish, Polish, Russian, Habsburg, or papal. Defense against these threats required constant vigilance, the maintenance of a disproportionately large military establishment, and – occasionally – preemptive strikes. All of the resources of the state were bent towards this end, but until the imposition of absolutism in 1680 those resources were not adequate to the task at hand. If commercial or economic motives played any role at all in the formulation of foreign policy, it was this: that the demands of the 'military state' necessitated an expansion of Sweden's resource base. Economic interests promoted military action only to the extent that Sweden's capacity to fight required a steady flow of cash. The Swedish crown never made war to get rich or to make its aristocracy rich; it made war to obtain the resources necessary to fuel its military establishment, which in turn was vital to safeguard the security of the state. It all boiled down to one dominant priority: the defense of the state by military means.

Prior to 1611, however, Sweden was just beginning to embark on its career as an imperial power, and its motivations were far less complicated than they would be by the middle of the seventeenth century. Three main factors conditioned Swedish foreign policy under the early Vasas. First was Sweden's territorial encirclement. Denmark, through its possession of Norway, the Scanian provinces, and therefore the Sound, walled Sweden in from the west and south; Poland controlled the southern and southeastern Baltic rim; Russia, especially under the aggressive leadership of Tsar Ivan IV (1533–84), encroached on Swedish territory from the east. The second factor was the decline of the Hanse and the collapse of the Teutonic Order. The death of the Order in the 1550s left a dangerous power-vacuum in Livonia and Estonia, a vacuum that Russia, Poland, and Denmark all aspired to fill. It was a development that Sweden could ill-afford to ignore: the port-towns of Riga and Reval were among the most important commercial entrepôts in the Baltic, and moreover their possession by Denmark, Poland, or Russia would further tighten the territorial noose around Sweden. The third factor was the growing importance of the Baltic trade to international commerce. That trade was absolutely vital to England and the Netherlands, and for that reason it drew the attention and ambitions of the major western powers, including Spain and France.[21]

Denmark presented Sweden with its greatest threat, or at least was its most implacable foe. For all their similarities in culture, language, religion, and even the structure of society and government, there was little feeling of kinship between the two monarchies. Kings Frederik II (1559–88) and Christian IV (1596–1648) both aspired to the re-creation of the Kalmar Union at one time or another; the northern border between Sweden and Danish Norway, in the desolate Finnmark, was never clearly resolved. Danish possession of the Sound was perhaps the most sensitive issue, since it allowed the Danish kings to levy tolls – the 'Sound dues' – on all maritime traffic passing into or out of the Baltic at the port of Helsingør, and potentially restricted Sweden's commercial access to the West. These conditions, in addition to Denmark's interest in Livonia, led to the bloody Seven Years' War of the North (1563–70). Wealthier Denmark held the upper hand for most of the conflict, but neither kingdom was capable of inflicting a decisive defeat on the other. In the end, the war caused too many problems for western and central Europe. Frederik II repeatedly closed the Sound to international traffic, effectively shutting down the Baltic trade, and the close ties between Scandinavia (particularly Denmark) and the German states threatened the fragile tranquility of the Holy Roman Empire. A group of foreign potentates, including those of France, Poland, Saxony, and the empire, mediated a peace settlement between the two Nordic rivals at Stettin (November 1570), which forced Sweden to pay Denmark a 150,000 *riksdaler* 'ransom' for the return of the port of Älvsborg, then in Danish hands. Denmark and Sweden observed an uneasy *détente* for the remainder of the century. The peace lasted until 1611, when the unresolved issues of the Sound dues and the Arctic border brought Karl IX and Christian IV to blows in the Kalmar War of 1611–13.[22]

The Polish and Muscovite threats were more nebulous but no less real. The clash with Russia began in earnest in 1561, when the Estonian port of Reval appealed to Erik XIV for protection. During the Seven Years' War of the North, Russia, Sweden, and Denmark all competed for control of Livonia. The Stettin settlement of 1570 ended Danish ambitions there, but since Emperor Maximilian II (1564–76) failed to

intercede in Livonia as he had promised to do at Stettin, only Sweden
was in a position to contest Tsar Ivan IV's ambitions in that embattled
territory. With Polish assistance, Swedish forces held off the Russians,
and by 1581 were firmly entrenched in Estonia. Fighting in the region
raged through the 1580s. Poland, under the rule of King Stefan Bathory
since 1575, continued to provide the Swedes with a measure of help, and
Russia's constitutional troubles gave Sweden the upper hand. The death
of Ivan IV in 1584, and the succession of the ineffective Boris Godunov,
weakened the Muscovite War effort. A truce in 1592 ended the conflict
for the time being; the Peace of Teusina (1595) confirmed Swedish possession of Estonia. Teusina brought only a temporary end to the rivalry
with Russia. The death of Boris Godunov in 1605 plunged Russia into
the confused in-fighting of the 'Time of Troubles'. Karl IX and his
nephew Sigismund each attempted to place their sons on the Russian
throne, primarily with the intention of frustrating the political aspirations of the other. At Karl's death in 1611, Russia, Poland, and Sweden
were still sparring over Livonia.

Poland had been Sweden's ally during the earlier stages of the
Livonian War, but that tenuous friendship was not fated to last long.
The dynastic union of 1587 brought the two crowns together under
Sigismund; Duke Karl's civil war against Sigismund naturally drove
them apart. Sigismund never gave up his claim to the Vasa throne.
As Karl IX involved himself in the intrigues in Moscow and sought to
expand Swedish power in the east beyond Estonia, Sweden and Poland
came into direct conflict. Poland still dominated the eastern Baltic in
1611; in 1610, a Polish army had utterly annihilated a Swedish-Russian
force at Klushino. Throughout the *stormaktstid*, Sweden and the Polish
Commonwealth would remain on terms that were less than friendly, and
not infrequently were at war with one another.[23]

The sixteenth-century wars made painfully apparent Sweden's lack of
allies outside the Baltic region. It was not for lack of trying. Erik XIV
had endeavored, without success, to forge marriage alliances with
England, Scotland, Poland, Hessen, and Lorraine, but could attract
nothing more substantial than the support of a couple of minor rene-
gade German princes, like Erich of Braunschweig-Calenberg. During
his flirtation with Catholicism, Johan III negotiated with emissaries
from France and Spain. Although Catherine de' Medici expressed some
interest in gaining the Swedish crown for her son Henri d'Anjou (later
Henry III of France) after his brief career as king of Poland in 1573–74,
such a union – with the legendary perpetrator of the St Bartholomew's

Day Massacres – would have proven just as distasteful to the Swedish nobility as it was frightening to Lutheran Denmark. Conversely, Karl IX would attempt to find an ally amongst the Protestant states of western and central Europe; arguing that a Catholic Poland threatened to bring about a re-Catholicization of the North – something that the usurper genuinely believed – Karl tirelessly canvassed the Protestant courts, but without effect. At the end of the sixteenth century, after the defeat of the Armada in 1588 and the triumph of Henry of Navarre in France, Protestant fear of an international Romanist cabal had temporarily evaporated. Moreover, Karl was widely perceived as a usurper; and it would have been ill-advised for any state to alienate Christian IV's Denmark. Denmark still controlled the Sound, had close ties with the leading Protestant princes in Germany, and enjoyed a better reputation than its Nordic neighbor.[24]

The Vasa State in 1611

The sixteenth century had been a tumultuous experience for the fledgling Swedish state. Gustav Vasa and his sons had created a stable central authority where there had been none before. Under Erik XIV and his half-brothers, Sweden had confronted the enemies that encircled it. To be sure, there had been a fair share of defeats, but on the whole Sweden survived its confrontations with Denmark, Russia, and Poland, and in Estonia it had established a lucrative foothold in the eastern Baltic. Despite Johan III's efforts in the 1570s, the Vasa kings had thrown off the 'papal yoke', and Lutheranism was firmly entrenched as the state religion. All five of the early Vasa kings had come face-to-face with internal challenges to their authority. Two of them – Erik and Sigismund – had of course succumbed; nonetheless, the authority of the crown was undiminished when Karl IX died in 1611. Given the odds ranged against it, the most remarkable thing about the Vasa 'experiment' was that the kingdom survived intact to greet the new century.

That is not to say, however, that the Vasa state had survived unchanged, or that the problems that had confronted Gustav Vasa had been solved. Foremost among those problems was the dearth of a workable bureaucracy. 'Rule by secretaries' had proven to be universally unpopular, especially amongst the nobility. Under Erik XIV, Johan III, and Karl IX the native-born nobility clamored for a greater presence within the administration and in the leadership of the army; as a class, however, the nobility was not yet equipped to fulfill that role. Still, the nobility's demand for a larger share in governance, if only to control the despotic tendencies of the early Vasa kings, was the central constitutional problem facing the monarchy prior to 1611. In terms of membership and the distribution of wealth, the Swedish nobility was fundamentally the same as it had been a century before. The only significant structural change in the noble estate was the introduction of noble titles – 'count' (*greve*) and 'baron' (*friherre*) – proclaimed by Erik XIV in 1561 as a means of rewarding loyal nobles. But the political power of the noble estate had definitely diminished since the election of Gustav Vasa.[25] The aristocratic Council had consistently asserted its traditional right to counsel the king, but all three of Gustav's sons had beaten down that right. The Council in 1611 was but a shadow of its former self, and could not mimic its Danish counterpart in acting as a corporate counter to the royal prerogative. The *Riksdag*, on the other hand, was by 1611 a mature and powerful institution. Gustav Vasa, Erik XIV, and Karl IX relied heavily upon that institution, and in particular on the support of the lower orders.

Interestingly, the aristocracy did not contest this. Though the Council might occasionally gripe about the excessive wooing of 'Herr Omnes', or the favors showered on the peasants by their kings, even the most vocal proponents of conciliar authority conceded that the *Riksdag* was the proper voice of the body politic. The Vasa kings had paid lip-service to the Land Law's insistence on rule by law, but during the course of the century they had also departed from the constitutional model mandated by that Law by pushing the great magnates to the side. Only in one area had the monarchy suffered a setback: the 1570 Stettin settlement with Denmark made it much more difficult for either of the Scandinavian kings to go to war with each other, giving chief responsibility for settling Danish–Swedish disputes to the Councils of both states.[26]

The economic legacy of the early Vasa kings was a mixed one. Gustav Vasa's kingdom was underdeveloped and poor, but it was at least solvent. Continuous warfare since 1563 had changed all that. The wars with Denmark, Russia, and Poland consumed vast amounts of wealth; incidental expenses, like the Älvsborg ransom in 1570–71, and the prodigal spending habits of Johan III exacerbated the kingdom's negative revenue balance. By 1582, the annual gap between ordinary revenues and expenditures was 133,000 *riksdaler*. If extraordinary revenues and wartime expenditures are included, the deficit rises to 345,000 *riksdaler*. There were, however, signs of pending improvements. Thanks to Gustav

Vasa, Sweden was no longer trapped in a Hanseatic trade monopoly. The Stettin treaty of 1570, by allowing Swedish commerce free passage through the Sound, guaranteed at least a measure of commercial access to western Europe. Most important, the early Vasas had worked assiduously to exploit Sweden's mineral resources and to increase exports. Gustav Vasa and his sons had imported foreign entrepreneurs, artisans, and capital to bring Sweden's mining industry in the *Bergslag* up-to-date. As duke of Södermanland, Karl IX had focused his considerable administrative skills on improving iron and weapons production in the Närke region, so that by the end of the century Sweden was already close to being self-sufficient in the manufacture of armaments.[27] Iron and copper, both of very high quality, were now Sweden's most valuable exports, with England and the Netherlands the primary purchasers. To improve access to these resources for foreign merchants, Johan III and Karl IX sponsored the founding of new towns, most notably Göteborg (1607) near the harbor at Älvsborg. But for the peasantry, constant warfare brought with it a heavy and unrelenting burden of extraordinary taxes. This did not yet lead, however, to open, violent discontent in the countryside. At the end of the sixteenth century, the peasantry was thoroughly inured to the onerous demands of the state at war. The constitutional importance of the *Riksdag* undoubtedly helped to cushion the blow, and even a class struggle like the Club War in Finland stemmed more from the local governor's arbitrary exercise of power than it did from general despair over taxes and conscription.[28]

The Nordic Seven Years' War and the confessional histrionics of Karl IX brought the Vasa state to the attention of all Europe, but it could not be said that Sweden had yet established itself as a significant European power, nor even that Sweden had integrated itself into the main currents of European life. Nothing illustrates this better than the condition of 'high culture' in sixteenth-century Sweden. The Lutheran Reformation had dealt the level of learning in the kingdom, already modest, a serious blow through the closing of Catholic educational institutions. The early Vasas had little interest in improving the university at Uppsala, and not until the 1630s would the university recover any credibility. Swedish noblemen craving an education would have to seek it on the Continent; the clergy was utterly reliant upon Protestant universities in Germany (primarily Rostock and Wittenberg) for a supply of competent priests. To be sure, Johan III's artistic sensibilities and his willingness to spend on architecture lent the monarchy at least a thin veneer of cultural sophistication, and the growing presence of foreign craftsmen and merchants accelerated Sweden's cultural growth. But Sweden did not produce any scholars, theologians, artists, or musicians of note during the sixteenth century. The sole exceptions were the scholarly brothers Johannes and Olaus Magnus, whose fanciful chronicles of Nordic history gave rise to a popular myth of Sweden's distinguished roots in antiquity, as well as a species of proto-nationalistic fervor known as 'Gothicism'. In contemporary European estimation, Sweden remained a cultural backwater, a bleak and barbaric land. It was a perception that would remain for sometime: when Gustav Adolf led Sweden to war in Germany in 1630, Emperor Ferdinand II referred to him derisively as a 'snow king'.

In one area, however, Sweden excelled, and that was perhaps the most important of all: the ability to make war for long periods of time with limited means. Sweden's accomplishment in this regard was made all the more noteworthy by the kingdom's obvious poverty. Sweden's enemies, especially Denmark, made extensive use of paid mercenaries. This was a luxury that Sweden simply could not afford for very long. The core of Sweden's land forces were native troops. By the end of the century, the noble 'knight-service' had proven to be unreliable, since the landed nobility went to extraordinary lengths to shirk this duty. The conscription of native foot-troops (known as the *uppbåd*), while hardly unique to Sweden, was better developed there than in the rest of Europe. Every fifth man in the province of Småland, and every sixth in the remainder of the kingdom, was liable for military duty to defend the nation. Gustav Vasa had asserted his right to summon the *uppbåd* during the *Riksdag* of 1544, but the act that distinguished the Swedish system from other medieval militia levies was the implementation of *utskrivning*, or registration, in the late 1550s. All eligible men were registered for conscription in their home parishes, thereby lending some efficiency to the *uppbåd*. Since war was the normal state of affairs in Sweden after 1563, the act of registration was in fact the immediate precursor to actual recruitment; hence the term *utskrivning* came to refer to conscription itself.[29]

Utskrivning gave the Vasa kings a means by which they could raise large armies without having to lay out large amounts of cash; even more advantageous in the age of the 'military entrepreneur', the troops did not have to be paid off when their services were no longer required. There were, of course, many disadvantages to the Swedish system. The *uppbåd* was intended for national defense, and hence the conscripts were reluctant to fight outside their country's borders. Since Sweden was so sparsely populated, it could not bear indefinitely the economic disruption caused by recruitment. Worse still, the native troops were not tactically competent. Scholars of military history, enamored of the achievements of Gustav Adolf in the Thirty Years' War, have sometimes exaggerated the tactical proficiency of the Swedish armies before the great warrior-king set foot in Germany in 1630; but the fact remains that Sweden's armies were inferior in this regard prior to the 1620s. Erik XIV, hailed by Michael Roberts as a tactical genius of sorts, tried unsuccessfully to introduce Western tactics, based around the use of pike-armed infantry, into the native levies. Under Karl IX, the famed tactician Johann 'der Mittlere' of Nassau-Siegen – cousin of Maurice of Nassau and proponent of the Dutch tactical reforms of the 1590s – gave up in frustration after attempting to teach the Dutch 'method' to a stubbornly unwilling Swedish soldiery. Even had these attempts proven successful, it is doubtful that they would have made a real difference. As Robert Frost has so lucidly demonstrated, conventional European infantry tactics would not have been very effective against Polish armies, which emphasized the heavy use of cavalry and were better suited to the terrain of the southeastern Baltic region. Karl IX's disastrous defeat at Kirkholm (September 1605) provided sufficient evidence of that. Still, the native Swedish troops were hardy, reliable, and above all cheap.[30]

Sweden was a respectable second-rate monarchy in 1611, no mean accomplishment for a state with such humble beginnings. There was nothing, however, to suggest potential for national 'greatness', that Sweden might make its influence felt in European politics beyond the Baltic. And even in the Baltic world, it was overshadowed by Poland and Denmark. For all of the commercial labors of its kings, Sweden remained an impoverished state, and the constitutional fissures that had begun to open wide after 1587 hinted at an impending crisis over the nature of political authority. No intelligent observer could have foreseen the chain of events that catapulted the Swedish state from its tenuous seat on the periphery of Europe to a central position in the disputes of the great powers of the Continent.

Chapter 2: The Reign of Gustav II Adolf

No Swedish sovereign has equaled Karl IX's son and successor, Gustav II Adolf (1611–32), in overall reputation. Indeed, few European monarchs of the seventeenth century – with the exception of Louis XIV – rival Gustav Adolf in this regard. Even among the most casual students of the early modern period, Gustav II Adolf is one of those few statesmen who enjoys instant name-recognition. Long before the appearance of the twentieth-century biographies of the king by Nils Ahnlund, Günter Barudio, and – most eloquently – by Michael Roberts, Gustav Adolf's immortality within European historiography was assured by a plethora of biographies, some of them more akin to hagiography than they are to serious historical literature. To his nineteenth-century admirers, Gustav II Adolf was simultaneously Old Testament warrior-king, practitioner of *Realpolitik*, and savior of European Protestantism. Even in recent survey texts of the early modern period and of the history of Western Civilization in general – genres that tend to brush off Scandinavian developments as 'peripheral' – Gustav Adolf is practically the only major Scandinavian figure who appears with any regularity. In short, Gustav Adolf has become, in Western eyes as well as in Swedish popular historiography, synonymous with the apogee of Swedish power and with seventeenth-century Scandinavia in general.

Regardless of the hyperbolic excesses of his earlier biographers, Gustav II Adolf largely deserves his elevated historical reputation. It was under Gustav Adolf's direction, and primarily because of his direction, that Sweden became a European power of the first rank. He did not establish anything resembling an 'absolute monarchy' in Sweden. He did manage, however, to rally the nobility and the commons behind him, even though the costs of his rulership were high. In foreign policy, Gustav Adolf was the first Swedish sovereign to assert himself successfully in European international politics outside the Baltic region. But his legacy would be a mixed one. Though not manifest when the king's life was cut short at Lützen in 1632, Sweden's career as a European 'great power' would prove to be brief, expensive, and painful.[1]

The Reconciliation: King, Nobility, and Nation

None of this, of course, was apparent when the young king – the second of Gustav Vasa's grandsons to hold the office – ascended to the throne upon Karl IX's death in October 1611. The Kalmar War with Denmark had begun only seven months before, and already its outcome did not appear to be favorable to Sweden. Worse still was the constitutional legacy of Karl IX's reign. The king's 'parliamentary despotism' and his often cruel autocracy had alienated the great families of the aristocracy. The 'bloodbath' at Linköping eleven years before had not been forgotten, and many of the leading families had ties to the Swedish political refugees at Sigismund's court in Poland. The aristocracy was in disarray, but not as yet broken, and the death of their unpopular and domineering master, before his successor had reached his majority, gave these families the opportunity they needed to reassert their power and restore Sweden to constitutional rule. The aristocracy stood by the 1604 *Riksdag*'s decision to recognize Gustav Adolf as Karl's heir apparent but with one qualification. Meeting at Nyköping in December 1611 and January 1612, the *Riksdag* offered their new sovereign, who had just turned seventeen, immediate acknowledgment as king, provided that he agree to abide by the terms of a coronation charter. The terms of that charter, promulgated on New Year's Day 1612, were far more restrictive than anything to which the earlier Vasas had been subjected. Seeking to protect the nobility – and the state – from the unconstitutional excesses of Karl IX, the authors of the charter required that the new king would have to obtain the consent of the aristocratic Council before levying new taxes, conscripting troops, passing laws, or making major foreign policy decisions. Moreover, membership in the Council would be restricted to native-born members of the nobility, as would possession of all significant offices both civil and military. Embroiled in a potentially disastrous war that was not of his own making, and needful of the goodwill of the landowning aristocracy, Gustav II Adolf had no choice but to submit.[2]

The result, however, was neither a diminishment of royal authority nor a period of protracted bitterness between king and Council. For this remarkable achievement, as well as for the spectacular rise of Sweden to prominence in European affairs over the next two decades, the loyalty and restraint of the Swedish aristocracy as a whole must take some of the credit, but in the main the achievement was Gustav Adolf's. Whatever Karl IX's personal and political flaws, the old king had prepared his son well, and Gustav Adolf was perfectly suited by temperament to his new role. Simultaneously both pragmatic and wildly imaginative, he did not share the predisposition towards brutality and vengeance displayed by his father and grandfather; though possessed of fine cultural sensibilities, he was not an impractical aesthete like his uncle Johan III. Karl IX had chosen the learned Johan Skytte as the prince's tutor. Under Skytte's capable tutelage, Gustav Adolf acquired considerable eloquence in Latin, native fluency in German, and working knowledge of a whole host of modern languages, including – unusual for his day – both English and Scots.[3] He was thoroughly familiar with history and with law, theology, and classical literature. From Skytte and from the accomplished Swedish general Jakob De la Gardie he learned the art of war, both in theory and in practice. In religion, Gustav Adolf was perhaps not so broadly irenic as many of his biographers would make him out to be, but neither was he so rigidly orthodox in his Lutheranism as his own clergy or his rival Christian IV. He was deeply influenced by the Gothicism of Olaus Magnus, which imparted to him a militant sense of purpose and mission as a national leader. Most important, he had seen his father at work, and was familiar with the mechanics of early Vasa kingship, but manifested little desire to rule in Karl's style. Perhaps the gentle patriarchalism of James VI/I's *Basilikon Doron*, translated explicitly for the prince by Skytte's brother, had its intended effect.

The Charter of 1612 was more a reconciliation than a confrontation between crown and aristocracy, and both parties to the agreement looked upon it in this fashion. Though restrictive in its terms, the Charter marked the beginning of a long-standing honeymoon not only between king and nobility, but between king and *nation*, a honeymoon that would last for the full twenty years of the reign. Like very few of his contemporaries, Gustav II Adolf managed to rule by a genuine consensus, smoothly integrating Council, *Riksdag*, administration, and the military establishment in a common effort to achieve the goals that the king would set out over the next fifteen years. Perhaps Gustav Adolf's most significant move in this regard was in his choice of a right-hand man.

Axel Oxenstierna (1583–1654), scion of one of the most distinguished families in the conciliar aristocracy, had led the movement to force the Charter upon the new king, and had been one of that document's chief authors. Potentially the leader of the aristocratic opposition to preroga-tive rule, he was nonetheless elevated by the king to the position of chancellor in 1612. The partnership of king and chancellor was a nearly perfect one. In choosing Oxenstierna, Gustav II Adolf demonstrated to the nobility his commitment to redressing their grievances, but Oxenstierna was no mere means to a constitutional end. He was sober, pragmatic, and calculating, a perfect compliment to the sometimes reckless and ambitious king. By the time of Sweden's greatest trial of the century – the intervention in the German War in 1630 – the two men not only worked well together as politicians, but were also trusting friends. It could be said that Oxenstierna functioned as a royal favorite, but such a characterization would not be entirely accurate. At no point in the reign did Oxenstierna dominate the king, nor did he ever shy away from complete candor in his dealings with his royal master. Despite the chan-cellor's intense dislike for some of the king's other ministers, notably the former tutor Johan Skytte, Oxenstierna was a thorough professional, not allowing his personal prejudices to stand in the way of his service to the state. The chancellor did not use his position for undue personal gain, and did not monopolize patronage at court in the manner of a Buckingham or Richelieu. The working relationship between king and chancellor was a purely personal one, and its attendant political harmony would not last beyond the king's death in 1632, but while the king lived it helped to impart to Swedish political life a stability that was sorely lacking in most of Sweden's European contemporaries.[4]

The rapidity with which crown and aristocracy reconciled was key to the success of the regime, for in 1612 Sweden was in dire straits. The Polish–Russian threat, of course, had not abated, but the most pressing issue was the war with Denmark. In Denmark the war effort was produc-ing visible political and financial strain; Sweden was faring much worse. Kalmar, a major stronghold of considerable strategic importance, had fallen to Danish forces early in the conflict, and all Swedish attempts to reconquer it were in vain. The port city of Älvsborg fell to the Danes once again in May 1612, closing Sweden's only window on the North Sea and neutralizing a large portion of Swedish naval strength. There were no pitched land battles worthy of the name, only an indecisive but destruc-tive 'war of posts' along the Scanian frontier. But Sweden's peasant army was no match for Christian IV's mercenaries, and at sea the Danish fleet held sway. Sweden's only substantial defense was its inhospitable and desolate terrain, which presented an insurmountable logistical obstacle to invading armies. Both Christian IV and his council eagerly accepted an English proposal to end the conflict by mediation. The resulting Peace of Knäröd (January 1613) made the war a decisive strategic victory for Denmark. Gustav Adolf was compelled to give up his father's claims in the Arctic, and to allow the Danes to continue their use of the Three Crowns in the national arms.[5] The treaty confirmed Sweden's exemption from the Sound dues at Helsingør, and allowed the Swedes limited rights to levy tolls off Riga, but the advantages accruing therefrom paled in comparison to Denmark's gain from the war. Denmark would continue to hold Älvsborg, plus some adjoining territory, until Sweden paid an indemnity of 1 million *riksdaler*. Sweden would be given until January 1619 to pay this second Älvsborg ransom; if it defaulted, the captive territories and the port itself would remain in Danish hands. This was a huge sum, and Christian IV expected the exhausted and nearly bankrupt Swedes to default. Since the days of Erik XIV, the Vasa monarchs had endeavored to break out of the territorial encirclement that threatened Sweden's very existence as an autonomous state. The Kalmar War, conversely, had only made this danger loom more menacingly than ever before. The Knäröd settlement created a Swedish state hemmed in at the far north and the west by Denmark, while the Polish-Muscovite threat continued unabated.[6]

Constitutional and Administrative Reform

Gustav II Adolf's enviable reputation as a monarch stems primarily from his achievements as a military leader, strategist, and tactician. This is unfortunate, if for no other reason than the fact that historians tend to overlook the significant domestic reforms that characterized the reign. The reform of the judiciary and fiscal apparatus of the state is far less dramatic than the story of the brilliantly executed campaigns in Germany in 1631–32; but an understanding of these reforms is of an equal or greater importance to an understanding of the process by which Sweden managed to assert itself as a great power in European affairs. For, in a way, to separate the domestic reforms of Gustav Adolf's reign from the making of foreign and military policy (as I do here) is to create a false dichotomy. These reforms served the same ultimate purpose as the king's extensive reform of Sweden's military establishment: to make it possible for Sweden to marshal its meager national resources and allow the state to make war almost continuously, while keeping the state in good working order at home. This is why historians of the early modern period – from Otto Hintze, through Michael Roberts, to the more recent scholars of the Scandinavian 'power-state project' – have looked to Sweden as a model of the 'military revolution' in action in the seventeenth century; the need to prepare for and make war drove the evolution of the Swedish polity throughout the century. The same could be said, of course, for most of the significant European monarchies of the period, but the link between constitutional/administrative reform and the conduct of warfare is especially evident in late Vasa Sweden. Extreme poverty – both economic and demographic – both drove the need for reform and shaped the course of reform. It was not simply a question of asserting the authority of the central government over a contentious landed elite, as was the case in France under Richelieu and Mazarin. France was wealthy, and Sweden was not; in France provincial liberties and a powerful nobility acted as a barrier to any assertion of royal authority, but in Sweden regional identities were not so well defined and the landed aristocracy not nearly so capable of resistance. A comparison between Vasa Sweden and Oldenburg Denmark also highlights the role of warfare as a catalyst in the reform process: the two states employed very similar administrative systems and subscribed to very similar constitutional ideologies at the beginning of the century, and both states would adopt absolute monarchy in the last half of the century; but in the interim the pace of administrative growth and streamlining was much more rapid in warlike Sweden than in Denmark.[7]

We should not assume that the Swedish reforms of Gustav II Adolf's reign were more 'modern' than similar reforms on the Continent, or that the king himself was a man of almost superhuman ability and vision. None of the major reforms were completed during his reign; moreover, Gustav Adolf himself was not the sole author of these reforms. Much of the direction and impetus for reform came from the demands of the Swedish nobility for a greater role in governance, and in particular from the administrative common sense of Axel Oxenstierna. And while the restructuring of the central administration, the creation of a system of royal appeals courts, and the streamlining of the state fisc originated during the reign of Gustav Adolf, none of these changes came to full fruition before the king's death in 1632. All of them, including the revolutionary introduction of the 'collegial system' in the Form of Government of 1634, would have to wait until Oxenstierna brought them into being during his regency in the period 1632–44. Even then the reforms were incomplete, for Sweden did not possess the resources, financial or cultural, to carry them out to the extent desired.[8]

Military necessity was not the only factor compelling constitutional and administrative reform. As we have seen, the Swedish nobility as a whole demanded a greater role in the governance of the state. The Charter of 1612 was the final and binding expression of noble discontent with the misgovernance of Erik XIV, Johan III, and Karl IX, which the nobility blamed on 'rule by secretaries' as much as they did on the abuse of the royal prerogative. The nobility, especially the leading families of the power elite, felt that these abuses would be curbed if the native nobility were to have a monopoly over civil offices and governing bodies. They achieved this, in a way, through Gustav Adolf's acceptance of the 1612 Charter, but the king's very readiness to work with the aristocracy in a consensual manner meant – ironically – that the need for reform was even greater after 1612 than before. Since Gustav Adolf ruled – in Michael Roberts' words – 'with the grain' of the Vasa state rather than against it, the nobility acquiesced to his authority, and no real opposition to the king ever emerged. The nobility was loyal to the king, and dependent upon him for direction. Fortunately, Gustav Adolf was both dedicated and attentive to the needs of the state. The brief constitutionalist movement of 1611–12 did not consider how Sweden would deal with an indolent or careless monarch, like Johan III, much less how it would survive during an interregnum. Even Gustav Adolf's dedication had its limits, for after 1621 the king was frequently absent on campaign, and hence was physically distant from the administration of the state.

All this pointed to one inescapable truth: that the style of personal governance and administration practiced by Gustav Vasa and Karl IX was no longer possible by the 1620s. The king's military and diplomatic duties abroad precluded his direct supervision of the workings of the state, and the growing complexity of state affairs meant that a single man, no matter how competent, could not handle the crushing daily burden of paperwork that accompanied the minutiae of governance. Oxenstierna and the king recognized this early on, and during the years of relative calm between 1613 and 1621 the pair began to apply common sense to the most important divisions of the administration. The judiciary came first, for in this area Sweden was particularly backwards. A series of ordinances in 1614 and 1615 created a supreme court, the *Svea hovrätt*, consisting of several members of the Council and a handful of assessors. On the surface, it appears very similar to the system prevailing in Denmark, in which the king sat in judgment with his Council once annually as the court of final appeal, but it was in reality very different: it employed men trained in the law, several of whom were commoners, and it was to be permanently established at Stockholm, where it was to convene five months every year. It could not possibly meet all that was expected of it, however, and over the next two decades three regional appeals courts were established. In 1618, Oxenstierna turned to the state fisc, creating a treasury board with some independent authority. Six years later, with the appointment of an auditor-general, the treasury began to employ double-entry bookkeeping, a considerable advantage for financial planning. Nor did the chancellor neglect his own peculiar province, the Chancery, which he expanded and re-organized as the most important organ of administration in his ordinances of 1618 and 1626. The Chancery now had the ability to carry on the day-to-day duties of governance even in the absence of the chancellor himself, which became imperative as Oxenstierna found himself pressed by duties outside Sweden after 1626.[9]

Local administration came in for its share of restructuring as well. Prior to Gustav II Adolf's succession, local bailiffs (*fogdar*) had functioned almost independently of royal authority, and wealthy local magnates found it easy to ignore the royal will at pleasure. Enforcement of royal authority in the provinces required a king who was willing and able to maintain a peripatetic court, traveling from province to province to make sure that his edicts were enforced, troops levied and taxes collected. Such a task was well beyond the capabilities of the monarch by the second decade of the seventeenth century. That would have to change if the king were to devote much of his time to war and foreign policy. By 1621, Sweden enjoyed the advantages of having well-defined administrative districts, under the direction of provincial governors (*ståthållare*). The governors – and their provincial treasuries – were directly answerable to Stockholm, and the bailiffs were subordinated to the governors. By the mid-1620s, the bailiffs served much the same function as did the *intendants* in Richelieu's France, marshalling resources for war at the local level. It should be noted, however, that while this did constitute an unprecedented extension of royal authority into the far reaches of the Vasa state, it did nothing to suppress the strong democratic traditions of village government, common throughout Scandinavia.

All of these reforms looked very good on paper, and functioned well enough to allow Swedish armies to perform as brilliantly as they did during the Thirty Years' War. But that is not to say that they were without flaws. As always, the chief drawback with the expansion of the bureaucracy at all levels was the lack of funds and – given the nobility's resistance to foreign-born bureaucrats – the dearth of qualified office-holders. 'A few can be found in the service of the Church who are useful and competent, but in the civil administration there are simply no useful or educated persons,' Gustav Adolf complained in 1620; 'the greater part [of the magistracy and office-holders] are so ignorant that not even a [significant] portion of them can write their own names.' The king would find the lack of diplomats with even a rudimentary command of Latin, let alone of other modern languages and rhetorical skills, highly embarrassing, and to this end he launched into a thoroughgoing reform of Sweden's educational institutions. Starting in 1618, the king – certainly a man who appreciated higher learning – began to pump increasingly large sums from royal coffers into the university at Uppsala, expanding the size of the faculty and providing stipends for students from less privileged backgrounds. After 1623, the king also began to fund new secondary schools, the 'gymnasia,' to provide secular education for those interested in pursuing careers in state service. The results were not felt immediately within the administration, but it was at least a beginning, and one that would pay off in the decades after the king's death.[10]

The reign of Gustav Adolf differed from those of his predecessors in its constitutional character as well. After having lost so much influence under Johan III and Karl IX, the aristocratic Council had imposed its authority upon Gustav Adolf in the 1612 Charter. Yet Gustav Adolf's governance did not witness a complete reversal of the traditional Vasa style of kingship. Instead, both institutions would play a significant, possibly equal, role; both were also made more formal and rigid. In accordance with the demands it had made in 1611–12, the Council was now a body of purely native aristocrats from the leading families, but its greater prominence transformed it from serving as the guarantor of noble privilege to a governing body made up of the foremost servants of the state. In earlier decades, it had met irregularly and in different locations; the vast size of the Vasa state made regular meetings at a central locale all but impossible for landed magnates in the provinces. Twin developments in 1625–26 changed this forever. First, the king decreed that while he was absent from the kingdom, the entire Council – not just a few individuals – would serve as regency, and would be permanently constituted in Stockholm. Second, a royal ordinance on the 'house of the nobility' (*Riddarhusordningen*), approved by the *Riksdag* of 1626, formally divided the nobility into three subrankings; the foremost of these, the conciliar aristocracy, would no longer take part in the *Riksdag*. The lines between Diet and Council, once blurred, were now distinctly drawn, and the Council was a separate body closely identified with the 'establishment.' And since the king was so frequently absent between 1626 and 1632 – and permanently absent during the interregnum of 1632–44 – the members of the Council were now well-established components of a permanent central administration at Stockholm.[11] Considering the persecution and humiliations suffered by the Council during the previous reign, the relationship between king and Council was a remarkably cordial one, yet the king was still master. On the few occasions when Gustav Adolf lost his temper or his patience with them, the councillors invariably refrained from protest and instead sought to mollify their sovereign with abject apologies.[12] Gustav Adolf had transformed his power elite into an administrative class, distinct from the nobility at large, as surely as Louis XIV would dampen the contentiousness of his nobility with the construction of Versailles.

The *Riksdag* was slated for reform, too, though not in quite so drastic a fashion. The earlier Vasas, even Erik XIV, had depended on their charisma, oratorical skills, and common touch when dealing with the *Riksdag* to gain the popular support they had required for their policies. The *Riksdag* was still, at Gustav II Adolf's accession, a disorganized and poorly defined body, its meetings not regulated by any standardized procedural rules. The king changed this with a special ordinance in 1617, which officially set the number of estates at four (nobility, clergy, burghers, and peasantry), and provided a procedure for joint meetings of all orders with the king. This provided Gustav Adolf with the opportunity to use his charm and oratory to maximum advantage, something that would prove to be of significant value as the costs of war grew drastically during the course of the reign. By the 1620s, the king had also come to rely on the expedient of meeting with select groups from each order, and in 1627 the king began to make use of 'secret committees', composed of a handful of representatives from the three higher orders, for discussing foreign policy issues of an especially sensitive nature. The *Riksdag* was as important as ever, but under Gustav Adolf it was even more responsive to royal authority than it had been under the king's grandfather.[13]

A final component, often overlooked, in the new administrative scheme of Gustav Adolf's regime was the clergy. The Lutheran Reformation had given the Swedish monarchy – as it had other states that adopted the Lutheran faith – the manifold political advantages conferred by state control over the episcopacy and the lesser clergy. In Sweden, however, the relationship between king and clergy was particularly close because of the enhanced administrative role that fell upon the ordinary parish priests. The clergy, as the collectors of local demographic intelligence, were absolutely necessary for the success of Sweden's military efforts, since they maintained the parish registers, that allowed both taxation and especially conscription to be conducted in an orderly manner. In short, the local clergy acted as the 'draft boards' of their parishes, passing on to secular authorities vital information regarding all those who were eligible for military service. They performed another valuable role as well – that of the mouthpieces of royal policy. Gustav II Adolf was not the only, not even the first, Protestant sovereign to make use of his clergy in this fashion. He did, however, probably use this device to greatest effect. Royal directions to the episcopacy, and thence to individual priests, gave explicit instructions to present the king's foreign policy aims in a favorable light to ordinary parishioners. The constant repetition with which such messages appeared in annual 'prayer-days' qualify them as royal propaganda, designed to gain the acquiescence of those who would be paying most of the extraordinary taxes and supplying soldiers to Sweden's armies. In doing so, Gustav Adolf used the clergy, intentionally or not, to attain a broader end: to accustom the far-flung population of the state to the habit of obedience to the central authority. The relationship between monarchy and clergy, however, was not entirely one sided. The parish priests accepted their new political duties with reluctance, and their close ties with the local populations they served meant that they also represented the interests of the peasantry in dealings with the crown. In the levying of taxation and conscription the clergy acted more as mediators, brokering relations between crown and village, rather than mere instruments of the king's policies.[14]

Military Reform

Despite the importance of his political reforms at home, reforms that were essential to Swedish military success during and after the reign, Gustav II Adolf is known first and foremost as a soldier and military reformer. To be sure, Gustav Adolf was not the tactical and strategic 'superman' he is made out to be in popular military literature. As a strategist, he was no better than his contemporaries, and probably inferior to his greatest opponent, Wallenstein. In the conduct of his campaigns in Poland and Germany, the king did not transcend the logistical constraints that limited the scope of strategic maneuvre in pre-Frederician warfare; he was just as subject to these vicissitudes as his opponents were. The king was, however, a skilled tactician, an inspiring leader of men, and above all a brilliant organizer. He applied to his military and naval establishments the same brand of administrative commonsense that characterized his civil reforms. By the end of the reign, Sweden possessed a fleet that was on par with that of Denmark, and an army that equaled – in tactical skill and efficacy – the much larger armies of the great continental powers.

In the basic direction of his military reforms, Gustav Adolf did not differ substantially from his predecessors, especially Erik XIV and Karl IX. Like his father and uncle, Gustav Adolf sought to increase the numerical strength of the native army, render more efficient the process by which native troops were levied, and to provide those troops with a tactical model that emulated the prevailing tactical doctrines of the continental armies. The most important achievement of the reign, where it came to military institutions, was the creation of a truly national army in Sweden. This was something that the earlier Vasas had endeavored to do, but in a less permanent sense. There was little difference between the native conscript armies of Gustav Vasa and his immediate successors and the feudal levies of western Europe, except in frequency of use. Peasants called up for service, haphazardly and as needed, were by nature poorly trained and ill-disciplined, and they clearly demonstrated their inferiority during the Kalmar War. Gustav Adolf managed to bring about drastic changes in this regard with a new ordinance on conscription around 1620. According to this ordinance, all peasant men, from age fifteen and up, were to be registered for military service and grouped into local *rotar* of ten men each (twenty for peasants living on nobly owned lands), from which soldiers would be drafted as the need arose, one from each *rota*. At the provincial level, the governor and the regimental colonel would supervise the process as commissars. The selection itself, however, was entrusted to community 'draft boards', consisting of the local bailiff, six leading parishioners (*sexmännen*), and the parish priest. The conscripts would be organized into provincial regiments, units that were simultaneously tactical and administrative. The conscription system applied only to infantry, for Gustav Adolf was no more successful than his father had been at enforcing the noble obligation to provide heavy cavalry, the *rusttjänst*; cavalry was recruited, not conscripted. In wartime, the crown would pay and support the soldiers through royal revenues, but in peacetime individual soldiers would be quartered on local farms, with officers receiving their own farms in lieu of cash. Such a system had immense advantages over the hiring of mercenary troops. It did not require a significant outlay of cash, except perhaps in wartime, and that could be deferred or even covered by other means, as the campaigns in Germany would demonstrate. The organization of provincial regiments as tactical and administrative units took advantage of existing regional identities and loyalties, and gave to the individual units an important moral advantage that they would not have enjoyed if more haphazardly mustered. Perhaps most important, the soldiers raised by this system were both soldiers and subjects; their king was at once their commander and their sovereign. The peasants' collective identity as free subjects of the crown undoubtedly facilitated this process. The irritating and often disastrous negotiations over pay and arrearages that plagued the relationships between European governments and mercenary captains were thereby dispensed with. The native Swedish army was truly a royal army.[15]

Gustav Adolf's tactical reforms merit some mention. Like Erik XIV and Karl IX, Gustav Adolf based his new tactical 'system' on prevailing Western notions, but with greater success. These reforms have been written about extensively elsewhere, so there is no need to dissect them in detail here. In brief, the king built upon the Dutch tactical reforms instituted by Maurice of Nassau in the 1590s, which emphasized smaller tactical and administrative infantry units, a higher proportion of officers and non-commissioned officers (NCOs), 'thinner' formations in line of battle, and constant drill that effectively transformed soldiers from individual warriors into automatons. The Dutch reforms, according to many proponents of the 'military revolution' concept, had restored some flexibility to pike-and-musket tactics, balancing the shock value of massive pike formations with the increased firepower provided by better-trained and more widely deployed musketeers. Gustav Adolf, who undoubtedly had a keen mind for tactical details, carried the Dutch system to its logical conclusion, further elongating his infantry units, training his musketeers to fire more rapidly, and teaching his infantry – through constant exercise – to change formation or front with astounding alacrity. By introducing lightweight 'battalion pieces' the king made the flexible use of field artillery much more practicable, and by forcing his cavalry to rely upon the sword rather than the pistol in battle, the Swedish horse was transformed into an offensive arm of great effectiveness by Western standards. Intensive theoretical training coupled with experience earned in foreign wars – the wars in the Low Countries after 1572 served as a training ground for warlike Swedish noblemen as they did for young noblemen throughout Europe – helped to develop a thoroughly professional ethos and demeanor in the Swedish officer corps before 1630. The significance of the Gustavian reforms within the history of the art of war has been greatly exaggerated by the king's admirers and biographers, most notably Michael Roberts, but it is indisputable that Sweden's military forces by the late 1620s were far superior to those fielded by the earlier Vasa kings, and battalion-for-battalion were more effective than the armies of Sweden's contemporaries in the Thirty Years' War.[16]

The navy, too, was in for its share of reform, but in this area the changes were less obvious. In the main, they amounted to smoother and more efficient administration. The earlier Vasas, Karl IX in particular, had not neglected the fleet and in Karl's day the fleet had indeed nearly equalled in numbers and in weight of ordnance to that of Denmark. A good fleet, after all, was essential to Sweden's survival given its geopolitical position. Danish control of the Sound presented the Swedish admiralty with nearly insurmountable strategic problems, for the Sound effectively split the Swedish navy in twain. The fleet did not make a spectacular showing in the Kalmar War, and had indeed lost much of its strength when the Danes took Älvsborg in 1612. Reconstruction of the fleet commenced immediately after the Knäröd settlement the following year, despite the financial exigencies imposed by the Ransom. It was largely due to the administrative and fiscal competence shown by the Admiral of the Realm, Karl Karlsson Gyllenhielm, and especially by his assistant, Klas Fleming, that the Swedish fleet improved so dramatically in quality, discipline, and leadership. Although not yet capable of taking on the Danish fleet directly at the end of the reign, it was more than sufficient to protect the Swedish coastline, and to fulfill its most important role during the later 1620s and 1630s: to safeguard the passage of Swedish troops across the Baltic and to ensure the security of the logistical lifeline between northern Germany and the Swedish homeland. Without a strong fleet, the herculean task of transporting an entire army from Stockholm to Usedom, the act that began Sweden's intervention in the Thirty Years' War in 1630, would not have been possible.[17]

The reforms, by providing Sweden with military forces that were simultaneously professional, native, and easy to mobilize, paid immediate and handsome dividends. When Swedish and Danish councillors confronted one another in the tense showdown at Knäröd in 1624 (see Chapter 3), it was Sweden's ability to mobilize its forces at a moment's notice that made possible a diplomatic victory over wealthier Denmark. Sweden's military strength in 1630, however, should not be exaggerated. No matter how well organized and trained, Sweden's military manpower was not up to the task of conducting extensive operations overseas. Sweden and its dependent territories did not have the manpower to support a large army on prolonged campaigns outside the borders of the Vasa state. In 1630 the Swedish army was significantly watered-down with foreign – mostly German, Scots, and Irish – mercenaries as it prepared to move out of Pomerania and deep into the empire; within a few years, native Swedish troops formed no more than the elite core of Gustav Adolf's army. The existence of that core was vital to Swedish successes in the 1630s, but it should not be assumed that Sweden's campaigns in Germany were conducted solely by a purely native, loyal, and well-trained army that placed minimal financial demands on the state treasury.

In terms of domestic politics, however, the reform of the Swedish military pointed to a development that was indeed revolutionary: the creation of what has been termed a 'military state' in Sweden. Sweden's geopolitical vulnerability, as we have seen, made the constant conduct of war necessary, and the earlier Vasas were not unmindful of this unpleasant fact. The reign of Gustav II Adolf, however, witnessed the restructuring of Swedish society and the Swedish economy solely for the purpose of preparing for and making war. Perhaps Gustav Adolf did not have the coarser despotic tendencies of his father and grandfather, but under his direction the state attained a degree of control over the disparate elements of society that his predecessors could not. Yet Sweden was not thoroughly 'militarized'; the state and the military were not one and the same, and ultimate control over the institutions of the state was still firmly in civilian hands. Noble families did seek military commissions for their sons, but mainly in field command and in the cavalry regiments. Swedish noblemen, as a group, had no interest in captaincies in the infantry regiments.[18] Certainly the nobility was not dependent upon careers in the military. Sweden was, however, a state whose very existence seemed to be predicated upon warfare and towards mobilizing its meager resources towards that end. And, in turn, constant preparation for war gave the central government a degree of control over the most private details of its subjects' lives that far exceeded the abilities of its contemporaries in the older, more established powers of Europe. The ordinary subject of the Swedish crown, far more so than his French, English, or Spanish counterpart, would find it all but impossible to remain 'invisible' to the inscrutable eye of the state.

Chapter 3: Sweden on the World Stage: The Foreign Policy of Gustav II Adolf

Sweden had been an imperial power, intentionally or not, ever since it acquired Estonia during the reign of Johan III. It was the reign of Gustav II Adolf, however, that marked the point at which Swedish foreign policy actively sought the creation of a Baltic empire, and at which the Vasa state first demonstrated the capability to pursue such an aim with success. It was also the point at which Sweden became a great power in contemporary estimation. Prior to this, in the eyes of European statesmen, other states had held the honor of being perceived as the primary Baltic power: first Poland–Lithuania, then Denmark. By 1629, Denmark's star had fallen visibly; by 1632, Gustav Adolf would be hailed as the new champion of Protestant Europe; by 1644, there was no question that Sweden ruled the northeast. The groundwork for this latter development can be attributed directly to Gustav Adolf and Axel Oxenstierna.

Historians of seventeenth-century Europe, as we have seen, still debate the motivations behind Sweden's embarkation on the path towards territorial expansion around 1630. The history of the debate has itself become a subject of interest to Swedish historians.[1] In recent years, the debate has faded somewhat, at least within the Swedish historical community. Sven A. Nilsson, among others, has written that the question of *why* Sweden became an imperial power is impossible to resolve with any certainty, and like many of his colleagues decided to focus instead on the question of *how* Sweden evolved into a great power, or *by what means* it was able to do so. The latter is indeed an important question; it should, however, not become the focus of historical attention to the exclusion of the former. Analysis of motive in the study of foreign policy and warfare is a difficult thing, especially when dealing with a society whose hopes, aspirations, values, and fears are so remote to us today, but such methodological problems are not wholly insurmountable.

Foreign Policy Goals

The debate over the motivations behind Swedish foreign policy during the *stormaktstid* has generally focused on the events surrounding the most momentous act of Gustav Adolf's reign: the decision to intervene in the Thirty Years' War by invading the Germanies in 1630. It was, after all, a watershed in European diplomatic and military history, the point after which Sweden could no longer be casually dismissed as a secondary power. In terms of scope and daring, it was indeed a revolutionary departure in Swedish foreign policy, but it should not be regarded as exceptional. This act was entirely consonant with Sweden's geopolitical goals of the entire *stormaktstid*, and the arguments over Gustav Adolf's motivations in this case can be applied with equal validity to Swedish foreign policy during the age as a whole.

Gustav Adolf's admirers and apologists from an earlier age saw the king as a secular Protestant savior and even as a proponent of German princely liberties. Modern historians who have studied the problem generally fall into one of the three categories discussed in the first chapter. 'Old School' political historians – Ahnlund, Roberts, and Günter Barudio, for example – see in Swedish expansionism a means of ensuring the security of the 'encircled' Vasa state. The non-Marxist economic historians (like Heckscher and Attmann) view Sweden's imperialism as an attempt to gain foreign markets in the Baltic and expand its commercial empire. Finally, there are those scholars who view Swedish foreign policy in terms of class interests: either that Swedish expansionism was crafted to meet the economic desires of the aristocracy (Peters), or that preparing for and making war gave the ruling elite the excuse it needed to subject the lower orders to the central authority purely for its own political ends (Lindegren) – what Michael Roberts has called the exertion of 'control . . . for control's sake'. To scholars in the latter two groups, Gustav Adolf's public justifications of his involvement in the German War, which emphasized the necessity of defending Protestantism on the Continent before an aggressively

Catholic Habsburg imperium could sweep down upon Sweden itself, were mere rhetoric, 'propaganda' designed to win the acquiescence of the hard-pressed population of Sweden to continued taxation and conscription. Recently a fourth 'thesis' has emerged, argued quite eloquently by Erik Ringmar, a social scientist rather than a historian. Dismissing all of the previous interpretations, Ringmar has suggested that Sweden's newfound assertiveness in international politics came from the desire of the monarch and other ruling elites to prove Sweden's strength before the world, to forge a new identity as an independent, viable, and thoroughly Protestant great power. Sweden was a new state, and Gustav Adolf the son of a usurper; intervention in the Thirty Years' War was a way of making sure that Sweden was taken seriously as a major 'player' on the world 'stage'.[2]

Any interpretation of Swedish foreign policy during the reign of Gustav II Adolf, and indeed for the remainder of the century, must take all of these interpretations into account. While all of these arguments cannot be entirely reconciled, they are not mutually exclusive. Still, the bulk of the available evidence seems to give precedence to the 'encirclement' theory, at least for Gustav Adolf's reign. Perhaps Sweden was not in any real danger of invasion by Catholic hordes in 1630, and perhaps its main enemies (except Denmark) had all been neutralized or cowed by that time, but that is an observation that can only be made from the vantage point of retrospect. During the reign of Gustav Adolf, enemies – real or imagined – lurked everywhere, and this condition would not cease magically with the Westphalian settlement in 1648. It was a recipe for overextension and eventual disaster, for this species of diplomatic paranoia was almost impossible to placate. As the Russian Prince Gortchakoff remarked in 1864 about European imperialism, 'the greatest difficulty is to know when to stop'. Ringmar's 'identity' thesis actually works quite well with this interpretation, for the international reputation of the state was in itself a bulwark against foreign encroachment and a means of attracting allies. To argue that commercial motivations alone, or that the state's 'need' to exert control over the lower orders, gave Gustav Adolf and his successors the impetus for expansionism is, however, to put the cart before the horse. Such arguments ignore the ideological component of international politics in the post-Reformation age, and in particular the Swedish kings' very real and tangible fear that their kingdom was ripe for the plucking by hostile and more-powerful polities. War and territorial expansion drove the need for commercial gain and social control, and not the other way around.

The Eastern Threats: Russia and Poland

The potential threats facing Sweden in 1613 were the same that had troubled Gustav Adolf's father and uncles: Poland, Russia, and Denmark. Denmark was the greater and the nearer of the three. As long as Christian IV held Älvsborg for ransom, the Danish threat was never far away. Indeed, to Christian and to most outside observers, the chances that Sweden would be able to pay off the ransom appeared slim. Ultimately, through a combination of painful extraordinary taxes at home and generous loans from the Dutch, Sweden managed to ransom Älvsborg by the terminal date of January 1619, robbing Christian IV of the chance to seal Sweden off from the North Sea. Even in the intervening years between 1613 and 1619, however, the fear of a Danish conquest was temporarily pushed aside.[3] Far more immediate dangers loomed in the east.

Russia posed an indirect danger to Sweden. Deeply immersed in its own constitutional problems during the infamous 'time of troubles', the empire of the tsars was in no condition to mount any kind of attack against Swedish territory, but its very instability was fraught with peril for the Vasa state. Since the death of Tsar Boris Godunov in 1605, both Poland and Sweden had endeavored to place one of their own on the Muscovite throne: Sigismund hoped to secure the Russian crown for his son Władisław, and Karl IX sought to do the same for his second son Karl Filip. Sweden did not enjoy much success in this venture. Karl Filip's candidacy was not taken seriously in Moscow, and at any rate his chances of securing a Russian patrimony ended with the election of Michael Romanov in 1613. Even then, Russia remained divided and weak, but Gustav Adolf and Oxenstierna both felt that Russia's weakness made a strike against her imperative. The possibility that Sigismund might succeed in adding Russia to his realm could not be risked; a united Poland–Lithuania–Russia would have little difficulty in crushing Sweden. The king and his chancellor believed that Russia itself could not be trusted, and it would be far safer to deal with a weakened and divided Russia now than to face a unified and strong Russia later. Then, too, there were commercial benefits to be had in gaining some measure of control over the lucrative Russian trade. The security concerns were the most important considerations, however, and to this end Gustav Adolf attempted to obtain some territorial concessions from the Russians during peace negotiations at Viborg in 1613–14. Chief among the Swedish demands was the cession of Kexholm and Ingria, which would at least provide a buffer zone between Russia and Sweden's eastern provinces. The Russian negotiators rejected Sweden's immodest demands, and war ensued. Swedish forces gave a good account of themselves, and by the summer of 1614 much of Ingria was in Swedish hands, but beyond that the war was an indecisive stalemate. It dragged on long enough, however, to excite the worry of English and Dutch merchants, and between 1615 and 1617 English mediators helped to fashion a peace settlement between the two combatants. In the resulting Peace of Stolbova (1617), Gustav Adolf agreed to renounce his younger brother's claim to the Russian throne, but gained in return all of Ingria and Kexholm. Swedish possessions now ringed the Gulf of Finland; at one stroke, the Vasa territories in the eastern Baltic were secured from Russian incursions, and Russia was cut off from immediate access to the Baltic Sea.[4]

Peace with Russia gave Gustav Adolf the opportunity he needed to deal with Poland. The king did not linger to rest on his laurels, but immediately set to work to neutralize the Polish threat. Poland was more to be feared in 1617 than she had been in 1600, for the rivalry between the two Vasa kingdoms had taken on a frightening new dimension. Previously, the conflict between the two states revolved entirely around their competition over Livonia and the dynastic quarrel between Sigismund and his usurper uncle. By the mid-1610s, however, Poland once again became the center of Catholic intrigue in the North. Papal interest in the possibility of re-Catholicizing the Scandinavian kingdoms, dormant since Johan III's failed apostasy, returned with a vengeance after 1604. The Norwegian Jesuit Laurentius Nicolai, better known in Sweden as 'Klosterlasse', had been a regular fixture at Johan III's confessionally ambiguous court in the 1570s; in 1603, he returned to Scandinavia to help coordinate efforts to return all of the Scandinavian kingdoms to papal obedience. It is unclear to what extent, if any, confessional ambitions influenced Polish foreign policy, but in Copenhagen and Stockholm it was readily believed that Sigismund was driven by militant Catholicism. Rumors of a papal–Polish–Spanish invasion of both Sweden and Denmark circulated freely throughout the North in 1603–04. Such designs had little hope of succeeding, for the Catholic minorities in Sweden and Denmark were tiny and harmless, but they occasioned considerable fear in Stockholm and Copenhagen. Both Gustav Adolf and Christian IV were sufficiently concerned to issue severe anti-Catholic decrees. In a series of statutes promulgated at the Diet of Örebro in 1617, Gustav Adolf promised swift and brutal justice to Swedes who sought contact with Catholic Poland, attended Jesuit schools abroad, or converted to Catholicism.[5]

The Swedish–Polish conflict made the Catholic 'threat' to Sweden more palpable. Karl IX's actions in Livonia after 1600 had warmed the once-tepid support of the Polish nobility for Sigismund's dynastic claims; the militancy of the Counter Reformation Church fashioned these dynastic claims into something resembling a crusade for the faith. Although the conflict between Sweden and Poland had settled down into a nearly bloodless 'Cold War' by the time Gustav Adolf came to the throne, a confessional 'propaganda' war of sorts was just beginning to heat up. The willing participation of those Swedish nobles who had been exiled under Karl IX, not to mention the warm relationship between Vasa Poland and the Austrian Habsburgs, made this war all the more dangerous, at least from the perspective of Gustav Adolf and Oxenstierna. The Swedish crown let slip no opportunity to chip away at Polish strength. With local assistance provided by the nobility of Kurland, Swedish forces took the fortresses at Dünamünde and Pernau in 1617–18, and secured a new truce with Poland at Tolsburg in 1618. Sigismund, however, showed no sign of backing away from his claims to his father's throne or from his threatening posture towards his cousin; and when Poland became immersed in a war with the Turks, Gustav Adolf seized the opportunity to take yet another swing at the Poles. In the summer of 1621, Swedish forces laid siege to the Livonian city of Riga, forcing its capitulation. Riga, the wealthiest commercial *entrepôt* in the eastern Baltic, was now a Swedish possession, and would remain so until the collapse of the empire in 1721.[6]

The conflict with Poland illustrates two important points about Gustav Adolf's foreign policy in the 1620s. First, it is a clear vindication of those historians who see a 'quest for security' as the primary motive behind Swedish expansionism. Conquests like Pernau and Riga were indeed commercial assets to cash-poor Sweden, but to Gustav Adolf they were first and foremost bargaining chips, designed to entice Sigismund into granting a more or less permanent truce. Repeatedly, Swedish negotiators offered to return Pernau, Riga, and other Swedish territorial gains to Poland in return for Sigismund's guarantees that he would not venture to attack Sweden, but to no avail. Second, the war with Poland shows the extent to which confessional fear had entered into the king's diplomatic thinking. Although Sigismund's claims on the Swedish throne were disturbing enough, they were nothing new; but the success with which he refashioned those claims in confessional terms, possibly with Habsburg and papal support, added a frightening new element to Swedish fears of encirclement. Since that change coincided with the first really serious

outbreak of confessional and constitutional discontent within the Holy
Roman Empire, following the Defenestration of Prague in May 1618,
Gustav Adolf's manifest interest in the affairs of central and western
Europe was a foregone conclusion.

The Background to the German War

One of the most stubbornly persistent myths in seventeenth-century
historiography is that of the inevitability of Sweden's intervention in the
Thirty Years' War, and therefore of Sweden's rise as a power of the first
rank. This misinterpretation comes not only from the writings of Gustav
Adolf's admirers from the nineteenth century, but even from such careful historians as Michael Roberts. In Roberts' view, Sweden had proved
its worth and its power to Protestant Europe well before the taking of
Riga in 1621, and leading Protestant statesmen – in the Netherlands,
England, and the German states – gravitated towards an alliance with
Sweden early on, perceiving Gustav Adolf as a natural choice to serve as
a Protestant champion. Only the untimely interruption of Christian IV
of Denmark, jealous of Sweden's growing reputation and offering his
services at a hefty financial discount, held Gustav Adolf back from intervening in the German War. It would not be until Denmark had been
crushed by the weight of invading Imperial and Catholic League armies
that Gustav Adolf would manage to take up his predestined role as savior
of Protestantism and of the German 'liberties'. Unfortunately, such an
interpretation has little grounding in fact; it has become clouded by the
persistent 'cult of Gustavus' and, more precariously, the teleological
assumption that Sweden was destined to maintain a Baltic hegemony
over Poland and Denmark. This argument also does Sweden, her king,
and Chancellor Oxenstierna a regrettable historical injustice, for it trivi-
alizes the gape-mouthed surprise with which most European statesmen
greeted the initial successes of the Swedish invaders in 1631. Despite
Gustav Adolf's significant gains in the eastern Baltic in the 1610s and
1620s, few diplomats or sovereigns thought of Sweden as anything other
than a secondary power. In contemporary eyes, the honor of *dominium
maris Baltici* still belonged to Denmark, not Sweden; Christian IV ranked
far ahead of his Swedish rival in prestige, reputation, and perceived
might. With the benefit of hindsight, it is easy to see why Sweden would
succeed where Denmark had failed. But in the autumn of 1631, when
Gustav Adolf's army devastated a Habsburg-Catholic army at Breitenfeld,

it was the first sign that Sweden had eclipsed Denmark as the leading Protestant power on the Continent, a reversal that was totally unexpected rather than the predictable outcome of a development that was nearly a century in the making.

Gustav Adolf had perhaps focused his attentions on the pressing issues in the East, but he did not neglect Sweden's interests in the opposite direction. This was as unavoidable as it was natural. From the end of the Kalmar War, the newly independent United Provinces began to look to Sweden with cordiality and curiosity born of self-interest, both political and commercial. Sweden was an underdeveloped land, and the exploitation of its rich mineral resources owed much to Dutch entrepreneurs. Most important, Sweden could serve as a counter to Danish predominance in the Baltic. That predominance threatened the Dutch commercial lifeline through the Sound, as did Christian IV's attempts to control shipping on the Elbe and Weser estuaries. Denmark, in short, was untrustworthy and over-mighty. The States-General began to practice what would become the hallmark of their Baltic policy throughout the century: friendship with the lesser of the Baltic powers to curb the hegemony of the greater. In 1613, this meant backing Sweden, and in that year the States-General concluded defensive alliances with Sweden and several of the Hanseatic cities. Sweden needed the support of the Netherlands too. Despite desperate efforts to raise the funds for the ransom of Älvsborg, the Swedish government could not possibly produce enough tax revenues to pay off the huge sum on its own. Gustav Adolf turned to the Dutch for aid, and with Dutch loans amounting to some 250,000 *riksdaler* Älvsborg was ransomed at the expiry of the agreement with Denmark, in January 1619.[7]

Sweden's newfound friendship with the Dutch provided at least a measure of security against a Danish attack, but this relationship was not the reason for Gustav Adolf's growing interest in the Imperial crisis after 1618. That interest came from the confessional element that had entered into the cold war with Poland. It would be several years, however, before fear of Catholic Poland translated into a desire for involvement in the German conflict. Protestant activists within the Evangelical Union made an effort to open up channels of communication with Sweden during the 1610s; but their efforts were half-hearted, as were Gustav Adolf's responses to them. The rebellious Bohemian Estates also sought Swedish support after 1618; but then they had already solicited the backing of nearly every sovereign in Europe who might nurse a grudge against the Habsburgs, and their desperate pleas for help were no special mark of distinction. Gustav Adolf's marriage in 1620 to Maria Eleonora, sister of Elector Georg Wilhelm of Brandenburg, undoubtedly helped to turn the king's attentions towards the plight of the German Protestants. The marriage tied him to the Hohenzollerns, one of the most distinguished (if also indecisive) princely lineages in the empire, a house that was both fearful of Habsburg centralization and subject to Polish authority, through its possession of Ducal Prussia, a Polish fiefdom. The negotiations for the match also gave the young king the opportunity to make a tour of the Protestant courts of Germany, and therefore to familiarize himself with their fears, ambitions, and machinations.

As Protestant fortunes waned following the suppression of the Bohemian rebellion and the failure of anti-Habsburg forces in the empire during the early 1620s, international interest in acquiring Swedish support for the 'Protestant cause' grew accordingly. There were a few Protestant activists, notably the Palatine statesman Ludwig Camerarius, who openly distrusted Christian IV and looked to Gustav Adolf as the ideal leader for an international Protestant coalition, but in the main Sweden was perceived as being a useful secondary member of an alliance led by Denmark. The reasons for this preference for Denmark were manifold. Denmark was seen as the greater power, but there were other considerations as well. Christian IV had demonstrated a desire to stand up for the 'liberties' of the German princes since 1621; he was not distracted by other obligations, as Gustav Adolf was by Poland. To the German Protestants, even those who were jealous of Christian IV's successes in acquiring secularized German bishoprics as patrimonies for his younger sons, the Danish king had the advantage of being a *membrum imperii*, an Imperial prince by virtue of his possession of the duchy of Holstein-Segeberg. Christian was, in short, 'one of their own', who was just as concerned about the expansion of Habsburg power as they were; Gustav Adolf might have been connected by marriage to several German princely houses, but he was still an outsider.

Then there was the matter of political aims. Gustav Adolf perceived his quarrel with Poland to be part of the same problem that afflicted the Germanies – Habsburg centralization combined with Romanist aggression – and his proposals for allying himself with England, the Dutch, and the German Protestants envisioned a tremendous collective effort to attack the Emperor Ferdinand II and Poland simultaneously. It was a strategic plan that would require a vast outlay of men, ships, and funds. The price was too high for Sweden's potential allies in the West, but the plan was impractical on other accounts as well. Gustav Adolf demanded overarching control over the war effort, would only allow a minor role for Denmark, and was unwilling to work alongside Catholic France, which also hoped (or at least Cardinal Richelieu did) to play a part. Christian IV, on the other hand, was amenable to the aims of James I of England, which amounted to the restoration of the outlawed Elector Palatine, Frederick V, and of *status quo ante bellum*; he demanded a far smaller commitment in terms of men and money; and he raised no objections to either French or Swedish participation. Gustav Adolf's reluctance to work with Denmark is understandable. Christian IV had blustered and threatened Sweden since the taking of Riga in 1621, resulting in a diplomatic showdown between the two monarchs during a 'border-meeting' at Knäröd in the spring of 1624.[8] The event had been a diplomatic triumph for Sweden, since the Swedes were far better prepared for war than were the Danes, but it did nothing to ameliorate the long-standing tensions within Scandinavian politics. Subordination of a Swedish War effort to Danish direction was unthinkable; it would be a humiliating blow to national pride, and it ran the risk of making Sweden vulnerable to Danish aggression – a risk that neither Gustav Adolf nor Oxenstierna, who harbored a visceral hatred for the Danes, would contemplate. Christian IV took direction of German princely resistance to the emperor in the spring of 1625, beginning the so-called Lower Saxon War (1625–29). When the major Protestant powers met at The Hague late that autumn, Sweden's voice was not to be heard. Although Gustav Adolf did not 'hold aloof' from The Hague Conference as Michael Roberts has alleged, his emissary to the conference died *en route*.[9]

Since his strategic vision did not accord with that of the other Protestant leaders, Gustav Adolf had no choice but to turn to the more immediate threat that, he believed, emanated from Poland. Christian IV was, for the time being, busy in northern Germany; this would keep the Dane from making mischief in Sweden and hopefully keep the emperor and his adherents occupied as well, at least for a time. In the meantime, the Polish War recommenced with renewed vigor. Swedish forces took control of the remaining portions of Livonia, handing the Poles a stinging defeat at the battle of Wallhof (January 1626). That spring, the Swedes went even further, launching an invasion of Royal (West) Prussia. Despite some Swedish victories, the invasion was hardly an unqualified success; Gustav Adolf's forces were able neither to close off the Vistula to traffic nor even to force the city of Danzig into the Swedish orbit. By that time, however, events to the south and west had taken a sinister turn.[10]

The war in Lower Saxony was not going well for Christian IV. The Protestant army ran up against a much greater force than Christian had originally anticipated: not one army, but two – Count Tilly's army of the Catholic League and Albrecht von Wallenstein's Imperial force. The promises of Christian's allies had proven to be empty ones, and the Danish king had not even been able to obtain the support of his own nobility until it was too late. Deprived of significant foreign support and even his own kingdom's resources, Christian was outnumbered and out-classed. Defeat followed defeat, and by September 1627 Habsburg forces had pushed back the king's troops, invading and occupying the Jutland peninsula that autumn. As if this were not disturbing enough, the twin Habsburg courts at Vienna and Madrid were beginning to revive old ideas about the establishment of an Imperial fleet in the Baltic, which would not only tighten Habsburg dominion over the empire but also give Spain a means by which the Dutch could be subjugated. Denmark was cowed; and while Tilly occupied the Danish mainland Wallenstein expanded his control to the east, over Mecklenburg and the German Baltic ports. The so-called 'Baltic design' of the Habsburgs threatened Sweden and Denmark alike, and it added new urgency to Gustav Adolf's earlier plans of intervention. The apparent imminence of a Swedish War in Germany forced the king and his chancellor to take action at home. The situation in Baltic Germany was the main topic of discussion at meetings of the Council, the *Riksdag*, and secret committees in 1628–29. The king also took the opportunity to bring his grim message to the population at large through a well-organized propaganda campaign, conducted under the auspices of the clergy through special sermons and prayer-days. The popish threat was encroaching directly on Sweden, and Sweden could opt either to meet it on foreign ground or to await its brutal arrival on native soil, but there was no escaping it; 'either we wait in Kalmar or we meet them in Stralsund'. This careful cultivation of public opinion, far more effective than Christian IV's efforts to justify the war retroactively to his nation, was one of the distinguishing features of Sweden's involvement in the Thirty Years' War, and it paid hand-some dividends. The Swedish people, already heavily burdened by taxes and conscription, were at least prepared beforehand for the additional sacrifices their sovereign would demand of them. Unlike in Denmark, where the conciliar aristocracy never approved of their king's 'royal adventure' and the broader population was not called upon to support it until it was too late, in Sweden Gustav Adolf succeeded in gaining the acquiescence and even the hearty agreement of both. In January 1628, a secret committee of the *Riksdag* handed their king *carte blanche* to commence the war in Germany when and how he saw fit.[11]

Initially, since the war with Poland was far from being settled, Swedish involvement took the surprising form of cooperation with Denmark. Gustav Adolf and Christian IV signed a defensive pact in April 1628, and within weeks their troops jointly garrisoned the vital port of Stralsund against Wallenstein's forces, while Danish and Swedish naval forces collaborated in patrolling the Baltic. This collaboration helped Christian IV loosen the Habsburg grip on his territories, but it was short-lived. Christian was under too much pressure at home to end the war on whatever terms he could get. The spectre of Scandinavian solidarity was a frightening one in Vienna, and Christian used it to full advantage. By means of an anticlimactic personal meeting with Gustav Adolf at Ulvsbäck parsonage on the Scanian frontier – a meeting which Gustav Adolf hoped in vain would result in further cooperation – the Danish king played upon this fear, and managed to back out of the war with grace and with few losses in a peace treaty signed at Lübeck in June 1629.[12]

Denmark was out of the war for good, and while she emerged relatively unscathed this did little to comfort the proponents of the anti-Habsburg cause elsewhere. Through the generous terms granted at Lübeck, Wallenstein succeeded in isolating Denmark from Sweden, his chief concern in 1628 and early 1629. Now the members of the old Hague Coalition turned to Gustav Adolf in desperation; they had no choice if their cause were to survive. The king, however, was otherwise engaged. The war in Poland had settled into a bloody stalemate, and Sigismund stubbornly refused to cast away his claim to his Swedish inheritance. Fortunately for Gustav Adolf, the Poles never really cooperated with Wallenstein's Imperial army, and there was no dearth of statesmen seeking to resolve the war in Prussia. In France, Richelieu was anxious to bring about a Swedish intervention in the empire. It was a tremendous coup, therefore, when Richelieu's agent Hugh de Charnacé, aided by Gustav's brother-in-law the Elector of Brandenburg, helped to mediate the six-year Truce of Altmark between Sweden and Poland in September 1629. Gustav Adolf was now free to assert his nation's might.

The 'Lion of the North'

The outlook for Swedish success in Germany in that autumn of 1629 was not promising. Even after Altmark, when faced with the most momentous

decision of his life, Gustav Adolf vacillated, plagued by doubts both pragmatic and ethical. Was he about to embark Sweden on a path that would
lead to disastrous overextension of its abilities as a power? Such had happened to Christian IV, now humbled and greatly reduced in prestige.
And what, for that matter, was to prevent his Danish rival from seeking
compensatory glory through an attack on Sweden when all of Sweden's
resources would have to be dedicated to the war in Germany? Since
Gustav Adolf was not directly involved in the 'emperor's war', would
a Swedish intervention be just in the eyes of the world? Oxenstierna, the
Council, and the *Riksdag* continued to pledge their unconditional
support to their king, but the allies that Gustav Adolf expected to attract
were not so reassuring. Richelieu offered an alliance, but Gustav Adolf
was wary of becoming a French puppet, and it would be two years before
France would offer workable terms. England and the United Provinces
were now fully immersed in their own problems, and could not lend
significant aid to Sweden. Worse still, the German princes themselves
were either indifferent or hostile. Public opinion in Protestant Germany
was very much in favor of Gustav Adolf's leadership, already forming
the cult following that greeted the Swedish king as the prophesied 'Lion
of the North' who would save the true faith from the iniquity of Rome,
but this counted for little in military terms. Some of the lesser but more
radical German princes, like the Sachsen-Weimar brothers, pledged
what little strength they could muster to the Swede, but the princes of
middling or greater influence were not so warm. The most prominent of
them, Elector Johann Georg of Saxony, had demonstrated little more
than nervous apathy towards Christian IV. To the elector, Gustav Adolf
was much worse than Christian. The Danish king was at least a fellow
Imperial prince, but Gustav Adolf was a foreigner, and the elector
hinted broadly that it might be his duty to resist any foreign encroach-
ments on his beloved fatherland. Sweden was to enter the war without
a single ally.[13]

The opening stages of the Swedish intervention were at once dramatic,
awe-inspiring, and anticlimactic. The expeditionary force, some 14,000
men accompanied by a large battle fleet, departed Stockholm in mid-
June 1630, arriving on the Pomeranian coast at Peenemünde six weeks
later. It was a remarkable logistical achievement, one which demonstrated
graphically the value of Klas Fleming's naval reforms. But it did not
occasion any great, immediate changes in German politics, nor did it
attract much attention from anyone except the king's most dedicated adherents in the empire. Ferdinand II, whose attentions were

drawn for the moment to northern Italy and the succession dispute in Mantua, harbored utter contempt for this barbarous 'snow king' and his pitiful army.

Sweden had entered the war at a strange point in its development. The political situation in the Germanies had been very clear-cut when Christian IV had intervened in 1625: emperor and Catholic League stood together against the ragtag assortment of minor German princes and Protestant mercenaries who demanded the restoration of the outlawed Elector Palatine; Philip IV of Spain rendered some aid to the emperor while fighting his own war in the Netherlands; France, dealing with its own Huguenot problem and with an as yet unsteady Richelieu at the helm, remained aloof from the conflict. The Danish intervention might have kept the anti-Habsburg cause alive, but in 1629–30 the war settled into an uncertain quiet, a quiet that disguised an explosive political situation. The year 1629 had marked the triumph of Habsburg forces everywhere, allowing Ferdinand to issue his infamous Edict of Restitution, by the terms of which all Catholic ecclesiastical properties illegally 'secularized' since 1555 were to be returned to the Church. The Edict was the high point of Ferdinand II's success in the war, but pressure from the loyal princes, both Catholic and Protestant, forced the emperor to dismiss his brilliant if erratic general Wallenstein. Richelieu schemed to weaken Habsburg power by separating Bavaria, the heart and soul of the Catholic League, from the emperor. The bulk of the Protestant princes hoped to use the opportunity to curb the ambitions of their sovereign in Vienna, not by uniting behind Gustav Adolf but by standing on their own as a 'constitutionalist' bloc. With Sweden and France menacing the borders of the empire, these princes reasoned, Ferdinand could be taken down a notch, and the princes could breathe easier about the safety of their liberties. This was something that activist Protestant princes in the empire had sought to do since the 1570s. These princes made a promising beginning when they met at Leipzig early in 1631, but this accomplished nothing, since they would neither stand on their own to fight the emperor, nor would they offer anything to the Swedish king.[14]

For the better part of a year following the landing at Peenemünde, Gustav Adolf had neither plans nor allies, save Pomerania and the city of Magdeburg. Neither of these allies was especially helpful, though Pomerania at least allowed the Swedes to maintain a vital base of operations on the Baltic coast. Even those who favored Gustav Adolf, like Wilhelm V of Hesse-Kassel, hesitated to make themselves clients of a Swedish warlord. Only Richelieu, who hoped to use Sweden as a tool of French policy as he used Bavaria, offered any real support; in the Bärwalde treaty (January 1631), Richelieu's envoys promised a hefty annual subsidy (400,000 *riksdaler*) in return for Gustav Adolf's pledge to maintain an army of 36,000 men in the field. It was the beginning of a long, profitable, and ultimately troublesome partnership between the two states, but in strategic terms it meant very little at the time it was signed. It did not make up for the lack of clear-cut political objectives in Germany, and it did not rally the German Protestants to Sweden.

The event that forced Gustav Adolf to act was the assumption of Imperial field command by Count Tilly, the former commander of the Catholic League forces. Tilly, a thoroughly competent general, aimed to keep the Swedes bottled up in Pomerania, to punish those who sided with Sweden, and to enforce the Restitution edict. Early in 1631 his forces laid siege to the city of Magdeburg, a Protestant town that had allied itself with the Swedes. This was a test of Gustav Adolf's resolve to stand by his allies, but the king's failure to compel either Brandenburg or Saxony to conclude alliances with him tied his hands. Magdeburg fell to Tilly early in May 1631. Its notorious sacking by Tilly's troops made it an effective warning against those who would defy the emperor, and it did no good for Swedish prestige. To expiate himself for the disaster at Magdeburg, Gustav Adolf moved his army deeper into the empire, hoping that military victory might bring the diplomatic success he needed to achieve anything within the Germanies. His brother-in-law, Georg Wilhelm of Brandenburg, meekly allowed Swedish troops to be quartered in his territories as he had previously done for Danish and Imperial troops in earlier campaigns. As Tilly moved to the southwestern reaches of the empire to punish militant Protestant princes there, Gustav Adolf took advantage of Tilly's absence and left Brandenburg behind. By early July 1631 he had crossed the Elbe at Tangermünde. Tilly turned northwards to pounce on Gustav Adolf, but at Werben Tilly's army proved unable to either dislodge the Swedes or even inflict significant casualties. As the army gained momentum, so too did the king's political reputation. He managed to restore the dukes of Mecklenburg, deposed in 1628 by the emperor, to their lands and titles. The Danish king had not been able to save the dukes, but the Swedish king did, and that in itself was a symbolic triumph. Lesser Protestant princes began to flock to the Swedes. Fortunately for the king, Ferdinand II now made a grievous diplomatic error: he allowed Tilly to menace the borders of electoral Saxony, forcing Johann Georg into a weak but temporarily effective alliance with Sweden in order to survive. Enjoying numerical superiority for the first time since his landing at Peenemünde, Gustav Adolf allowed himself to be drawn into open battle with Tilly. On the field at Breitenfeld on 7 September 1631, a united Swedish-Saxon army of 42,000 men faced Tilly's veteran force of some 33,000. Tilly was a skilled general, and his troops did indeed succeed in driving the Saxon auxiliaries from the field. But the Swedish core of the army, 24,000 strong, held and destroyed Tilly's army in a brilliantly conceived counterattack. It was, for military historians at least, a graphic confirmation of the superiority of the Swedish tactical 'system'; most important, it was a tremendous blow to Habsburg morale and a great moral victory for the Swedish king. It served to convince Protestant Germany that he was indeed the 'Lion of the North' whose coming signalled the beginning of a new age.[15]

An Uncertain Goal

The unexpected victory at Breitenfeld filled the king with confidence just as it had filled the emperor with justifiable fear. Gustav Adolf decided not to pursue the remnants of Tilly's army and instead to move to the south and west, towards the Rhine and Main river valleys. This decision gave Tilly the opportunity to raise a new and larger army, but advancing south gave Gustav Adolf a real advantage. Central and southwestern Germany, all but untouched by the war, were also unguarded. Tilly, on the other hand, had retreated into the Lower Saxon and Westphalian Circles to the northwest, an area already ravaged by the passage of armies and therefore unable to supply reinforcements or sustenance. The Swedes had long since broken their logistical ties with their Pomeranian bridgehead, and were now supplying themselves through systematized plunder, a practice that has become euphemized as the 'contribution system'. Gustav Adolf's strategy, then, was driven more by logistical considerations than by any specific political goal after Breitenfeld.

And after Breitenfeld the reinvigorated Swedish army made spectacular gains. The army kept advancing, and there seemed to be no good reason to stop. In early October, Würzburg fell; in November, Frankfurt; the following month, both Worms and Mainz capitulated. By the end of 1631, Swedish forces garrisoned strategic strongpoints throughout half of the empire. As the army settled down in winter quarters, and Gustav Adolf set up his headquarters in Mainz, the king was at the apogee of his military and political career. He had come this far in eighteen months, and he had done it alone, without substantial help from any of his reluctant allies. Having done so, the imperious way in which he now treated the German princes and the emissaries of his newfound friends can perhaps be forgiven. The suddenness of the Swedish triumph had taken everyone by surprise. The king's political aims at this point were not clear to anyone, perhaps not even to the king himself, but Gustav Adolf certainly did not share the goals of the other would-be belligerents. Gustav Adolf did not have any patience for the arguments of the 'constitutional party', nor did he share their respect for the sanctity of the princely liberties. The king had no desire to limit himself to the avowed English goal of restoring the exiled Elector Palatine. The idea of a negotiated peace appealed neither to the king nor to Oxenstierna. Once again, the issue of security was the overriding concern, even if only vaguely formulated. As Oxenstierna expressed it, what the Swedes wanted was peace 'with our foot on their neck and a knife at their throat'.[16] It was an understandable sentiment, and one that was consistent with Vasa foreign policy up to this point, but it hardly translated into cogent or realistic policy.

Yet what Gustav Adolf had created was no less than a Swedish empire in Germany, whether or not he liked or intended it. And in order to maintain his garrisons and his troops in the field, and to coordinate the complicated network of 'contributions' from the German princes, he would have to establish a civil government of sorts. To this end he enlisted the aid of Axel Oxenstierna. Swedish governance in the conquered regions of Germany would function relatively well over the next sixteen years, but it was not a harmonious relationship. German princes who greeted the success of Swedish arms as liberation from the ambitions of an over-mighty emperor in Vienna were not happy to exchange a distant overlord for a more powerful and demanding Swedish one. In the north, the princes of the Lower Saxon Circle saw no advantage in being transferred from Danish domination to Swedish.

Sweden's unimaginably rapid success in Germany in 1631 meant entirely new relationships with its non-German allies too. This utterly transformed the nature of the alliance with France. Richelieu had hoped to use Sweden as a tool in French foreign policy, but Gustav Adolf would not play along with the subtleties of Richelieu's plans. In particular, Gustav Adolf refused to respect the neutrality of Maximilian of Bavaria, whose intentions he rightly regarded with suspicion and hostility. Nor did the king trust his primary German ally, Saxony, now that the danger of immediate retribution from the emperor was past. Elector Johann Georg continued to hope for an empire free of foreign influences and armies, and his own field commander Arnim would not subordinate himself to Swedish command.

The only way that Gustav Adolf could accomplish his vaguely defined goal of Swedish security in the empire was to destroy the forces of the emperor and his allies. This is precisely what he sought to do as he and his chancellor made their plans for the campaign of 1632. The king now had command of nearly 100,000 troops, organized into half a dozen separate field armies. Hoping that he could double that amount through recruitment, Gustav Adolf set about a strategic plan of startling audacity: to sweep through Bavaria, destroying Tilly's army in the process and removing Duke Maximilian from the war for good, then on past Vienna, and into the Habsburg hereditary lands. It was a wonderful plan, but in the final analysis proved impracticable. Breaking camp in March 1632, Swedish forces brutally ravaged Bavaria and accomplished a brilliant crossing of the river Lech in the face of Tilly's army. Though Tilly died from wounds shortly thereafter, his army remained intact at Ingolstadt. In the meantime, Ferdinand II had recalled Wallenstein into Imperial service, and the enigmatic *generalissimo* had spent the winter building up a new army in Bohemia. When Wallenstein broke loose and forced Arnim's Saxon army to flee Bohemia, Gustav Adolf was forced to deal with him in order to keep Saxony in the war. Attacking Wallenstein's prepared position at the Alte Veste, outside Nürnberg, in August, the Swedish troops met their first real defeat. As the army's supplies ran low and Gustav Adolf's troops faced the prospect of starvation, the king retreated towards Swabia and Bavaria. Wallenstein, now cooperating with yet another Imperial army under Pappenheim, continued to menace Saxony, and the Swedes moved northwards to counter this. The two commanders – Gustav Adolf and Wallenstein – blundered into one another near Naumburg early in November 1632, and battle ensued near the village of Lützen on the 6th. Lützen was a bloody but decisive Swedish victory, but one that came at a high price; for numbered among the Swedish dead was the lifeless, half-naked body of Gustav Adolf himself.[17]

Chapter 4: The Interregnum and Queen Christina, 1632–54

The death of Gustav Adolf at Lützen dealt a tremendous blow to the Swedish War effort in Germany. The king's death could not be said to have happened at his moment of triumph, for it came as his strategic plan for 1632 was clearly falling apart. Tilly was dead, Bavaria lay in ruins, and Saxony was safeguarded for the time being; but the enemy forces, in Bavaria and Saxony, were hardly destroyed. It was the king's ignominious end itself, however, that most hurt the Swedes and their allies. After Breitenfeld, Gustav Adolf had become the very personification of the Protestant and anti-Habsburg cause, and his death robbed that cause of its most celebrated champion to date. Conversely, Sweden's enemies had good reason to celebrate the king's passing, even if it came at the cost of a battle. Ferdinand II and his allies took heart at the news; and though Christian IV of Denmark may have lamented the passing of his old rival, it gave him the opportunity he craved to recreate a Danish imperium in the Lower Saxon Circle of the empire. Fortunately, Gustav Adolf had trained highly skilled subordinates, both civil and military, who would manage to keep the faltering military effort from falling apart over the next four critical years.

The political situation at home was equally precarious. Gustav II Adolf may have been a skilled administrator and a brilliant general, but he was a near failure in attending to his dynastic duties. His marriage to Maria Eleonora of Brandenburg had not only failed to deliver a meaningful alliance with the elector of Brandenburg, it was also domestically unproductive. The queen was neither highly intelligent nor stable. Gustav Adolf – and his foremost advisers – openly regarded her as shallow and silly. The king had not entrusted her with any political duties while he was alive, and her collapse into hysterical, paralyzing grief after the news of Lützen showed her to have no capacity for service as a regent. Worse still, the Brandenburg marriage had produced only one heir: Princess Christina, only 6 years old at the time of Lützen. Sweden was now deeply immersed in its most trying political commitment abroad, bereft of experienced royal leadership and in the hands of a mere toddler who would not be able to assume the duties of sovereign for another twelve years.

Although foreign observers might have seen Gustav Adolf and Sweden as synonymous, in reality this was not so. Sweden was reasonably well equipped to weather the crisis. In part this was due to a healthy dose of good luck, but in the main the credit for Sweden's continued success and stability over the next decade can be attributed to Axel Oxenstierna. Certainly Oxenstierna did not work alone. He owed much to the proven talents of generals like Horn, Torstensson, Banér, and Wrangel, men whose aptitude for war testifies to the efficacy of the Swedish 'system'. Nonetheless, the chancellor dominated the making of foreign and domestic policy. Though not a military leader, Oxenstierna had been the king's partner over the twenty years of the reign; in Germany, he had almost single-handedly coordinated Swedish civil administration and the logistical underpinnings of the war effort. He had been involved in strategic planning at the highest levels, and was dedicated in principle to victory on the Continent. As long as the Swedes had skilled generals, Oxenstierna's leadership and dedication would prevent the German adventure from complete dissolution.

Domestic Politics: The Regency and the 'Form of Government'

As Gustav Adolf's body began its long journey from the field at Lützen to lie in state in Stockholm, the Swedish central administration scrambled to assert its authority and to resume at least a measure of the regularity and steadiness with which it had conducted its business during the king's lifetime. It was primed for such an emergency, for Gustav Adolf's administrative reforms had been predicated upon the assumption that the king would be personally absent for much of his time in office, as in fact he was. The central government was therefore reasonably well prepared for the shock of being plunged unexpectedly into an interregnum.

The composition of Sweden's regency government of 1632–44 was perhaps unusual by European standards. Members of the royal family, no matter how high in rank, were accorded no place amongst the Regents. This had been the king's doing, not the aristocracy's; before his death, Gustav Adolf had excluded both his wife and his brother-in-law, Johann Casimir of Pfalz-Zweibrücken, from participation. Maria Eleonora would play almost no role at all even in the upbringing of the young Queen Christina. The central direction of the state was instead entrusted to Chancellor Oxenstierna and several members of the Council of State. Oxenstierna would serve as the head of the Regency, and though his close relationship to the late king made him the obvious leader, the role would tax his abilities and patience to the uttermost. The chancellor was already overburdened by his logistical and diplomatic responsibilities in Germany, which kept him away from home until 1636. The Regency and the Council continued to look to him for leadership, frequently asking his advice on the most trivial of domestic issues while he struggled to keep Sweden's armies fed and Sweden's allies in line. Oxenstierna, as Michael Roberts pointed out, had to be both Oxenstierna and Gustav Adolf simultaneously, reflecting the trust that most Swedish aristocrats had in the man. Still, factionalism within the conciliar aristocracy – kept muted while the king had been alive – began to show itself by the mid-1630s. By 1635, it had become apparent that the opportunities for quick success in Germany were now gone, and the aristocracy as a whole grew tired of the costly involvement in the German War. Oxenstierna's own irascibility, which grew sharper with age, did not ease his relationships with his fellow councillors. His circle of enemies in the administration grew larger, to include not only his old rival Johan Skytte but also some of the other leading figures in the Regency: Karl Karlsson Gyllenhielm, Per Banér, and even Oxenstierna's protégé, the diplomat Johan Adler Salvius. The group schemed sporadically for Oxenstierna's removal, but without success. Oxenstierna still had friends and – even more import-ant – family in Stockholm: his brother, Gabriel Gustafsson Oxenstierna, plus his cousins Gabriel Bengtsson and Bengt, were all members of the Council; Axel's sons Johan and Erik, as well as Gabriel Bengtsson's son Bengt, served as key diplomatic personnel on the Continent throughout the 1630s and 1640s. None of them approached Axel in administrative abilities, but all were competent and loyal.[1]

Oxenstierna's energies focused primarily upon the war effort in Germany, but the single greatest domestic achievement of the Regency must also be attributed to him: the so-called 'Form of Government' of 1634. The administrative reconfiguration of 1634 was by no means a sudden or unprecedented event; it represented instead the culmination of

twenty years of bureaucratic reform, and a goal towards which Gustav
Adolf had been striving in the years before the German War diverted his
attentions elsewhere. The Form of Government created a central administration consisting of several semi-autonomous 'colleges', divided by
'fields of responsibility and competence'.[2] The first colleges had already
been established before the end of the 1620s: the High Court in 1614–15,
the Treasury in 1618, and the Chancery in 1626. The High Court at
Stockholm had been expanded somewhat with the addition of three
regional appeal courts, at Åbo (1623), Dorpat (1630), and the *Göta hovrätt*
at Jönköping (1634). To these colleges, the Form of Government added
two others: the War College (*Krigskollegiet*) and the Admiralty (*Amiralitetet*).
And yet two more were added after 1634, the Mining College (*Bergskollegiet*,
1637) and the College of Commerce (*Kommerskollegiet*, 1651). Presiding
over each college would be one of the highest officers of state: the Marshal
of the Realm for the War College, the Treasurer of the Realm for the
Treasury, and so forth. The Steward of the Realm (*Riksdrotsen*) would
serve as president of *Svea hovrätt*, while each of the appeal courts would
have a member of the Council of State serving as president. Below each
president a group of 'assessors' and scribes carried out the day-to-day
functions of each college, men with experience germane to the competence of the college. In the War College, for example, the assessors
would include two Councillors, preferably with military experience,
four military officers, one field marshal of native birth, the Commissary
General, and the Inspector General.

The 1634 Form of Government was revolutionary in at least four
regards. First, it marked the beginnings of a truly professional administration. Prior to the 1634 Form, as in the central administrations of most
European monarchies, possession of office did not presume any particular
training, knowledge, or abilities; it was a civic duty to which the nobility
as a caste was bound. Although several offices encompassed by the Form
of Government were reserved for men of noble birth, and the preference
was clearly for native-born nobles, the emphasis of the new administration
was on competence, not birth. Moreover, as many of the positions within
the colleges were to be funded by certain earmarked revenues, the college
system gave rise to something resembling a salaried bureaucracy.
Second, the new administration was to be seated firmly and permanently
in Stockholm. Officials within the collegiate system could not be absent
without express permission. The Form of Government fixed meeting
times, locales, and even procedures, lending the new bureaucracy an aura
of permanence and efficiency that was rare in other European states.

Third, the Form sharply delineated the areas of competence of each college and each official therein. The Form assigned specific powers of authority to the office, not to the man; 'when members of the colleges left Stockholm to go elsewhere, their authority ceased'.[3] Fourth, the central administration would be linked smoothly to local governments, by means of extensive and exhaustive instructions given to each of the provincial governors (formerly *ståthållare*, now called *landshövdingar*).

There were limitations to the Form of Government, in practice and in theory. The tacit exclusion of non-nobles from the administration conflicted with its emphasis on expertise. As Leon Jespersen has observed, 'this combination of qualifications with the principle of noble descent contained a latent contradiction of which the other estates were fully aware'.[4] The actions of the Regency and of the Council, simultaneously scheming against Axel Oxenstierna and relying excessively upon his advice in trivial matters, went against the whole *raison d'être* of the collegial system and reduced its effectiveness. Despite the dictates of the Form, high officials were frequently absent without excuse.[5] It was nevertheless a remarkable system. For evidence of its efficacy, one need only look at Sweden's successful prosecution of the war in Germany during the Regency years for proof. It provided the Swedish government with a core of stability that only improved with time and experience. The collegial system, as is well known, would later serve as a model for Tsar Peter the Great's administrative reforms in eighteenth-century Russia, and was also considered briefly in Denmark in the late 1650s.[6] And in terms of Swedish state and society, it utterly transfigured the nature of the nobility. The presence of aristocratic councillors in the new system seamlessly tied together administrative and constitutional structures within the Swedish polity. Moreover, it transformed the native nobility from a class of provincial landowners, to whom administrative 'careers' were both secondary and part-time, into a class of professional and salaried civil servants, whose primary duties centered around their bureaucratic tasks in Stockholm.

Changing Goals in Germany

The labors of the indefatigable Oxenstierna and the administrative revolution of 1634 gave Sweden the capacity to hold her own in Germany over the next decade and a half, but they did not assure the attainment of the ambitious goals of Gustav Adolf. This was not entirely due to the death of the king, for Sweden's allies on the Continent were proving themselves troublesome well before Lützen. The friendship of Johann Georg of Saxony was unreliable at best; Georg Wilhelm of Brandenburg nervously held aloof from a commitment to Sweden; many of the lesser-to-middling German princes aided Sweden more out of fear than anything else. And Sweden could not maintain its commitment to the war indefinitely. Even with the assistance of several German states, and even following Gustav Adolf's dictum of 'war feeding itself', the costs of the German War to the Swedish economy had been staggering: around 20–30 million *riksdaler*, when the state's annual revenues in ordinary and extraordinary taxes and tolls came to a mere 3 million.[7] Foreign subsidies were not to be counted on; payments from the Netherlands were infrequent, and the French subsidies were due to expire in 1636. The means of paying for the war would have to be sought in other sources if the Swedes were to maintain their military presence on the Continent.[8]

The three years following Lützen witnessed a reversal of Swedish fortunes in the German War and elsewhere. Oxenstierna distrusted the French, and did his best to avoid partnership with Richelieu so that Swedish forces could enjoy a free hand in Germany. At first the prospects for this seemed promising. The Heilbronn League, constituted in April 1633 under Oxenstierna's direction, united Protestant German princes from three circles of the empire, pledging their military support until the German liberties were again secure; but that league, bereft of Saxon or Brandenburg participation, would not last long. Sweden's military forces soon lost their reputation for invincibility. At Steinau in Saxony, late in 1633, Wallenstein captured an entire Swedish army. The Bohemian *generalissimo* would be gone after February 1634, abandoned by Ferdinand II and assassinated by Imperial order, but the Habsburgs were still strong enough to take on the Swedes. The united armies of Ferdinand, king of Hungary (the son and heir apparent of the emperor) and the *Cardinal-Infante* Ferdinand of Spain delivered a fatal and humiliating blow to the Swedish forces under Gustav Horn and Bernard of Sachsen-Weimar at Nördlingen in September 1634. With Habsburg power in the ascendant, the Heilbronn League fell apart, and Sweden's allies deserted her wholesale. By the end of the year, Johann Georg of Saxony was negotiating a peace with the emperor at Pirna, and in May 1635 the two parties signed the Peace of Prague. The Peace turned Saxony and Brandenburg into open enemies of Sweden; most of the German Protestants followed suit immediately thereafter. The diehard supporters of

Sweden, like the Hessian landgraves, found themselves harshly punished for their disloyalty to the emperor. Sweden was assured of at least some financial support through the renewal of its subsidy agreement with France, and the formal French entry into the war in the spring of 1635 gave the Swedes some respite. But Sweden's waning military and diplomatic fortunes compelled Oxenstierna to give up the territorial conquests in Alsace and the Rhineland to French garrisons, a significant loss of the gains made in the halcyon days of 1631–32. Even with French assistance, Oxenstierna found himself hard-pressed to pay off the troops in Swedish service, whose pay was already months in arrears, and the discontented Swedish garrison at Magdeburg mutinied in August 1635 as a result.[9]

Sweden faced significant threats on the periphery of the German conflict as well. Indeed, to Oxenstierna, the possibility of attack from either Poland or Denmark was more to be feared than any disaster within Germany. The six-year Truce of Altmark with Poland was due to expire in 1635. For a time, Polish attentions were diverted elsewhere: Sigismund Vasa died in early 1632, to be succeeded by his son as King Władisław IV (1632–48); and shortly thereafter Poland was at war with both Russia (the so-called War of Smolensk) and the Turks. But both conflicts were resolved by 1634, and Swedish security in the northeast would depend upon the renewal of the cease-fire with Poland. With the aid of French mediation, this was in fact achieved. The Peace of Stuhmsdorf (1635) brought twenty years of peace between Sweden and Poland, but at a high price: the Swedish negotiators handed back to Poland all of Gustav Adolf's conquests in Prussia. They also recanted the right to levy tolls on shipping to and from the Prussian ports, a major source of funding for the Swedish war machine. These actions were probably necessary to avoid war with Poland, but they infuriated Oxenstierna. Sweden's vulnerability in Germany forced it to make concessions to her other 'unsleeping enemy' in the Baltic, Denmark. Taking advantage of the reversal of Sweden's fortunes in the empire, Christian IV managed to extract from Oxenstierna the recognition of his son Frederik as administrator of Bremen and Verden in 1634.[10] This reassertion of Danish influence in the Lower Saxon Circle was also a great diplomatic loss to Sweden. Worse still, the Danish king drew closer to the pro-Imperial, anti-foreign party within the empire. Relations between Denmark and Ferdinand II appeared to be warming, and in 1634 the Danish heir apparent married a daughter of Johann Georg of Saxony.[11]

Under such circumstances, it was hardly surprising that Sweden's war aims in Germany should be modified. Oxenstierna entertained no illusions about this. But something had to be gained from the incredible costs of the past two years of campaigning. Oxenstierna wanted a dignified withdrawal from the German morass, but with two goals in mind: *satisfactio*, or territorial recompense for Sweden's efforts on behalf of the Protestant and princely cause, preferably in the form of large cessions of land in northern Germany; and *assecuratio*, some kind of guarantee that Sweden would be protected from the Habsburg threat that had loomed in the Baltic. The two goals went hand in hand, for the best assurance of Swedish security would be the acquisition of a buffer zone in Baltic Germany. They would be necessary for less tangible reasons as well. Withdrawal from the German War without something to show for the effort would be a tremendous blow to Sweden's newfound reputation as a great European power, and could well trigger an unpleasant reaction from the heavily burdened Swedish population. Even these limited aims seemed unattainable in 1633–36. Swedish hopes for *satisfactio et assecuratio* were pinned above all on ownership of Pomerania, under Swedish occupation but claimed – legitimately – by the elector of Brandenburg, and this put Sweden squarely at odds with Brandenburg even before the the signing of the Prague agreement. The often contradictory directives of the Regency in Stockholm, which simultaneously demanded a rapid withdrawal from Germany and some territorial recompense, did not help the beleaguered chancellor. In June 1636, the Regency recalled Oxenstierna from Germany.

The war would not turn out quite so grimly as Oxenstierna had anticipated. The recovery of Swedish arms would require, however, something that Oxenstierna had tried hard to avoid: partnership with France. A Swedish victory at the battle of Wittstock in Brandenburg (October 1636) and an initially successful advance into Bohemia early the following year breathed new life into the Swedish War effort, and gave some hope that an alliance with France might not be necessary. Further military reversals later in 1637, as Swedish forces retreated back to Pomerania to fight a purely defensive campaign, soon demonstrated that Sweden still needed French gold to fight its battles. Following agreements made with Richelieu's emissaries at Wismar (1636) and Hamburg (1638), the Swedish armies in Germany made a remarkable recovery, pushing deep into Silesia in 1638. A new spate of mutinies amongst the infrequently paid Swedish troops, following the death of General Johan Banér in 1641, revealed once again Sweden's fiscal inability to wage war on its own. The predictable result was the Treaty of Hamburg (June 1641), which bound the two states together in opposition to the Habsburgs until war's end.

Richelieu needed Sweden to act as a diversion while it pursued its war with Spain in the west; Sweden needed French support in order to survive.[12]

Thus united, and facing a Habsburg coalition that was nearing exhaustion, the Franco-Swedish alliance had well-founded hopes for victory after 1641. It was not a cordial alliance, but it functioned well enough by 1643 to allow Oxenstierna to plan realistically for 'satisfaction and security'.

Brömsebro and Westphalia

In the midst of Sweden's final push towards victory in Germany came an event of no small political importance at home. Christina, the sole heir and child of Gustav Adolf, celebrated her eighteenth birthday in December 1644. The formal coronation would not take place until 1650, but still she had reached her majority and was therefore expected to take on her duties as queen. Christina had grown to young adulthood amidst her country's fluctuating fortunes on the battlefield and at the negotiating table. Oxenstierna, now past sixty years of age and understandably weary, had directed the war effort almost single-handedly since Lützen. Christina did not particularly care for Oxenstierna and his clan. In 1644–45 and again in 1645–48, she would side with those of her councillors who demanded a quick and lenient peace with Denmark and in the empire. But the ascension of Christina did not reduce Oxenstierna's primacy in the formulation of foreign policy, and the old chancellor would continue in state service until his death in 1654.

Refreshed by the renewed alliance with France, Sweden came back into the war with vigor. The new Swedish field-marshal, Lennart Torstensson, drove his forces deep into the empire and the Habsburg hereditary lands in the spring of 1642, smashing the Saxon army at Schweidnitz, capturing the Moravian capital of Olomouc, and moving back into Saxony to take Leipzig by siege that summer. Vienna quailed at the prospect of a Swedish assault; the allies of the Habsburgs, notably Bavaria, quickly deserted the emperor for France. Elsewhere the war went just as badly for the new emperor, Ferdinand III (1637–57). Spanish forces in the Netherlands were on the defensive against a new Dutch onslaught after 1637, the Dutch navy utterly destroyed a powerful Spanish fleet in the calamitous battle of the Downs two years later; the French general Condé administered a stinging defeat to the Spanish Army of Flanders at Rocroi (1643) while the 1640 revolt of the Catalans crippled Spain from the inside. But all parties were hard-pressed: the German princes and their subjects clamored for peace, and in both France and Sweden the populations grew despondent and even violent over their sacrifices in men and taxes. Spain and the emperor might have been forced to the peace table, but Sweden and France were just as anxious to join them there.

As Sweden's plenipotentiaries made their way to Osnabrück early in 1643 to begin the negotiations that would culminate in their 'half' of the Peace of Westphalia, Oxenstierna made the decision to deal once and for all with Sweden's 'wicked neighbor', Denmark. Christian IV, much older and careworn than in 1625, had tried since 1629 to regain a portion of his nation's former reputation and to maintain Denmark's neutrality. In walking a precarious diplomatic tightrope between Sweden and the emperor, the Danish king had managed to alienate virtually everybody. Christian's final stab at exerting influence in European politics was to establish himself as the primary mediator in the Osnabrück peace talks, a role that was accepted only grudgingly by the emperor and with suspicion by Oxenstierna. The old chancellor needed little convincing that Denmark was not to be entrusted with Sweden's future at Osnabrück. The Council agreed with him, and in June 1643, without a declaration of war, Oxenstierna secretly ordered Torstensson and Hans Christoff von Königsmarck to move their forces quietly from Bohemia towards Lower Saxony. In December they struck. Königsmarck overran the Danish-held bishoprics of Bremen and Verden, returning them to Swedish control, while Torstensson invaded Holstein and Jutland, and Gustav Wrangel attacked the Scanian provinces. Ferdinand III pledged his support to Denmark, but it was too late. The Imperial army, under the command of Matthias Gallas, failed to move north in time. Christian's limited land forces, caught completely unprepared, could do little to slow the Swedish advance. The Danish fleet – once the masters of the Baltic – put up a heroic defense, but to no avail. With a great deal of unofficial Dutch assistance, the Swedish fleet defeated the Danes in the battles of Kolberger Heide and Fehmarn, hence achieving naval superiority in Danish waters. By the end of 1644, Christian IV had no choice but to sue for peace.[13]

The so-called 'Torstensson War' and the peace treaty which ended it at Brömsebro in June 1645 marked a watershed in the history of inter-Scandinavian relations, in the constitutional development of Denmark, and in the story of Sweden's rise to great-power status. French and Dutch mediation prevented Oxenstierna from attaining his initial demands, which included the cession of Skåne, Halland, and Bleckinge to Sweden, which would have completely shattered Denmark's control over the Sound and thereby its claim to *dominium maris Baltici*. Sweden's actual gains, however, were damaging enough to its ancient rival: the surrender of the Norwegian border-provinces of Jämtland and Herjedälen, the islands of Gotland and Øsel, and unhindered and free passage for all Swedish shipping passing through the Sound. As collateral for this latter clause, Sweden was to hold the Danish province of Halland for thirty years. It was a clear sign of Denmark's precipitous decline as a great power. Denmark was still a dangerous enemy, and one with a cause for vengeance, but Brömsebro marks the point at which Sweden became the dominant Baltic power.[14]

Meanwhile, the peace talks at Osnabrück dragged on, but the outcome of the Torstensson War left little doubt that Sweden was not to be trifled with. Swedish forces in the empire made the point plainly, winning a stunning victory over Habsburg forces at Jankov (March 1645) in Bohemia; allied with the Transylvanian prince Georg Rákóczi, Torstensson prepared to lay siege to Vienna, a fate that was spared the emperor only because of the Transylvanian's forced withdrawal for financial reasons. Swedish garrisons held much of Lower Austria, and by 1647 were able to move practically at will throughout the Habsburg lands. In May 1648, the Swedes crushed the last Bavarian army at Zusmarshausen. Sweden's victory over the emperor was as complete as it could be, given the circumstances; Oxenstierna's plenipotentiaries at Osnabrück were in a position to demand and expect much in return.

This does not mean that Sweden was able to dictate the terms of its portion of what would become known as the Peace of Westphalia. Oxenstierna's negotiators had relatively little say in the resolution of the internal religious affairs of the empire, although Swedish pressure certainly helped the German princes obtain the revocation of the more odious restrictions on Protestant worship. The initial demands for *satisfactio et assecuratio* had to be modified as well. The Swedes demanded all of Pomerania, which belonged by right to Brandenburg after the death of the last, childless Pomeranian duke in 1637; skillful diplomacy by Brandenburg, aided by France, pressured Sweden into taking only the western half of the duchy (*Vorpommern*). Sweden also received the valuable port-city of Stettin, plus the bishoprics of Bremen and Verden in Lower Saxony, but not the portions of Mecklenburg it had claimed. A further Swedish demand – the payment of 30 million *Reichsthaler* as an indemnity, to allow the kingdom to pay off its vast armies – was exhorbitant, and in the end Sweden had to content itself with only 5 million. The treaty of Osnabrück was signed by all parties concerned in August 1648. That did not bring an immediate end to the German 'adventure'. No formal arrangement for the withdrawal of Swedish troops was made until 1650, and the last Swedish troops departed German soil (excluding Pomerania and Bremen-Verden) in 1654.[15]

Swedish gains at the Osnabrück talks were not as generous as Oxenstierna had hoped, and were not even commensurate with Sweden's considerable investment in the war, in terms of men, resources, and money. Osnabrück was still a triumph. Sweden had a significant foothold in the Holy Roman Empire, and a voice in Imperial affairs; a role as co-guarantor of the Peace; ports of great strategic importance in western Pomerania; and new sources of commercial wealth as well. At Brömsebro, Sweden had been the first European power to loosen Denmark's stranglehold on Baltic commerce. In short, Brömsebro made Sweden a great *Baltic* power; Osnabrück was the international acknowledgment of Sweden's emergence as a great *European* power. But Sweden was neither France nor Spain. It could not approach either in terms of available resources, despite its clever mechanisms for mobilizing such as it had. Its reliance on French support during the 1640s revealed a serious weakness: for much of the *stormaktstid*, Sweden would exhibit a tendency to look to France for guidance and aid. Its rapid rise to greatness created new enemies and further embittered its former adversaries. Even the Dutch, so vital in the development of Sweden's mineral resources and commerce, would begin to turn on Sweden as the latter displaced Denmark in Baltic affairs. Sweden had made a spectacular rise to power, but already visible – just dimly in 1648 – were the signs of an equally spectacular decline.

Christina: The Costs of War . . . and of Faith

Before 1632, the development of the Vasa state – in politics, diplomacy, the economy, and religion – clearly bore the personal imprint of the reigning sovereign. Recent Swedish historical literature has tended to overlook this, and even the writings of the *Maktstatsprojekt* focus on the history of administrative institutions and constitutional constructs. Nonetheless, it is impossible to divorce the history of Sweden between Gustav Vasa and Gustav II Adolf from the history of the dynasty itself; the two things are practically synonymous. An exception must be made, however, for Christina. Christina was neither lazy nor prodigal like her great-uncle, Johan III, nor did her personal eccentricities ever amount to the full-blown mental illness exhibited by Erik XIV. Neither was she a born administrator nor *Realpolitiker* like her father, grandfather, or great-grandfather. Intellectually gifted and possessed of an insatiable curiosity, she was indeed a remarkable woman, but never a remarkable ruler. She has attracted the attention of foreign biographers to a degree that no other Swedish sovereign has ever done; popular fascination with Christina has more to do with her femininity and her faith than it does with her abilities as a monarch. It was manifestly clear from the beginning of her reign that Christina did not have the passion for governance characteristic of most of her predecessors. Her passions lay elsewhere.[16]

Christina's upbringing had been an unusual one. She was never especially close to her flighty mother. She never knew her father, who had been absent on campaign constantly during the interval between her birth in 1626 and his death in 1632. Early on, however, she displayed striking similarities to Gustav Adolf, sharing her father's love for an active outdoor life, and preferring riding to more acceptable womanly pursuits. Christina was fiercely independent, and tough both physically and emotionally. Above all, Christina was brilliant and dedicated to her studies. She was a voracious reader, with a strongly humanistic bent. In her personal faith, despite her strictly Protestant upbringing, she was an ecumenicalist who would later develop strong sympathies for the Roman religion, and the queen chafed at the stultifying narrow-mindedness of the orthodox brand of Lutheranism espoused by Oxenstierna and the episcopacy. Like her ancestors, she had a very real thirst for power; unlike them, she found her homeland intellectually stifling.

This is not to say, however, that Christina was a failure as a ruler. From the time she assumed the mantle as queen regnant upon reaching her majority in 1644, she took direction of the state with a firm hand, and did not simply defer to Oxenstierna and the other dominant figures of the Regency. This first became evident in the formulation of foreign policy. Christina had little acquaintance with peace, but she knew well the deleterious effect of war on her realm, and she sought to give Sweden and its hard-pressed population some respite from the hostilities in which it had been engaged for the better part of a century. Sweden was not in imminent danger of attack from its enemies. At the end of 1644, Christina pressured Oxenstierna to conclude his vendetta against Denmark and negotiate a peace, and she was foremost among those at court who called for an end to the war in Germany in the late 1640s. Perhaps she hamstrung Oxenstierna's ability to obtain yet more favorable peace terms at Brömsebro and Osnabrück, but she also recognized what most of the kings of Sweden's *stormaktstid* failed to see: that Sweden might have been a great power, but given its limited national resources it would have been all too easy for the Vasa state to overextend itself in its quest for security.[17]

The most loudly voiced concern of the Swedish ruling elite at the time of Christina's accession, and for the remainder of the reign, was the queen's marital and procreative status. Her personal proclivities in this regard can easily be likened to those of Elizabeth I: while she enjoyed the attentions of potential suitors, she had little desire to share her power with a husband, nor to agree to a match that would weaken the power of the monarchy. The queen's romantic relationships were also complicated by her paralyzing fear of childbirth, and her own self-consciousness about her physical appearance; it was said of Christina that she 'hated mirrors because they had nothing agreeable to show her'.[18] As an adolescent, she developed an infatuation for Magnus De la Gardie (1622–86), son of the general and councillor Jakob De la Gardie. Magnus would become one of her chief confidantes, surpassed only by the queen's favorite Ebba Sparre in this regard, and Christina's affection for the dashing young aristocrat propelled him to membership in the *Riksråd* and the War Council. He was not, however, a serious contender for the queen's hand. That position was reserved for Karl Gustav, Count Palatine, son of Gustav Adolf's sister Katharina and Johann Casimir, and therefore Christina's first cousin. Karl Gustav and Christina were very good friends, but Christina made it clear that she had no intention of marrying the man. The queen did manage to find a solution that compromised neither her authority nor that of the monarchy. At the *Riksdag* of 1649, Christina successfully pushed through a succession pact, which bound the *Riksdag* to recognize Karl Gustav as king should Christina die without issue. To do this, she had to enlist the support of the non-noble estates. The nobility, including the conciliar aristocracy and especially the Oxenstierna faction, agreed only grudgingly. To them, the succession of Karl Gustav represented a potential diminution of the improved political position they had built up during the prolonged regency.

The disputes over the succession pact of 1649 eloquently illustrate both the primary problem facing Christina and the queen's chosen tactic for attacking this problem. It was fortunate that Christina was strong-willed and politically astute, for she faced social, economic, and constitutional crises at home that were worse than those which confronted her father in 1612. Despite the victories of the Swedish crown in Germany, the state fisc was not healthy. It would have been impossible to have paid off Swedish forces in the empire after Osnabrück without external assistance; hence Oxenstierna's insistence upon some sort of reparations from the German princes. French subsidies had not been enough to sustain the war effort on their own. Heavy taxes, heavier conscription, and frequent crop failures had reduced the Swedish peasantry to penury. Military conscription had depopulated entire villages, and although Sweden was not so thoroughly afflicted by internal unrest as was France, there were signs of increasing resistance to taxation and *utskrivning* in the countryside. In Värmland, burghers and peasants alike protested violently against property taxes, the capitation tax, and commercial duties in 1638–39. Even the local clergy openly denounced the heavy taxation from the pulpit. In the capital city itself, poorer burghers in 1650 protested vehemently against the 'oven tax' (see Chapter 5); the ringleaders were sentenced to death for their affront.[19] The nobility, however, had profited substantially from Sweden's wars. The leading field commanders had plundered vast amounts of wealth during their campaigns. The nobility grew rich in large part at the crown's expense. Bereft of the means of remunerating its generals in cash, the Regency had donated, sold, and mortgaged vast amounts of crown properties, in Sweden and in the recently conquered lands, to individual noble families, while foreign officers in Swedish service were frequently naturalized and also compensated with gifts of crown land.

In such a situation, it was hardly surprising that the lower orders, including the burghers and the lesser clergy, should raise their voices to the queen in protest. As the priesthood complained at the *Riksdag* of 1650, the nobility 'alone enjoyed [the fruits of] the peace that we have attained, but none of the other Estates, who certainly have sacrificed just as much, both in lives and property, and [who] now have been reduced to servitude and shall not taste the sweetness of peace'.[20] The lower orders demanded a radical solution: a *reduktion*, or a forced reclamation of alienated crown properties now in noble hands. The peasant House had proposed such a measure as early as 1644, but it was at the *Riksdagar* of 1649 and 1650 that the *reduktion* would become the rallying cry of all the unprivileged orders. At the latter Diet, the three commoner estates – the clergy, the burghers, and the peasantry – issued a formal 'Supplication' to Christina. Emphasizing their personal loyalty to the queen and their faith in a strong monarchy, the commoners bemoaned the inequitable social distribution of sacrifice and profit accruing from Sweden's wars. To ease their sufferings, they implored Christina to take back that which the crown had given away over the preceding decades.[21]

Whether or not Christina gave any serious thought to a *reduktion* is still a matter of debate. She never implemented the policy. But the bitter and vitriolic split between noble and non-noble, which reached its peak at the *Riksdag* of 1650, gave Christina the opportunity she needed to attain her other political goals, including the final resolution of the succession. In the Vasa tradition, Christina fashioned herself into a demagogue, successfully courting the support of the lower orders in opposition to the aristocracy. The implied threat that she might enforce a *reduktion* was enough to cow the nobility into giving its unconditional assent to the succession of Karl Gustav. The queen's policy of ennobling commoners should also be viewed in this light. Her reign set a record for the number of ennoblements in seventeenth-century Sweden. Some of Christina's appointments, including the elevation of the common-born career diplomat Johan Adler Salvius to membership in the Council, were intended to weaken the influence of the aristocratic Oxenstierna faction.

By exploiting the widening gap between the noble and commoner estates in Sweden, Queen Christina had restored to the monarchy unquestioned primacy over the nobility at the very moment when the nobility was strongest. This was no small achievement. Unfortunately, Christina did not make use of this opportunity to bring much-needed reform to her kingdom. The *reduktion* issue died quietly away, and the queen did not seek out alternative methods of solving the crown's fiscal crisis. Although she did not embark upon further costly military ventures, Christina did add further encumbrances to the already-burdened treasury. Up until her reign, the Swedish court at Stockholm had been a modest affair, sometimes embarrassingly so. After Gustav Adolf's death, the Council had refrained from inviting foreign guests to the king's funeral, for fear that the emissaries of distinguished foreign powers would see just how poor Sweden was.[22] Christina endeavored instead to bring her court up to contemporary Continental standards of splendor and elegance, hiring musicians, artists, and poets from all over Europe. The queen even brought René Descartes, with whom she had been corresponding for several years, to reside at court in 1649; her frequent and exhausting early morning meetings with the Frenchman, as has been often alleged, may well have brought about his death in Stockholm in February 1650. By the standards of the time, such luxuries were necessary for sustaining the international reputation of the monarchy, but they were luxuries which Sweden could ill afford.[23]

For the final three or four years of her reign the queen was absorbed in her own personal problems. Although Swedish elite culture prospered under her tutelage, Christina was intellectually restless, especially so in matters of religion. Her religious upbringing had been directed by the bishop of Strängnäs, Johannes Matthiæ, whose tolerant, irenicist brand of Protestantism stood in stark contrast to the increasingly exclusionist leanings of the orthodox Lutheran episcopacy and the Oxenstierna clan. Christina's close ties with Catholic visitors at court, like Descartes and the French ambassador Chanut, doubtless influenced her. Like Johan III, Christina found herself drawn to the liturgical majesty of the Roman rite, but without any inclination to return Sweden to papal obedience or even to make her personal piety a matter of public knowledge. Her secrecy in this matter makes it difficult to tell exactly when she made the decision to convert, but by 1651 she was definitely a practicing Catholic. Christina knew full well that, in accordance with the Örebro decrees of 1617, she could not remain as queen of Sweden if she were to convert; this helps to account for the urgency with which she approached the issue of the succession. She first mentioned the possibility of her abdication to the Council in 1651, but the final decision took a great deal of painful soul-searching for the queen. In an emotional ceremony at the Uppsala *Riksdag* in June 1654, Queen Christina, not yet 28 years old, set aside her crown and renounced her claim to the throne.[24] The remainder of her colorful life – her journey to Rome, her formal acceptance of the Roman faith – has little or no bearing on the history of Sweden; though Christina never lost her thirst for power, her break with Sweden was a clean one, and her ambitions were directed towards Poland and Naples rather than towards the land of her birthright. Her abdication, however, was followed immediately by two events of profound significance: the coronation of her cousin as King Karl X Gustav on the very same day as the abdication ceremony, and the death of Axel Oxenstierna shortly thereafter. The passing of the 71-year-old chancellor robbed the nobility of the last great constitutionalist of the century. To the conciliar aristocracy, the accession of Karl X Gustav may have seemed a troubling development. At age 32, the new king was young, ambitious, and warlike. Most important, it had been the aristocracy that had made difficult his path to the position of heir apparent. Karl Gustav owed nothing to his nobility.

Chapter 5: The Swedish 'Power State': Society, Culture, and the Burden of War

The seventeenth century is frequently described as an age of 'crisis'. Though historians have hardly come to any consensus as to what that entails, few scholars would deny that – for much of Europe – the century was characterized by economic contraction rather than growth. The salient features of the late sixteenth-century European economy – rapid population growth, a decline in agricultural productivity, rampant inflation – combined with the growing demands of the state and of war to produce a volatile economic situation by the middle of the next century. The result of this equation, together with the overall destructive nature of the Thirty Years' War, was considerable social and political upheaval.

Not all of Europe suffered in this way, however. The Netherlands, as has been well established, remained quite prosperous during this period. So, too, did Sweden, albeit in relative terms. Involvement in nearly continuous wars against Poland, Denmark, the Muscovite state, and the Habsburg coalition on the Continent put tremendous demands on Sweden's economy and population, burdens that the lower orders did not always accept with quiet obedience. But neither did the Vasa state crack under their weight. Of course, the Swedish population was already inured to the demands of a state at war, a factor that made the seventeenth century a bit more bearable for them. It was more than the resilience of the peasantry, however, that accounted for Sweden's ability to weather more than a century of constant warfare. The Swedish polity developed innovative and effective methods of funding its military exertions abroad, methods that accorded well with Sweden's traditional military institutions.

Paying for War: Economic Development and War Finance

Over the past two decades, historians of early modern Sweden have been less interested in the motives behind Sweden's 'bid' for great-power status than they have been in the physical means by which Sweden was able to attain and maintain that status.[1] For this reason, we have a clear and detailed view of the workings and capabilities of the state fisc in Sweden. Swedish state finances were extraordinarily primitive by Continental standards at the outset of the seventeenth century. Sweden, like Denmark, was what has been called a 'domain state' in that by far the largest source of state income came from the profits of the royal domain. The Reformation, of course, had substantially enlarged the size of royal landholdings during the sixteenth century, assuring the crown of a significant income from this source, but there were notable disadvantages to reliance on domain income. The most obvious draw-back was that domain incomes, drawn largely from the rents of peasants living on royal lands, were paid 'in kind', that is in agricultural and other produce like tar, wheat, fish, and butter. As such, they were not easily transformed into cash. The Swedish crown did not enjoy a reliable source of cash income, certainly nothing that could compare, either in volume or reliability, with the Danish Sound dues. Heavy reliance upon revenues collected in kind made it impossible for the central government to hire large mercenary armies and made paying the salaries of its bureaucrats a difficult and embarrassing process. It was this very lack of liquid income that prompted Christian IV of Denmark to demand the rapid payment of the 'Älvsborg ransom' in 1613.

Dependence on incomes in kind was not entirely devoid of advantage. Unless it hired mercenaries, the Swedish crown did not have to scrape together the cash necessary for the mustering and demobilization of foreign soldiers, and revenues paid in kind were perfectly suited to meeting the needs of a native conscript army intended for national defense. Still, the financial demands of the war with Poland in the 1620s, and even more so those of the German War after 1630, would require a far more extensive mobilization of national resources than at any other point in Sweden's history heretofore. And fighting an offensive war overseas required a steady flow of cash; as Michael Roberts observed, 'you cannot pay an army with butter or tar'.[2] The hiring of mercenaries was now unavoidable, as Sweden did not have a population large enough to maintain several native armies in the field and still protect the fatherland. After Breitenfeld, it is doubtful that native troops made up more than 20 percent of the field armies in Germany. There were, of course, foreign subsidies, most important of which were the cash payments from France that started with the Bärwalde treaty in 1631, but even these were insufficient to cover all of Sweden's enormous military expenditures. The German War cost Sweden approximately 20 to 30 million *riksdaler* in total; the unreliable French and Dutch subsidies, according to one recent estimate, covered no more than about 1 to 15 percent of annual expenditures in the war. Success at war, in the German War as in later campaigns, would require changes in the economy and a restructuring of the state fisc.[3]

Scandinavian historians have portrayed the economic development of seventeenth-century Sweden as a three-stage process: first, as a 'domain state', with the largest source of state revenues coming from the royal landholdings; second, after 1620, as a 'tax state', as the central government sought to bankroll its military commitments through a mixture of tax revenues, credit, partial self-sufficiency of its armies, and donations of crown land; and third, after 1680, a return to domain-based revenues, as King Karl XI reclaimed alienated crown lands in a sweeping *reduktion*. The transition to the second stage concerns us here, as it helps to explain Sweden's success in sustaining its most extensive and successful conflicts as a great power. Most of the changes that brought about this transition had their beginnings in the last decade of Gustav Adolf's reign, and many can be attributed directly to the policies of that king and Axel Oxenstierna.

Sweden's ability to finance its wars after 1626 owed in part to a drastic expansion of the tax structure and a more thorough exploitation of already existing taxes. The reform and expansion of the Treasury and of the local administration allowed for more efficient collection of domain revenues and 'ordinary' taxes than had been the case under the earlier Vasas. The bulk of the taxes collected during Gustav Adolf's reign and up until 1680 came from extraordinary levies, something that had been practiced only sporadically before. The first significant wave of extraordinary taxation began in the wake of the Kalmar War and the Älvsborg ransom, when Gustav Adolf called upon all Swedes – the nobility as well as *all* peasants, and even the royal family itself – to pay a graduated annual tax for the sole purpose of paying the ransom. This four-year grant, later expanded to six years, established a precedent not only for long-term extraordinary taxation, but also for breaching the nobility's exemption privilege. A host of new taxes approved by a reluctant *Riksdag*, intended to cover the costs of war in Poland and the possible upcoming campaigns in Germany, appeared during the 1620s: a tax on all livestock and cultivated land (1620), the 'Lesser Toll' on all goods brought to be sold at market towns (1622), the Excise (1622, including a tax on bake-ovens), a tax on all grains brought to grist (1625), a capitation tax (1625), and the highly unpopular 'Three Marks Aid', a fixed poll tax introduced in 1628. All Swedes were liable, with few exemptions; the nobility agreed to pay, and their peasants – normally allowed a 50 percent exemption from extraordinary levies – had to pay in full. Even those peasants living in close proximity to noble manor houses, within the so-called 'mile of freedom' (*frihetsmil*), were denied their customary exemption. The fiscal crunch of the 1650s likewise inspired the introduction of new levies, like the tax on ground grain (*kvarntull*) of 1656, and a doubling of the Excise in 1651. The most significant features of the new extraordinary taxes were their permanence – the capitation (*mantalspengar*) of 1625 became a regular annual tax in 1634 – and the manner in which they were levied: under Gustav Adolf, the basis of tax assessment, like that of conscription, shifted from the farmstead to the individual. The 1625 Mill Tax, for example, was levied on every Swede over the age of twelve. Extraordinary taxes were becoming ordinary and personal.[4]

Domestic commercial revenues first became a significant source of state income during the 1630s, thanks to the Vasa policy of importing foreign entrepreneurs to assist in developing Sweden's mineral resources. Merchants in Stockholm exported 373 English tons of high-quality bar-iron (*stångejärn*) to Britain in 1648; in 1659, that figure increased to 3443, and would more than double again over the following decade.[5] The dramatic growth of the copper and iron industries after the 1620s meant that crown income accruing from export duties would likewise grow in importance, especially after the initial stages of the German War. As commerce blossomed, so too did both the urban population and the number of towns, enlarging the state's tax base. Stockholm, with a population of 6000 in 1550 and perhaps 10,000 in 1600, had bloomed by 1650 into a respectable city of 50,000 inhabitants, although it should be noted that the presence of the central administration there contributed greatly to this spurt; civil servants far outnumbered artisans and merchants throughout the seventeenth century. Not all commercial duties came from ports in Sweden and Finland, however. Swedish naval ascendancy in the 1620s allowed Gustav Adolf and Oxenstierna to levy tolls on maritime traffic sailing to or from the major Baltic ports from Prussia eastward in 1627. The Prussian tolls levied off Danzig and Pillau were the most lucrative, tendering more than half a million *riksdaler* in 1629 alone; their loss, conceded at Stuhmsdorf in 1635, was a major blow to the state fisc.[6]

Taken together, the income generated by commercial duties, ordinary taxes, and extraordinary taxes was substantial, but it was hardly adequate to cover the expenses of a large, mostly mercenary army fighting an offensive war on foreign soil. National resources were stretched to the limit; the difference would have to be made good elsewhere, and foreign subsidies were neither predictable nor extensive enough. Gustav Adolf's answer to the problem would become the byword of Swedish military logistics and war finance up to 1660: war should 'feed itself' (*bellum se ipsum alit*). The so-called 'contribution system', in which armies in the field supported themselves through the levying of systematic, coerced drafts of money and provisions taken from local populations in their theaters of operations, was a distinctive feature of logistics in the Thirty Years' War. It did not originate with the Swedes or with Wallenstein, as military historians have sometimes been wont to suggest; indeed, it was a predictable response to the unprecedently prolonged campaigns of that war and the primitive nature of logistics in seventeenth-century warfare. Christian IV, for example, had made frequent use of 'contributions' in the campaigns of the late 1620s. It was the Swedes, however, who perfected the system: conquered territories, allied princes, and neighboring cities paid regular instalments in cash or in kind. Frequently the system amounted to nothing more than a kind of orderly extortion, but it worked. The 'contribution system' made particularly good sense for the Swedish armies fighting in Germany after 1630. The lines of supply for the Swedish forces, extending from Stockholm and Kalmar to German ports like Stettin and Stralsund, and thence to the seat of the war further south, were too long and tenuous to be maintained for long, especially as the recruitment of mercenaries in Germany swelled the ranks of the army. Intelligent application of the contribution system allowed the Swedes considerable strategic freedom: to break loose from their bases in Pomerania and Brandenburg, maintaining only small garrisons along the way, and to push deep into the empire without overwhelming fear of losing logistical support. Living off the land also offered the opportunity to deny vital provisions to hostile armies, and to punish or intimidate enemies or neutrals, as illustrated by the operations around Bavaria in 1631–32. To Jan Glete, this systematic mulcting of the German territories was the most significant achievement of the *stormaktstid*; it was nothing short of the creation of a Swedish 'fiscal-military state' in Germany.[7]

In the short term, the doctrine of *bellum se ipsum alit* offered great advantages. By the time of the battle at Lützen, 'contributions' and plunder covered most of Swedish expenditures on the war in Germany, and their annual amount outstripped the ordinary revenues of the kingdom by a factor of ten or more. Military successes after Breitenfeld permitted the Oxenstierna regency to lessen the burden of taxes on the Swedish population and to reclaim their exemption privileges; by war's end, the annual costs of the German War absorbed only about 4 percent of the state's annual budget. Without the systematic application of this principle, Sweden could have hardly maintained its forces in the Germanies for as long as it did, and it certainly would help Karl X Gustav to keep an army of occupation in Denmark in the late 1650s without unduly straining his ordinary budget and – even more remarkable – without stripping the Danish countryside bare. There were, however, attendant drawbacks. Few areas on the Continent could boast the level of agricultural productivity necessary to support large armies indefinitely, and operational planning therefore had to be predicated upon a particular region's ability to feed the troops. Gustav Adolf may have enjoyed logistical freedom of maneuver, but the need to feed his troops off the land restricted his options at the same time. Moreover, the system required the presence of a large bureaucracy; certainly it absorbed nearly all of Axel Oxenstierna's energies during the 1630s.[8]

Historians outside of Sweden, by focusing on the benefits of the 'contribution system', have neglected the Vasa state's employment of financial strategies that were more typical of the age, credit in particular. Without credit, all of the aforementioned incomes would not have sufficed to cover the costs of the state at war. The sources of this credit were manifold: loans raised on the basis of expected commercial duties and copper exports, usually provided by Dutch financiers involved in the Baltic trade, bankers in German towns like Hamburg, members of the central administration in stockholm, and Dutch or German entrepreneurs like the arms merchant Louis de Geer. Field Marshal Königsmarck personally lent at least 1.1 million *riksdaler* to the crown before his death in 1663.[9] Non-payment of wages, to high-ranking officials as well as to common mercenary soldiers, was also a common stop-gap measure. Sweden would not be overwhelmed by debt as so many of its contemporaries were, and would only rarely resort to outright cancellation of debts. In the years immediately following Westphalia, the state debt amounted to some 4 million *riksdaler* – substantial in light of the fact that ordinary revenues before 1630 amounted to about 1.5 million annually, but not crippling.

The Westphalian *satisfactio* covered most of the costs of demobilization in Germany, but the central government took care of its other debts in a fashion that would later emerge as the most vexing constitutional question in the second half of the century: through donation of crown lands. Starting with the last years of Gustav Adolf's reign, and peaking during the regency and the rule of Christina, the crown gradually acquired the habit of alienating portions of the royal domain and even mortgaging tax-rights to the farms of freeholding peasants as a means of paying creditors and of rewarding loyal administrators and generals. As a temporary measure, it made good economic sense. It was both a way of ensuring the loyalty of the nobility and of remunerating entrepreneurs and commanders without unduly straining the state fisc. Alienation may even have increased the profitability of the former crown lands, as noble landowners made a real effort to 'colonize' deserted farms, thereby expanding the tax-base. Sweden was moving away from dependence on domain revenues, and closer to reliance on direct and indirect taxation.

Swedish Society at War

War made Sweden wealthy and poor at the same time. Swedish iron, copper, and naval stores were in demand as never before; the spoils of war brought almost unimaginable wealth to the Swedish nobility, both to older established families and to recently ennobled, foreign-born mercenary captains. But to the bulk of the population – the peasants, whether *frälse* or *ofrälse*, whether in Finland or in the Swedish heartland – the wars in Poland and Germany brought unmitigated misery. Since the war was not fought on home soil, the peasantry did not experience the horrors of war first-hand as did their counterparts in much of Germany. Their misery was imposed from above, by their own government, and not at the hands of ill-disciplined foreign armies, through conscription and heavy taxation rather than through contributions and violent encounters. The government-sanctioned 'prayer-days' might have softened the blow – at least the Swedish peasants were given a reason for their sacrifices – but even the most eloquent state propaganda could not hide the fact that the

cost of asserting and maintaining Sweden's newfound great-power status
was a high one, and that a summons to service in the king's armies was
tantamount to a death warrant.

No single element of Swedish society profited so much from the wars
on the Continent as did the nobility. The accession of Gustav II Adolf in
1611 marked the beginning of a 'golden age' for the Swedish nobility.
The reconciliation of 1612 assured the noble estate that they no longer
had to fear the 'rule by secretaries' of the earlier Vasa kings, and the
reforms of Gustav Adolf and Oxenstierna gave them a near monopoly
over the upper ranks of the central and local administrations. The wars
of the 1620s, 1630s, and 1640s, which created a demand for a constantly
growing bureaucracy as well as military leadership, provided the nobility
with almost limitless opportunities for careers in state service.

The territorial conquests of the period 1626–48 also brought opportunities for profit besides administrative careers. The conquered lands,
once added to Sweden's Baltic empire, became *latifundia* for Sweden's
foremost generals and administrators. Others were rewarded with
donations of alienated crown lands within Sweden and Finland in lieu of
pay. By 1654, the nobility was by far the largest collective landowner in
the kingdom, with nearly 63 percent of all cultivated land in Sweden and
Finland in noble hands; royal tenancies became almost a negligible
quantity. Nearly two-thirds of the tax-rights to the farms of *skattebönder*
were nobly owned as well. The wealth amassed by individual noblemen
could be staggering. Hans Christopher von Königsmarck, who was
naturalized rather than native, left behind him at his death in 1663 a
fortune of some 1.6 million *riksdaler*.[10] The 1640s and 1650s also marked
the beginning of a period of conspicuous consumption within the noble
estate. Successful generals, most notably Karl Gustav Wrangel, returned
to Sweden with vast fortunes, art collections, and entire libraries plundered
from Bavaria, Austria, and the Habsburg hereditary lands. It was the
high point of noble opulence in the Vasa state, characterized by construction of grandiose manor houses throughout the countryside.[11]

The Swedish nobility also increased in size. A noteworthy new feature
in the relationship between the monarchy and the noble estate was the
ennoblement of foreigners and non-noble Swedes who had distinguished themselves through loyal service to the state. Prior to the
German War, the conciliar aristocracy had stubbornly resisted the elevation
of either commoners or foreigners to noble status. The financial pressures
of war, however, broke down this resistance. The granting of patents of
nobility was the natural reaction of a central authority that was desperately

seeking new sources of short-term income, as well as ways to compensate foreigners who had rendered invaluable services as administrators or as mercenary captains. This was not part of a royal plan to create a client base within the noble estate, for the period of the most intensive ennoblement came during the 1640s, when the power of government rested more with Oxenstierna and the Regency than it did with the young Christina. Between 1640 and 1649, 243 commoners were elevated to membership in *Riddarhuset*, more than twice the number ennobled during the entire period 1610–39.[12] By 1650, a full 50 percent of all adult noblemen came from 'new' families.

These new ennoblements ultimately would serve to exacerbate deepening rifts within the noble estate. Gustav II Adolf, it will be remembered, had introduced the formal ranking of noble families represented in *Riddarhuset* by dividing the nobility into three sub-groups: the titled aristocracy of counts (*greve*) and barons (*friherre*), the non-titled conciliar aristocracy, and the lesser nobility. A handful of distinguished generals and administrators – men like Wrangel and Banér – managed to gain entry to the elite first group. The vast majority of those elevated during the 1630s and 1640s, however, including those foreign military commanders who were ennobled for their services, were relegated to the third rank; a few would succeed in climbing up to the first or second ranks. Of the 34 noblemen appointed to Council membership during Christina's brief reign, exactly one-half came from the lower nobility. The lesser nobility far exceeded either of the other two groups in numbers. But since voting in the *Riddarhus* was done by group, with any decision requiring the assent of two of the three chambers, the members of the older, established conciliar aristocracy could draw together to defend themselves against the lesser nobility of the third rank. The potential for constitutional conflict within the noble estate was high.[13]

It should be pointed out that the rise in the fortunes of the nobility did not signal a commensurate decline in the power or prestige of the monarchy. The compromise of 1612 and the 1634 Form of Government gave much greater constitutional freedom and power to the noble estate; the minority of Christina, the negotiations for the succession of Karl Gustav, and later the minority of Karl XI in the 1660s all gave the nobility the opportunity to reduce the royal prerogative in the absence of a strong ruler like Gustav Adolf. Yet the nobility did not do so. The Swedish nobleman saw himself as a servant of the state, possibly because of the solidarity between monarch and aristocracy forged during the war years under Gustav Adolf. Even a man like Axel Oxenstierna saw no inherent contradiction in simultaneously acting as the protector of noble privilege and as the promoter of state interests.

Sweden's new role as a great power wrought changes within the non-noble orders as well. The growth of export industries and the greater degree of urbanization that accompanied it predictably resulted in a corresponding expansion of the urban mercantile classes (*borgare*). Some, as we have seen, were ennobled as a reward for their services or loans to the crown during the German War. War and commerce may have brought wealth to the larger towns and social prestige to the mercantile elite, but the burghers as a group opposed the intrusion of an ever more oppressive central authority into urban life. As the central administration relied increasingly on trained royal appointees rather than local elites to serve as mayors (*borgmästare*) in the larger towns, the burghers oftentimes resisted – sometimes actively – the heavier tax and customs obligations imposed upon them from above. Fortunately, as in its relationship with rural society, the crown did observe a measure of government by consensus, and disciplined or removed those royal officials whose actions inspired constant grievances from the urban populations.[14]

The same industries that brought profit to the *borgare* also enlarged the wealthier rural sub-class of peasants who engaged in iron-smelting, weapons manufacture, or the distilling of tar. This incipient industrial working class had an overall higher standard of living than their 'pure peasant' neighbors, and enjoyed other significant benefits like exemption from conscription, but as these industries were confined to a few specific regions their numbers were not sufficient to cause any significant change in the social climate of the realm. The rural population, as Per Brahe remarked in 1636, was the real backbone of Swedish power, as it was from the peasants that Sweden drew the bulk of its tax revenues and the conscripts for its armies.[15]

The conditions of life did not change dramatically for those peasants who had been shifted from royal to noble residency as a result of alienation. Peasants on the alienated lands still continued to pay their taxes, now to a bailiff of the noble landlord rather than to a royal bailiff; such peasants were called *skattefrälsebönder*. Nor did the alienations result in any greater degree of noble control over the peasantry. Only in Skåne, taken from the Danes in 1660, did the nobility exercise complete legal jurisdiction over their peasants. Skåne was an exception only because the nobility there continued to observe Danish law, and soon they too were forced to conform.[16] Local studies have suggested that the shift in land-ownership patterns did not result in higher taxes for individual peasants or a noticeable worsening of noble–peasant relations. The grievances of the peasant estate, presented at the *Riksdag*, do not reflect any particular animus against noble landlordship.[17]

The living conditions of the peasant 'fourth estate' as a whole, however, worsened after the 1610s, and the persistence of wartime conditions after the early 1620s tested the endurance of even the hardiest Swedish peasant. The spate of new extraordinary taxes, beginning with the Älvsborg ransom contributions and resumed during the 1620s, was particularly onerous. Their collective weight, however, should not be exaggerated. Of all of these taxes, only the grist mill tax and the Three Marks' Aid were truly unfair; the mill tax was assessed arbitrarily, and made the grinding of grain at home illegal, while the Aid made no distinction between rich and poor. The involvement of the individual communities in the assessment of taxes, however, prevented the worst excesses. Until 1680, the central government was generous in granting exemptions to those who pleaded impoverishment. The absorption of military expenses through the contribution system in Germany likewise reduced the urgency for tax revenues, bringing down the demand for taxes earmarked for the German War from 2.4 million *riksdaler* in 1630 to about 128,000 three years later.[18]

The most crushing burden heaped upon the shoulders of the peasantry came from conscription. Gustav Adolf's military reforms had increased the intensity of *utskrivning*, and the demands for manpower in the Polish and German campaigns necessitated even sterner measures. Prior to 1627, the government drafted peasants at the level of one conscript from every *rota* of 10 royal or freeholding peasants, and one from every 20-man *rota* on nobly owned lands. The same spirit of universal application regardless of social status evident in taxation was soon employed in conscription as well. From 1627 to 1633, noble peasants were drafted on the same basis – 1:10 – as all other peasants were. Fortunately for the peasantry, this practice did not last for long. In 1635, the ratio was dropped to 1:30 (noble peasants) and 1:15 (all others), and thereafter the old 1:20 and 1:10 ratios were restored. Oxenstierna's regency government made a further concession to the badly used peasants in 1642, by changing the basis of the *rota* from the number of men to the number of farms, but maintaining the old ratios. In other words, one man from every 20 farms (nobly owned) or one from every 10 farms (all other peasants) would serve; since a farmstead might have several male residents, this significantly lowered the number of men drafted for service in a single conscription. It should be pointed out, however, that conscription was not necessarily an annual procedure. In some years, there might not be any conscription at all; in others, two or three conscriptions might be decreed for a single year.[19]

Initially, the needs of the army could be met by drafting the less desirable elements in the villages, but by the 1630s the central authorities permitted few exemptions. It became difficult for drafted peasants to hire substitutes; teenagers, those gainfully employed, and even the only sons of wealthier peasants could not escape service. Only those engaged in vital industries or those physically incapable of active service managed to avoid the draft. The demographic costs could be very high. In the parish of Bygdeå, 230 men were called to military service between 1621 and 1639. Of this number, only ten returned home unscathed; 215 died in service, and five others were maimed. The resultant decline of the adult male population in the parish came near to 40 percent, and females outnumbered males by a factor of 3:2. As Swedish historians have recently demonstrated, Bygdeå's experience may not have been typical, but neither was it unique. It is clear that Sweden's wars occasioned catastrophic losses.[20]

The response of the Swedish peasants to this burden appears to have been relatively docile. Sweden was part of what some historians have termed a 'low-pressure zone' in terms of peasant rebellion. To be sure, Gustav Vasa had had to contend with a number of grass-roots insurrections, and there was some concern that the much greater burdens of taxation and conscription in the mid-seventeenth century would prompt more of the same, but by and large the Swedish peasantry under the later Vasas accepted its unenviable lot with grim fatalism. There were a couple of minor incidents of violent resistance to conscription and taxation, but they were insignificant, localized, and easily suppressed; they were bereft of noble support. Swedish peasants did not dare to undertake anything on the scale of contemporary revolts in France. The *Riksdag*, which the ruler or Regency often consulted before issuing a conscription order, at least gave the peasants a voice and perhaps some leverage in negotiating concessions on other issues. They would give vent to their protests quite eloquently, with the clergy's sympathetic support, at the *Riksdagar* of 1649 and 1650. On the other hand, the peasantry did not always comply in due obedience. Peasants who wished to avoid *utskrivning* could do so by going into hiding or by fleeing their parishes altogether, and the desertion of conscripts remained a problem throughout the century. In the Finnish community of Säminge, for example, less than one-half of

1600 men conscripted between 1620 and 1679 actually served; in the more prosperous community of Kalajoki, however, a full 800 of 900 total conscripts – 89 percent – faithfully answered the call to military duty.[21]

One should not exaggerate, however, the degree to which the state was able to force its will on the lower orders. Conscription was never as heavy as it appeared on paper in Stockholm; the central administration did not simply pluck men, money, and produce from a powerless rural population. The communities themselves were directly involved in the assessment of taxes and conscription. Local officials and especially the rural parsons, who were instrumental in executing *utskrivning*, were sympathetic to the plight of their peasants, and acted as a filter between the state authorities in Stockholm and the peasant communities themselves. The mobilization of resources might have been brutally intense at times, but it required negotiation between center and periphery, and hence it was consensual rather than a one-sided process.[22]

The development of Swedish society around mid-century reflects the accomplishments, capabilities, and limitations of the 'power state' at its height. The nobility, though increasingly divided, embraced its post-1612 role as an administrative class without having to be first reduced to political or social impotence by the Vasa monarchs. As a group, the nobility was an asset, not a liability, to the central authority in Sweden. In turn, the central administration created by the Vasa kings, by Gustav II Adolf in particular, had shown itself capable of mobilizing national resources, particularly with regard to military conscription, in a way that few contemporary polities on the Continent could imitate. But the very success of the Vasa achievement demonstrated at the same time the inescapable poverty of seventeenth-century Sweden. The peasantry was too poor to bear the burden of continuous and onerous taxes. More importantly, Sweden's limited manpower base could not long support the kind of losses that villages like Bygdeå suffered during the 1620s and 1630s. The Vasa state was considerably wealthier in 1650 than it had been in 1600, but even with the addition of new territories, subject populations, industries and commerce, it did not have the requisite 'sinews of power' to maintain its status for very long.

Cultural Life in the Stormaktstid

In the two decades following Breitenfeld, Sweden did indeed prove itself to the world, demonstrating that it was a power to be taken seriously. The grudging respect earned by the Vasa state's ability to wage war beyond its means, however, did not mean the same thing as widespread esteem for Sweden as a nation of letters. To be sure, individual Vasa kings – particularly Erik XIV, Johan III, and of course Gustav Adolf – earned well-deserved reputations abroad as learned men, but in this sense they were also regarded as oddities, cultured men who emerged from a barbarous people. The educated elite of western and central Europe tended to view Scandinavia and the Baltic region as peripheral to the mainstream of European culture. This view was patently unfair when applied to Poland, slightly less unfair with regard to Denmark; but in the case of Sweden it was not far from the mark. Vasa Sweden was a military powerhouse, but it was also a cultural backwater, even at the middle of the seventeenth century.

This is not to say, however, that Sweden had not yet begun the process of integration into European intellectual and artistic life. The transition to the Lutheran faith in the sixteenth century highlighted the urgent necessity of revamping institutions of higher education, to meet the needs of the new clergy if for no other reason. Duke Karl had reopened the university at Uppsala in 1593, but the school demonstrated little real improvement over the next twenty years. It remained an institution for the instruction of priests, and not a very good one at that. Thoroughgoing reform of educational institutions in Sweden would be left to Gustav Adolf and Oxenstierna. The king had compelling reasons to improve and expand secondary and university education in Sweden: not only did countering the Catholic threat require a theologically sophisticated priesthood, but the expansion of the central bureaucracy, staffed by native-born Swedes, presupposed the existence of a well-educated administrative class. Questions of prestige undoubtedly played a role as well. Gustav Adolf wanted the world to take him and his nation seriously; the university was a visible reflection of Sweden's cultural sophistication, and in this regard it had been sorely lacking. The king increased the number of faculty severalfold, and donated over three hundred manors from the royal domain to provide for its upkeep. Starting in the early 1620s, new secondary schools, *gymnasier*, were established in each episcopal seat, and additional universities emerged to serve the needs of the far-flung empire: at Dorpat in 1632, Åbo in 1640, and Lund in 1668.[23]

The universities were open to men of all orders. A university education offered the prospect of some upward mobility, usually within the clergy, to sons of peasant families. Roughly a third of all students at Uppsala were of peasant origins. As the nobility assumed its place as the primary administrative class after 1611, however, it required and demanded educational opportunities tailored to fit its particular needs. Gustav Adolf sought to address this through the founding of a noble academy, the *Collegium Illustre*, at Stockholm in 1626. The *Collegium* was intended to provide the sons of noble families with a thorough grounding in classical and modern languages, rhetoric, and in the 'manly arts' of riding, fencing, dance and music. The *Collegium Illustre*, however, was not a success, and it closed its doors soon after its establishment. Nonetheless, noble families of sufficient means were sending their sons on the 'grand tour' in increasing numbers by mid-century. This, along with the travels of Swedish officers on the Continent during the German campaigns, lent something of a cosmopolitan flair to Swedish noble culture in the middle decades of the century; it gave them a taste for continental art, architecture, and music, while enhancing their connexions with European civilization at large. The plundering of monasteries and noble estates in Catholic Germany and Bohemia transformed rough Swedish nobles into avid art collectors and bibliophiles.[24]

Despite the growing complexity of their ties with the mainstream of European cultural life, at mid-century the Swedish nobility remained inward-looking. A common ethos bound them together, and bound them to their nation and king as well: *Gothicism*. Gothicism originated as a means of promoting the solidarity (and moral superiority) of the native-born nobility in the face of foreign, especially Danish, rule. Given its greatest literary expression in Johannes Magnus' *Historia Gothorum Sveonumque* (1554), Gothicism persisted and had begun to take on royalist and, later, imperialistic overtones by the time of Gustav Adolf. Gothicism claimed that Sweden was the oldest of all kingdoms in the world, and that its inhabitants still spoke the closest approximation of mankind's original language; that it was the ancient Goths (in Sweden) who brought civilization to the ancient Greeks and Romans. Gustav Adolf and his successors embraced this ideology enthusiastically, as did their nobilities. Gothicism deprecated Sweden's enemies, while justifying Swedish attempts at Baltic dominion and even Swedish claims on the Imperial throne. Such pretentions to superior lineage were commonplace in seventeenth-century Europe, at least within court culture; but while the 'Imperial theme' might be trotted out from time to time as a symbolic element in court masques held at Whitehall, the Louvre, or even Copenhagen Castle, in Sweden it was an active ideological force, even within the universities, that bound king and nobility together in something very much like nationalistic fervor. In this regard, its only true parallel elsewhere in Europe was the phenomenon of Sarmatianism in contemporary Poland.[25] And for all its flaws as a theory of history, Gothicism promoted a deep interest in Sweden's past amongst the educated, leading to the appointment of a *riksantikvarie* (antiquarian of the realm) in 1648 and the founding of the *Antikvitetskollegium* eighteen years later.[26]

Regardless of the 'sueco-centrism' implied by Gothicism, Sweden was indeed becoming – if slowly – an active participant in European elite culture. It was the royal court, above all other factors, that set the pace for this growing sophistication. Gustav Vasa had eschewed elaborate ceremony and opulence at court. His sons, however, did not. One of the chief complaints of Johan III's nobility was that their king spent huge sums on the 'importation' of artists, architects, musicians, and skilled craftsmen in the luxury trades to Stockholm. Sweden could not afford a lavish court in the 1570s, but by the 1640s the country could not afford to do without one if it were to be considered worthy of great-power status. Gustav Adolf himself had neither cash nor time to spend on his court – he was rarely in Stockholm after 1626 – and so the task was left to Christina. The young queen, who yearned for the refinements of court life in the larger monarchies, introduced such artistic forms as the 'court ballet' into Sweden; popular painters from the Continent, such as the Frenchman Sébastien Bourdon, frequented Christina's court. The erection of impressive public buildings – such as the *Riddarhus* complex in Stockholm – and the aristocracy's mania for constructing elaborate manor houses, like Wrangel's Skokloster and Magnus De la Gardie's Läckö, brought to Sweden such luminaries of Baroque architecture as Nicodemus Tessin. Leading intellectuals, like Descartes, came to the Swedish court as well; not because Sweden itself had any great attractions to offer, but because of the reputation and generosity of its monarchs.[27]

The trend towards opulence at court and in the manor houses of the nobility had little impact on the common Swede, except perhaps indirectly through the tax burden it entailed. Whatever access the Swedish peasantry had to European culture came through the medium of the state church. The local parish priest was the only contact that most Swedes had with the world outside their villages; the role of the clergy as local servants of the crown, probably better developed than was the case anywhere else in Protestant Europe, was invaluable to the Vasa kings and their Caroline successors, and must be counted among the most important factors behind Sweden's rise to power. The clergy justified and explained government policies to the population at large, and they maintained the demographic information necessary for the efficient collection of taxes and the entire *utskrivning* process. Gathering this information meant that the lesser clergy was omnipresent in the everyday lives of each and every subject of the crown, registering births, deaths, baptisms, and confirmations, and making themselves familiar with the most intimate details of their parishioners' lives. And, of course, the clergy were the enforcers of 'social discipline', compelling attendance at church, punishing moral transgressions, and looking after the poor.

The Lutheran clergy were also the enforcers of conformity, and successful ones at that. Regardless of the confusion caused by the irenical leanings of Johan III and the almost puritanical Protestantism of Karl IX, by the time of Gustav Adolf's reign Lutheranism in Sweden was exceptionally homogeneous. In keeping with current trends in Denmark and northern Germany, the Swedish state church was exclusively orthodox, or 'gnesio-Lutheran', in its theological outlook. Sweden was not a confessionally tolerant state. Despite the occasional 'Catholic scares' caused by the papacy's inexplicably persistent interest in promoting a *missio suecica* during the first three decades of the seventeenth century, Catholics remained a tiny minority, made temporarily visible only through the favor that Christina showed to Catholic visitors. Heterodox Protestants were likewise insignificant, and the only sizeable religious minority was the Eastern Orthodox community in Ingria. The clergy themselves must take much of the credit for this achievement. The ferocity of their persecution of suspected witches – which would intensify during Sweden's real 'witchcraze' in the last half of the century – demonstrates their dedication to suppressing confessional and social deviance.[28]

It is easy to see why a cosmopolitan humanist like Queen Christina would find Swedish Lutheranism so intellectually stifling. It was intolerant, utterly humorless, and not even intellectually active; Swedish Lutheranism produced no theologians of note during the entire century. But Sweden's confessional homogeniety was important nonetheless, for it served as a kind of social cement, one of the few things that held the kingdom – if not the empire – together as a unified society. Michael Roberts remarked that 'Sweden was the Lutheran Spain'.[29] Perhaps this is an exaggeration, but the advantages bestowed on Sweden by its single-minded attachment to orthodox Lutheranism should not be underestimated. The crown did not have to waste time or effort on combatting troublesome religious minorities, nor on adjudicating endless disputes within a factionalized clergy. Nor did the personal piety of the Vasa monarchs after Karl IX ever trouble the relationship between ruler and subjects. Christina wisely maintained an outward devotion to Lutheranism even after she had made the decision to defect to Rome; the news of her conversion after her abdication came as a great shock to her former subjects.

Chapter 6: Proto-absolutism or 'Military Monarchy'? The Brief Reign of Karl X Gustav, 1654–59

The dynastic shift that came with Queen Christina's decision to abdicate in 1654, without an heir of her own body to continue the Vasa line, did not result in any great political crisis. That it did not do so owed, in part, to the loyalty of the nobility, who saw state service and not political self-interest as their primary obligation; in equal measure, it owed to the sturdy dependability of the lower orders, who despite the deep and justified grievances which they aired at the 1650 *Riksdag* were still obedient subjects, whether that obedience stemmed from the populist traditions of the Vasa house or because habits of deference had simply been beaten into them by the exigencies of a state at war. Christina herself must take some of the credit, too. She was not, perhaps, quite so dedicated to the welfare of the Swedish state as her father had been or her chancellor was, but she was conscientious and responsible enough to ensure that she would have a competent and popular successor.

Indeed, Karl Gustav, Count Palatine, had been groomed for power for years before he ascended the throne on the day of Christina's abdication in June 1654. As a general serving under Torstensson since 1642, and as commander-in-chief of the army in Germany in June 1648, the Palatine had been instrumental in the Swedish diplomatic and military successes of the late 1640s and Sweden's successful extrication from its military commitment in Germany by 1651. Although the circumstances surrounding his succession had been difficult, he was universally well liked amongst the conciliar aristocracy; once crowned, the nobility rallied loyally to his side. The new king offered the promise of a broader popularity as well, for in so many ways he seemed to resemble his uncle, Gustav Adolf. His love of the soldier's life, not just as commander but as an active partici- pant in the tumult of battle, was the only most obvious parallel between Karl Gustav and the 'Lion of the North'. Karl Gustav also had the kind of heroic flair that caught the imagination of biographers like Samuel Pufendorf. He was well educated; knowledgeable in theology, multilingual, and refined, he was hailed by at least one eighteenth-century chronicler as the most learned of Sweden's kings, no mean tribute given his company in that erudite category. He appears to have absorbed that common touch and gift for oratory that had proven to be such a valuable asset to the preceding dynasty. The 32-year-old Karl Gustav was well prepared for rule, in character as in military and administrative experience, when he became King Karl X Gustav in 1654, and Sweden accordingly faced brighter prospects, perhaps, than it would have had Christina married and given birth to an heir of her own line.

Karl X Gustav was not bestowed by nature with a long life. He could not possibly have accomplished in his less than six years as king what Gustav Adolf had in twenty-one years. Accordingly, he is the least studied of all Swedish monarchs of the seventeenth century. The reign of Karl Gustav, nonetheless, had a significance that belies its brevity. He was the last successful conqueror-king in Sweden's history, and through his wars with Poland, Russia, and Denmark brought the Swedish empire to its greatest territorial extent. Although he did not live to witness Denmark's humiliation at Copenhagen in 1660, he was directly responsible for Sweden's usurpation of the Dane's former *dominium maris Baltici* and Sweden's finest moments on the battlefield. He managed to accomplish all this, moreover, without sacrificing harmony and stability at home. Under Karl Gustav's direction, cooperation between king and Council reached its high point, with little constitutional confrontation between king and aristocracy, despite the unremitting demands of war. In short, Karl X Gustav's governance represents the apogee, in terms of external expansion and of constitutional functionality, of the Swedish empire.[1]

Though it would not become apparent until after 1660, the greatest significance of Karl Gustav's kingship was what it did *not* resolve, the problems that it could not repair and perhaps even exacerbated. The late 1650s mark the point at which the Swedish empire had begun to overextend itself and overtax its resources. The wars of Karl Gustav may have swelled Sweden's prestige amongst the nations of Europe; but the wars were of questionable necessity, burdening Swedish administration and society – already severely strained by the Thirty Years' War – almost to the breaking point. They earned for Sweden the hostility of the Dutch Republic and the newly reborn Brandenburg, and made any kind of *rapprochement* with Denmark impossible. Conversely, Karl Gustav's military commitments increased Swedish dependency on France, a relationship that would bear bitter fruit in the decades to come. The constitutional legacy of Karl Gustav's reign was a mixed one as well. Swedish historians have debated the relationship between crown and nobility under Karl Gustav in light of the constitutional 'revolution' of 1680. To some, Karl Gustav's reign represents a return to 'dualism', a partnership of near equals, involving the king and the Council; to others, the smooth cooperation of king and Council was a mere accident of personalities and circumstances. It has also been maintained that Karl Gustav 'emancipated' the crown from the fetters imposed by the noble estate. Since the reign was such a short one, the debate means little outside the narrow confines of the 1650s. No matter what precisely was the reason for this political harmony at home, it is undeniable that Karl Gustav was able to make policy, foreign or domestic, virtually unopposed. Karl X Gustav's success in upholding and expanding the royal prerogative not only imposed additional burdens on all elements of Swedish society, it also ultimately backfired in constitutional politics. It resulted in an aristocratic backlash after Karl Gustav died, leaving behind a mere infant as his successor, and giving the nobility the opportunity to free itself from an overbearing monarchy. This, in turn, helps to account for the particularly vengeful manner in which Karl Gustav's successor, Karl XI, reasserted the powers of the crown in 1680. There is a link, albeit an indirect one, between the unintentional 'proto-absolutism' of Karl X Gustav and the very real, institutionalized absolutism of Karl XI.

The Polish War

At heart, Karl X Gustav was a soldier, and this makes it more difficult to pin down the general motivations behind his foreign policy. Since the king loved a good fight, it is tempting to view the wars of the late 1650s as acts of unadulterated aggression, stemming from a mixture of thirst for territorial conquest and a desire for glory in battle. We must, however, also take into account the mentality that permeated earlier and later acts of aggression by Swedish sovereigns, including the Seven Years' War of the North, the Livonian wars of Karl IX, the Polish and German campaigns of Gustav Adolf, and the multi-front conflict launched by Karl XII in 1700: the fear – or, more accurately, paranoia – of territorial encirclement. Although the leading aristocrats in the Council might debate the wisdom of Karl Gustav's timing in initiating hostilities, and though they might bemoan the possible social consequences of prolonged taxation and conscription, they did not question the necessity of making war. It appears, in other words, that the aristocratic outlook on the general goals of Swedish foreign policy was not fundamentally different than that of the king. Given the sacrifices required to support Karl Gustav's ambitions in the Baltic, this suggests that both the aristocracy and the sovereign himself saw the Baltic wars of the late 1650s as imperative for maintaining the security of the state.

Sweden's reputation as a military powerhouse exceeded its actual military capabilities when Karl Gustav came to the throne in 1654. By and large, Swedish forces in the empire had succeeded in fulfilling Gustav Adolf's mandate – making war feed itself – but even then the large numbers of mercenaries in the ranks required that the war in Germany be fought increasingly on credit. With the end of the war in 1648, the monarchy faced the prospect of having to make good on loans of staggering size which Sweden could not pay off. It could no longer draw on the resources of its allies and subjugated populations in Germany beyond Pomerania and Bremen-Verden. Its own resources were inadequate for the task at hand: too much royal land had been alienated, and the decline of copper prices on the international market further restricted the government's cash flow. High wartime taxes and conscription levels were giving rise to visible tensions within the lower orders, as demonstrated by the debates at the 1649 and 1650 diets.

At the same time, Sweden was not yet wholly secure. Danger loomed not only from the empire, but also from the seemingly endless wars between Poland and Russia. The Smolensk War of 1632–34, in which Russia – instigated in large part by Gustav Adolf – attacked Poland, had not ended well for the Muscovites. It was a victory for the Poles, but in 1648 Poland suffered a tremendous setback with the outbreak of rebellion in the Ukraine. The Polish Commonwealth practically dissolved over the next six years: Władisław IV died, to be replaced in the 1648 election by his brother Jan Kazimierz (1648–68) even as the Ukrainian rebel army invaded the Polish heartland; the new king not only faced the hostility of many of his most powerful magnates, but also the prospect of a senate paralyzed by the infamous *liberum veto*, a recent innovation. Poland's enemies, chiefly Russia, were not slow to seize the opportunity.

In January 1654, Alexis Romanov promised Russian support to the rebels in the Ukraine. The reinvigorated and enormous Muscovite army made rapid progress. By the end of the 1654 campaign, the Russians had taken Smolensk and a series of weaker Polish garrisons; by the following summer, they controlled much of Lithuania.[2]

From the perspective of Karl X Gustav and his Council, this war represented not an opportunity but a crisis. Poland had been Sweden's greatest enemy in the east, but Russian territorial gains were more threatening to the eastern territories of the Swedish empire. The volatility of the situation in Poland–Lithuania prompted Karl Gustav and his Council to make preparations for war at the end of 1654, hiring foreign mercenaries and reintroducing wartime levels of conscription. Since neutrality did not appear to be a viable diplomatic option, Sweden would have to go to war – but against whom? Karl Gustav's first inclination was to ally himself with Poland and attack Russia, despite the pitiful performance of Polish armies so far. Jan Kazimierz, however, would not or could not accept the price Karl Gustav demanded for his friendship, a price which included renunciation of Polish claims on the Swedish throne. Karl Gustav saw little choice in the situation; he decided to cast his lot with Russia, as an indirect means of precluding a Russian threat to Swedish interests in the eastern Baltic. In the summer of 1655, while Alexis Romanov led Russian forces into Lithuania, Swedish armies under Magnus De la Gardie and Arvid Wittenberg set forth from Livonia and Swedish Pomerania, respectively, with the goal of taking Polish Prussia. The Polish defenses, such as they were, melted before the Swedish advance. Polish and Lithuanian magnates defected by droves to the Swedish king. In August, Poznań was in Swedish hands; by September, Karl Gustav had entered Warsaw; the following month, Cracow surrendered to the Swedes, as did several field armies.

Karl Gustav and his generals had achieved a stunning victory. Most of the Commonwealth's significant cities were under Swedish control, and although Danzig evaded subjugation, Swedish forces held the rest of the Vistula. Unlike Gustav Adolf's triumphs in the empire in 1631–32, however, the conquest of Poland did not bring Sweden universal acclaim on the Continent. Emperor Ferdinand III feared the proximity of the Swedes in southern Poland to the vulnerable Habsburg hereditary lands, nor were the German princes any happier with the Swedish victory. Sweden, after all, was a guarantor of the fragile Westphalian settlement. In Denmark, the prospect of further Swedish gains in the southeastern Baltic caused consternation, as it did in the United Provinces, which since

Brömsebro had been inclined to favor weaker Denmark over a Sweden that threatened the freedom of their commerce in the Baltic.[3] Most important, the population of Poland rallied behind their defeated king. Swedish excesses – particularly against properties of the Catholic church, recalling the horrors of the 1630s in Germany – turned the Poles against their invaders. Polish peasants initiated a disruptive *petite guerre* against isolated Swedish garrisons. By early 1656, Jan Kazimierz was riding high on a wave of popular resistance, and most of the generals and magnates who had deserted him the year before flocked to his defense. Karl Gustav had at his command an army that was well trained and far superior to that which Gustav Adolf had led in 1626, but it was not large enough to hold on for long under such circumstances.[4]

The next year witnessed a gradual but grudging withdrawal of Swedish forces from Poland. Karl Gustav still hoped for a more enduring victory, and there were reasons to hope for one. In June 1656, Swedish negotiators concluded a truce at Marienburg with Friedrich Wilhelm of Brandenburg (1640–88), granting the elector sovereignty over Ducal Prussia as a Swedish vassal. Quickly the 'Great Elector' rushed troops to the king's aid; together, they crushed Jan Kazimierz's reassembled army in a vicious two-day battle outside of Warsaw (28–29 July 1656). The rest of Europe, however, seemed to turn against Sweden all at once. The Russians defected; after concluding an alliance with Jan Kazimierz in May 1656, Alexis Romanov sent his armies against Livonia, Estonia, Kexholm, and Ingria. Swedish defenses held strong, but the Russian onslaught was a powerful one, and the Muscovites managed to take Dorpat before withdrawing, exhausted, from Livonia at the end of 1656. Alexis did not continue the fight, and the two adversaries arranged an armistice in 1658, but Russian hostility was a major cause for concern. To the south, Karl Gustav accepted the support of the prince of Transylvania, Georg Rákóczi, in return for recognizing Rákóczi as king of Poland. The Transylvanian brought a large army and rendered valuable service to the Swedes, but he also brought with him – because of his ambitions in Hungary – the spectre of Habsburg intervention. At the end of 1656, Emperor Ferdinand III promised a token force to assist Jan Kazimierz, but in May of the following year Ferdinand's successor, the Emperor Leopold I (1658–1705), sent a much larger contingent to aid Jan Kazimierz against the Swedes. Even Karl Gustav's only legitimate ally, Brandenburg, turned against him. In a brilliant demonstration of diplomatic *Realpolitik*, the Great Elector cast his lot with Poland in September 1657, receiving in return Jan Kazimierz's recognition of

Brandenburg's possession of Ducal Prussia. The Swedish armies in Poland could accomplish nothing more. Even before Brandenburg's defection, Karl Gustav had begun to withdraw the bulk of his forces towards Pomerania. This withdrawal was not panicked, nor was it even an admission of defeat, for Karl Gustav had found another, more vulnerable target: Denmark.[5]

The Danish War, 1657–60

The Danes had not forgotten the humiliation of Brömsebro a decade before. The marriage of Karl X Gustav to Hedwig Eleonora of Holstein-Gottorp compounded that humiliation. Alliance with the duchy gave Sweden a strategically valuable base of operations on Denmark's southern frontier, but it was a blow to Denmark's prestige as well: it was ruled by a cadet line of the Oldenburg dynasty, its dukes the direct descendants of Frederick I of Denmark, and relations with the Gottorp dukes had been a thorny issue for Christian IV.[6] The constitutional upheaval in Denmark that followed Christian IV's death in 1648 made Sweden's former overlord even more dangerous. Christian's son and successor, Frederik III (1648–70), was the victim of an aristocratic reaction in Danish politics after 1648. His powers had been severely curtailed by a coronation charter forced upon him by his Council of State. Sweden's problems in Poland presented Frederik III with a promising opportunity, both to recoup the losses incurred at Brömsebro and to improve the king's standing at home. In 1656, Danish naval forces joined a Dutch fleet sent to protect Danzig from the Swedes, but Frederik III did not openly show his hand until Leopold of Austria did first. As soon as he knew that Austrian troops were on their way towards Poland, Frederik III and his Council declared war on Sweden and concluded an alliance with Poland. In June and July 1657, a Danish army overran Bremen, while Danish troops in Norway moved into Jämtland and Västergötland.[7]

It was a disastrous mistake. The Danish War of 1657–59 would be, in many ways, a re-enactment of the Torstensson War, only this time the losses and the resultant humiliation would be much greater. Reacting with stunning alacrity, the Swedish king sent Karl Gustav Wrangel to attack the Danish heartland from the south. Wrangel recaptured Bremen, sweeping into Holstein and Jutland. By August 1657, Swedish forces had taken Kolding in central Jutland, and had invested the formidable new fortress at Frederiksodde (modern-day Fredericia); by the end of October, Frederiksodde had fallen and the entire peninsula was occupied. Native Danish troops put up a pitiful defense of Jutland, and the local nobility fled the mainland in terror. The victory was stunning but not decisive, and Denmark was not yet defeated. Frederik III still had a respectable navy at his command; despite the disparity between Swedish and Danish land forces, the two Scandinavian rivals were still about evenly matched in naval strength. A strong Danish navy, and a series of powerful fortifications built during the 1640s and 1650s, protected the Danish islands from attack.

Serendipity intervened on behalf of the Swedes. Foul weather had kept the Danes from making effective use of their fleet during the autumn months; the harsh winter of 1657–58 would prove to be outright disastrous for Denmark. For the first time in recent memory, the waterways that served as the most important defensive feature of the Danish islands – the *Lillebælt*, separating Jutland from the central island of Fyn, and the *Storebælt*, which lay between Fyn and Sjælland – froze over. This bizarre occurrence simultaneously prevented the Danish fleet from defending the islands and allowed the Swedish army to move about the kingdom at will. In early February 1658, Karl Gustav and his army crossed the narrow waters of the *Lillebælt*, taking thinly defended Fyn within days. Less than two weeks later, the king – against the advice of his generals – marched his army across the untested ice of the *Storebælt*, approaching Sjælland from the south and east. The Danish forces defending the island were taken by surprise. Though the Swedish force in Sjælland was not a large one, its mere arrival in Vordingborg, dangerously near to Copenhagen, was enough to frighten the Danes into submission. Frederik III sued immediately for peace. The resulting treaty, signed at Roskilde on 8 March 1658, was a catastrophe for Denmark. Brömsebro had already brought about the cession of Jämtland and Härjedalen, plus the pawning of Halland, to Sweden; Roskilde built upon these gains. Halland was now a permanent Swedish possession, to which were added Blekinge and Skåne. The three Scanian provinces were Denmark's richest farming lands, and without them Denmark could not control the Sound. More Norwegian territory, including Bohuslän and Trondheim, was ceded to Sweden, effectively splitting Norway in two and giving Sweden yet another valuable North Sea port. Frederik III was also forced to disgorge the island of Bornholm, Denmark's easternmost outpost, a concession that would be of great strategic importance for Swedish fleets operating in the south central Baltic. In addition, Denmark would be obligated to help prevent the passage of foreign fleets into the Baltic, to provide Karl Gustav with two thousand troops, and to provision the Swedish occupying force in Denmark until May 1658. Brömsebro had brought Denmark's *dominium maris Baltic* to an end, but Roskilde destroyed the last shred of the Oldenburg monarchy's pretensions to that dominion. Sweden had vanquished its former overlord, and never again would Europe perceive Denmark as anything other than a second-rate power.

Roskilde also marked the point at which most European statesmen began to view Sweden as a nuisance and not as the heroic champion of the anti-Habsburg cause. Gustav Adolf had been a hero; Karl Gustav was an unprincipled aggressor. The wars against Poland and Denmark had alienated nearly all of Sweden's potential allies and enraged her traditional enemies. The Polish Commonwealth had recovered from its ignominious defeat in 1655–56, and was preparing to seek vengeance on Swedish holdings in Livonia and Estonia. Habsburg Austria was wary of Karl Gustav for his actions in Poland, as was Russia. Karl Gustav dared not attack any of these opponents; the campaigns of 1656–57 had demonstrated that even a fresh, well-disciplined army could not hold onto Poland for long, and any action against Austria ran the risk of alienating the German princes. Brandenburg had already turned against Sweden. Oliver Cromwell had courted Sweden, but the closure of the Sound to foreign fleets was not welcome news in England, and anyway both Cromwell and his Protectorate would be dead shortly.[8] The Dutch, too, quailed at the prospect of a closed Sound and of an over-mighty Sweden. Only Mazarin's France, of all the leading powers, had not entirely deserted Sweden, and Mazarin had in mind uses for Sweden other than involvement in a drawn-out Polish War.

Karl Gustav was faced with a painful dilemma: the overwhelming strength of his enemies, and the ferocity of Polish hostility, meant that he could not disband his forces, yet Sweden could not sustain a battle-ready mercenary army on its own soil. Karl Gustav contemplated an attack in Prussia, both to seize the duchy and to avenge himself upon the Great Elector. Much to the surprise of his contemporaries, the king settled on an easier target. Denmark had already been defeated, but the Copenhagen government was not proving to be very cooperative in executing the terms of the Roskilde treaty. In mid-August 1658, without a word of warning, Karl Gustav set out by sea from Kiel and landed his army on Sjælland, laying siege to Copenhagen yet again. Denmark was no more prepared, perhaps even less so, for the audacity of its old enemy than it had been the year before, but this time Denmark had powerful friends. Although the Swedes had already taken the town of Helsingør and its imposing fortress Kronborg, giving them control of the Sound, a huge Dutch fleet forced its way into the Sound to relieve beleaguered Copenhagen. In the well-fortified capital, the once-unpopular Frederik III stood shoulder-to-shoulder with the town militia and the garrison, holding off the Swedish besiegers and making himself a national hero in the process. Most disturbing, a large Imperial–Brandenburg–Polish army moved rapidly into Holstein and Jutland in the autumn and winter of 1658–59. The combination of threats wrecked Karl Gustav's plans. By the end of 1659, Swedish forces were trapped in Denmark, with no obvious means of escape by land or by sea, and they were in full retreat in Prussia.

Sweden managed to extricate itself from this potential nightmare purely by accident. Shortly after returning to Sweden to attend to his affairs there, Karl X Gustav took ill and died, reportedly from pneumonia, on 23 February 1660. As the king had no adult successor to take up his leadership – his son, now King Karl XI, was but a boy of 5 years – the untried and understandably nervous regency government was eager to make peace. Fortunately for Sweden, its enemies were divided by faction, and in no condition to prolong the war for much longer. The conditions of peace, set forward in three different treaties in 1660–61, were accordingly lenient: the Peace of Oliva (May 1660; Sweden, Poland, Austria, and Brandenburg) re-established the *status quo ante bellum* of 1655, but gave formal recognition to Swedish claims to Livonia and revoked the claims of the Polish kings to the Swedish throne; the Peace of Copenhagen (June 1660; Sweden and Denmark) returned Bornholm and Trondheim to Danish rule, but otherwise kept intact the terms of Roskilde; the Peace of Kardis (1661; Sweden and Russia) brought about the return to Sweden of territories taken by the Muscovites since 1656. It was not, perhaps, a settlement that Karl Gustav would have found to his liking two years earlier, but it was more than Sweden had any right to expect. Sweden did not lose any of its pre-war possessions, and its conquests from Denmark were for the most part sustained. The settlements at Oliva, Copenhagen, and Kardis were collectively, in Robert Frost's words, a 'lucky escape' for Sweden, but Sweden itself had suffered considerable damage. Sweden would once again be in a position to launch an equally ambitious war on several fronts, but it would take the better part of four decades – and a fundamental reorganization of the state – before it could do so.

Karl X Gustav and the Swedish Constitution

Swedish historians remain divided in their verdict over the constitutional legacy of Karl X Gustav's reign. Although this first king of the Pfalz-Zweibrücken line ruled for less than six years, much changed for Sweden – both internationally and domestically – during his brief reign. Despite the king's failure to achieve his avowed foreign policy goals, he had accomplished a great deal, most notably a defeat of Denmark that came close to entailing Denmark's incorporation into the Swedish empire. Such gains, however, came only with great sacrifice on the part of all orders of Swedish society, and the necessary sacrifices were not made willingly. When Gustav II Adolf had been compelled to ask his subjects to pay higher taxes and tender more conscripts for the German War, the people of the Vasa state – though inured to hardship – were still relatively fresh and undeterred by the prospect of conflicts to come. When Karl X Gustav did the same in 1654–55, the Swedish population was in much worse shape. The lower orders had already come close to threatening resistance at the 1650 *Riksdag*, and made it clear that they were no longer willing to accept wartime levels of taxation and conscription unless the nobility made parallel sacrifices. Maintaining Sweden's status as a great and influential power in the mid-1650s was a much more difficult proposition than first asserting that influence had been in 1630.

The task that confronted Karl X Gustav throughout his reign would require administrative, constitutional, and social change, and for that reason Swedish scholars have been tempted to find in his reign the tell-tale precursors of absolute monarchy in Sweden. The explicit imposition of absolutism would not come until 1680, when Karl XI found both the chance and the justification for doing so, but Karl X Gustav's actions during the late 1650s have led several historians – including Stellan Dahlgren, Hans Landberg, and Göran Rystad – to posit that it was the father, not the son, who first endeavored to free the monarchy of the constitutional shackles with which the nobility held the crown in check. On the surface, the evidence these historians summon to defend their argument is compelling. Karl Gustav rarely consulted with his Council as a group, and only summoned two full meetings of the Diet during his reign; he did not feel compelled to seek the assent of the *Riksdag* when imposing new taxes, demanding more intensive conscription, or when concluding alliances or peace treaties. The king kept for himself the right to make administrative appointments. Occasionally he neglected to fill important positions at all; when Erik Oxenstierna, who had followed his father as chancellor in 1654, died in 1656, Karl Gustav did not bother to appoint a successor.[9] The most damning piece of evidence is Karl Gustav's determination to drive through a *reduktion*, the compulsory return of the extensive crown properties alienated to noble families under Gustav Adolf and Christina. Only a would-be absolutist would countenance such actions; and Karl Gustav, who coincidentally admired the writings of Bodin, seemed to fit the bill. In the words of Hans Landberg, Karl X Gustav 'emancipated' the crown from the fetters of the nobility in general and the Council in particular.[10]

As Michael Roberts pointed out in one of his last essays on seventeenth-century Sweden, such conclusions confuse cause and effect. Of all the Swedish monarchs who ruled before 1660, Karl X Gustav was probably the most sensitive to the feelings of his nobility and the most conscientious in his dealings with the Council. He strove to follow the example of his illustrious predecessor Gustav Adolf: to work with the Council and the *Riksdag* in order to mobilize Sweden's resources to their fullest. This is particularly evident if we examine the king's relationship to the Council. It is true that Karl Gustav did not meet regularly with the Council *as a body*, for that would have been virtually impossible given the duration of the king's absences and the fact that so many councillors had other pressing administrative or military duties. Nonetheless, the king kept in close contact with the Council even while on campaign, and met with at least a small core group of the Council during his short visits to Stockholm. When he did meet with them, he was open to suggestions and encouraged debate, without resorting to the forcefulness or high-handed imperiousness with which both Gustav Adolf and Christina had sometimes treated their Councils. For its part, the Council served the king loyally, and not merely out of fear. Karl Gustav's Council worked well together as a team, with little open factionalism. But they also worked well with the king himself. The councillors might have looked to Per Brahe, a leading advocate of noble privilege during Christina's regency, for leadership, but above all they sought to please their king. In trivial matters of day-to-day administration, the Council might take independent action in the king's absence, but in the main they deferred to the king, and sought to pursue his instructions to the letter. The Council made it abundantly clear that while they expected to play some role in the mobilization of resources for war, they left to the king's judgment all major decisions affecting foreign policy – with whom to fight or to conclude alliances, and when to make peace. In short, Karl Gustav and his Council enjoyed uncommon solidarity, which in turn derived from the nobility's traditional emphasis on service to the state. The king usually got what he wanted when he wanted it, and the Council went along, not because of any kind of royal intimidation, but out of a kind of noble patriotism.[11]

It is also true that Karl Gustav was not terribly assiduous in consulting with the Diet as a whole. In part, this owed to the limitations that command in the field placed upon his availability. It also stemmed from the recognition that it was the lower orders, not the nobility, that objected to his policies. The nobility did not question the necessity of their king's military commitments, but the peasantry and the burghers were not happy to bear the high costs of continuous warfare. The conscription levels of 1642 – 1:20 for noble peasants, 1:10 for others, assessed by number of farms – were insufficient to meet wartime demands. The quotas had been changed in Christina's last years to 1:16 and 1:8 respectively, though this grant expired in 1656. The following year, Karl Gustav reintroduced conscription by headcount, with ten men to a *rota*, even on noble-owned lands. The need for manpower was so acute between 1657 and 1658 that Karl Gustav carried out four conscriptions. The king, however, did not feel compelled to summon the *Riksdag* for each and every change in conscription quotas, nor to consult with them regarding the introduction of heavier taxes, which affected the nobility as well. And yet this makes Karl Gustav neither an absolutist nor an innovator. Gustav Adolf, for example, had not troubled himself to meet with the *Riksdag* when he imposed new taxes as he prepared to intervene in Germany prior to 1630. And Karl Gustav – and his Council – *did* seek a broader popular mandate for increases in taxation and conscription; not through meetings of the entire *Riksdag*, but through 'secret committees', smaller gatherings of representatives from all four estates, and through provincial diets. The latter proved to be especially valuable, since they allowed the central government to make special deals with individual regions, while at the same time precluding the possibility of having to face an organized, national resistance to royal policies.[12]

It should be pointed out that Karl Gustav did not attempt to use the support of the lower orders as a weapon against noble power. Though a common tactic of the Vasa monarchs, Karl X Gustav did not employ it. At the *Riksdag* of 1655, when the king made the first formal proposal for a *reduktion*, he could count on the support of the lower orders, but by then the Council had already steeled itself for the sacrifice. There were no open confrontations between the nobility and the lower orders supported by the crown, as there had been in 1650. If the nobility, and therefore the Council, were rendered more pliable by fear of a repeat performance of the 1650 *Riksdag*, then so much the better for the king. For his part, however, Karl Gustav did nothing to encourage such fears.

The question of the *reduktion*, which will be addressed in detail later, requires at least a word of explanation here, for the *reduktion* would be the hallmark of Swedish absolutism two decades later. Karl Gustav had decided to pursue this course of action even before he ascended the throne in 1654. It would not be implemented during his reign, and would become a dead letter in the period between his death and the end of the Scanian War in 1679. The king did not approach it as a means of weakening the nobility or of increasing the wealth of the monarchy at the nobility's expense, though the *reduktion* inherently entailed both of these developments. To Karl Gustav, it was a fiscal imperative. The state debt at the end of Christina's reign was horrendous, and the necessity of preparing for war in 1655 would require additional sources of income. There were no foreign subsidies as in the 1630s; there were no Prussian port-tolls as there had been under Gustav Adolf. All other resources had been tapped: some of the most lucrative export duties, including those on copper and the ancient 'Great Toll', were pawned to several creditors in 1655. Alienation may have made royal properties more productive, farm for farm, but it also robbed the state fisc of much of its ordinary income: by the time of Karl Gustav's succession, about 60 percent of that income went to private landowners, and nearly two-thirds of Sweden was now tax-exempt.[13] Karl Gustav was committed to seeing the *reduktion* through, creating a special college within the administration solely for this purpose, under the direction of councillors Herman Fleming and Gustav Bonde. The king did not force this upon his nobility. He aired the proposal to the Council in the spring of 1655, and then pointedly absented himself from their deliberations, allowing them to come to the (albeit grudging) conclusion that it was the nobility's patriotic duty to give up at least some of the lands they had acquired from the crown. Only then did the issue pass before the *Riksdag*. The support of the lower orders at the 1655 *Riksdag* was important for the king, for they – like Karl Gustav – insisted on an immediate restoration of one-quarter of all land donations made since 1632. The non-noble estates also argued that any *reduktion* should be considered a process without a specific timetable, and not a one-time and final act on the part of the nobility. This final question was not resolved before the king's death. In the meantime, the nobility would have to pay the rents accruing from the lands eligible for *reduktion*. The nobility, in the *Riddarhus* and on the Council, only gave in to the policy of *reduktion* when faced with less attractive alternatives and in the hope that acquiescence would secure their other financial privileges. But it was also the nobility – speaking through the Council – that allowed the *reduktion* to become policy, by agreeing to it in principle without coercion from king or *Riksdag*.[14]

In constitutional terms, then, the reign of Karl X Gustav was a period of close partnership between king and nobility. This is not to say, however, that the nobility, or even the Council, would have tolerated the king's ambitious foreign policies any longer than they ultimately had to. After the short-lived peace settlement at Roskilde in 1658, the Council – heretofore exhibiting nothing but unquestioning loyalty to their royal master – recognized that perhaps the king had gone too far in his ambitions by provoking the enmity or jealousy of nearly all Europe. They saw what would become apparent at the end of the century, that Sweden was on the threshold of imperial overextension, and at that point they did not hesitate to tell the king that they were now reluctant to lend their support to his every whim in matters of foreign policy. This Karl Gustav accepted with good grace, and at any rate his death early in 1660 spared Sweden the possibility of a confrontation between king and Council over this issue. Karl X Gustav did not attempt to crush, sidestep, or intimidate his nobility, but the effect was the same after his death. Concerned that an unrestrained monarch would lead Sweden to disaster, the ruling elite in the aristocracy was determined not to allow this to happen again. And the fact that Sweden faced the prospect of another regency, made necessary by the youth of the as yet uncrowned Karl XI, allowed the aristocracy to take the requisite measures to protect itself from the royal prerogative.

Chapter 7: The Swedish Empire in Louis XIV's Europe, 1660–79

Had the plans of Karl X Gustav come to full fruition, they would have amounted to something bordering on a diplomatic revolution. If Denmark had succumbed to the post-Roskilde onslaught, it could have been incorporated into the Swedish empire; if the war with Poland had ended favorably, the Swedish spoils in the south central Baltic rim would have included Royal Prussia at the very least. But Sweden could not attain either of these goals; the forces ranged against it were simply too great. Nor was Sweden able to maintain its tentative footholds outside Europe. The 'New Sweden' colony established in 1638 along the banks of the Delaware, in the present-day American states of New Jersey and Delaware, had failed shortly after Karl Gustav's succession. The colony had expanded and prospered, albeit modestly, under the capable direction of Governor Johan Printz. When Printz's successor, the more aggressive Johan Rising, attempted to seize Dutch settlements encroaching on the Delaware Valley, he sealed the fate of New Sweden. Dutch colonial forces retaliated in 1655, taking the main settlement at Fort Christina and dissolving the colony. The tolerant Dutch administration allowed, even encouraged, the Swedish settlers to stay, and most of them did so; but New Sweden, as a crown colony, was no more. Cabo Corso, an outpost on Africa's Gold Coast seized from Portugal by Louis de Geer's Swedish-based trading company in 1655, fared no better, and fell to the Dutch in 1663.[1]

Regardless of these setbacks, the Swedish empire was at its greatest territorial extent in 1660–61. The peace settlements at Oliva, Copenhagen, and Kardis secured Sweden's conquests in the eastern Baltic and in

Germany. The possessions in Livonia now had international recognition, and Sweden held most of the Scandinavian peninsula; it had robbed Denmark of its most prosperous regions and its stranglehold on Baltic commerce. With Denmark vanquished, and neither Poland nor Russia capable of maintaining a significant naval presence, the Baltic was in effect a Swedish *mare nostrum*. The population of the Swedish empire in 1620 did not exceed 1.25 million souls; by 1660, it numbered around 2.5 million. Sweden had doubled its population in forty years purely through conquest, something that none of its contemporaries on the Continent could match.[2]

The Burden of Empire

Unfortunately, the Swedish government could not rest on its laurels. Creating an empire through the triumph of Swedish arms was one thing, maintaining it and protecting it entirely another. Perhaps war could feed itself; but Gustav Adolf's optimistic *dictum* appeared to have been proven false during the Polish War of the late 1650s. Peace, to be sure, could *not* feed itself, not for a state which had to be constantly on its guard on so many fronts, and for which the material demands of national security were so overwhelming. For Sweden, sustaining an empire in peace would prove to be far more vexing than creating an empire in war.

The Swedish empire in 1660 was a diverse conglomeration of lands. Confessional homogeneity was a distinct advantage in an age of heightened religious tensions – Lutheranism predominated throughout the empire – but the territories and subject populations that made up the Swedish empire represented a myriad of languages, customs, and laws. German had been the *lingua franca* of the Baltic region in diplomacy and commerce, and so it became the administrative language of the Swedish empire as well; forcing an alien language upon several subject populations would have proven all but impossible when Sweden could barely provide enough bureaucrats to fill the needs of the kingdom itself. A very few regions, like Ingria, were sparsely populated and hence easy to re-shape to Sweden's mold. Indeed, Gustav Adolf had sought to populate the region with German and Dutch 'colonists', and – failing that – with Swedes and Finns. But much of the remainder of the conquered lands had well-established, prosperous, and cultured populations. Bremen and Verden were the best examples of the latter type. Bremen had been among the wealthiest of the Hanseatic ports, clearly exceeding Stockholm in seniority and in cosmopolitan sophistication.

Only the Lutheran faith held the Swedish empire together culturally; perhaps that could be a strong bond in itself, but it was not enough to suppress the barely disguised hostility with which some of the conquered populations regarded the Swedish presence in their lands. Keeping the empire safe from outside attack was difficult, to say the least, when so many of its outposts chafed under Swedish rule. Proud Bremen and Verden particularly resented their status as Swedish provinces, a status that had been imposed upon them by force. To be sure, they had also resented their previous possession by Denmark, but the Danish administration there had not been nearly so intrusive and demanding as the Swedes were. In Skåne, Blekinge, and Halland, the problems presented by collective regional pride were perhaps the worst. In these former Danish lands – provinces, not possessions, of the Oldenburg monarchy, which some of the most important Danish aristocratic families called home – loyalty to the old motherland persisted. During the Danish War of 1657–60, Skåne had been a hotbed of popular resistance to Swedish rule, as the peasant leader Svend Poulsen carried out an annoying *petite guerre* against Karl X Gustav. The Scanian lands were not distant frontier outposts. They were contiguous with the Swedish heartland; their rich agricultural economy was an asset that the Swedish kings had long coveted, and their ports and shipbuilding facilities were of vital strategic importance to the empire.[3]

Resentment of Sweden within its conquered lands paled in comparison with the hostility of the neighboring powers that had lost territory, prestige, and resources as a direct result of Sweden's rise to power. Denmark had suffered a permanent and crippling setback, but the Danes' thirst for revenge – not just among the ruling elite, but throughout all levels of society – was palpable and dangerous after 1660. The Swedish partnership with Holstein-Gottorp directly threatened Denmark from the south and constituted a blow to Oldenburg dynastic pride. And the Danes now had the backing of the Dutch. Earlier in the century, the Dutch Republic tended to side with Sweden against Denmark, since the latter was the greater threat to the security of Dutch commerce in the Baltic; but the tables had turned, and Sweden's grip over the Baltic was tighter than Denmark's had ever been. Brandenburg smarted over the loss of Pomerania, and feared Swedish ambitions on Prussia. Resentment of Sweden was nearly universal throughout the Holy Roman Empire. Gustav Adolf may have been initially greeted as the liberator of Protestant

Germany in 1630–31, but the damage wrought by Swedish armies after that point, and the heavy exactions demanded by Oxenstierna between 1632 and the early 1650s, gave rise to a pervasive ill will towards Sweden that persisted well past the end of the war, in Protestant territories as well as Catholic. During the wars of Karl X Gustav, the bulk of German princely support seems to have been squarely with Brandenburg and Austria. To the east and southeast, the outlook for acquiescence to Swedish dominion was no better. Poland might have been crushed, and in power and influence a mere shadow of what the Commonwealth had been a century before, but it was still a dangerous foe. The threat presented by Russia was incalculable. Only internal political strife held back the tsars from contesting Sweden's position in the eastern Baltic, and it would not be long before that obstacle would be at least partially removed. Ironically, the empire built to protect Sweden by breaking a perceived territorial encirclement created a situation in which Sweden really was encircled by hostile states, collectively powerful and bent on revenge.[4]

The ruling elite in Sweden was not unaware of the problems that faced it both within its empire and without. Nearly all political discourse within the Swedish polity – whether it took the form of debates over fiscal policy or strained relations between the classes – derived in some way from the larger question of how to run the empire. One of the most vexing problems confronting the Swedish crown and Council during the course of the seventeenth century involved the relationship between center and periphery. Should the newly acquired territories be given the status of Swedish provinces, enjoying the same rights of Swedish law and participation in the political process as Sweden and Finland? Or should they be treated as subject lands, paying tribute to Stockholm but left to their own devices in matters of local administration? The earlier Vasa kings had aspired to the former solution. Extending the rights of free Swedes to the conquered populations – in essence, making them *Swedes* – made practical sense. By emphasizing uniformity and standardization, it would make administration less difficult, while broadening the state's tax-base and supplying more warm bodies to the Swedish war machine through application of the *utskrivning*. The rapid expansion of the empire after 1630, however, rendered such an approach difficult. The Swedish bureaucracy was not up to the task, at least in numbers, of imposing Swedish institutions, law, and administration on such a diverse assortment of territories. It was simpler to maintain troops and a handful of administrators to supervise established local governments, to promote trade with the motherland, and to exact the taxes necessary for the upkeep of a mercenary army. The self-interest of the Swedish nobility must also be taken into account. A true incorporation of the conquered lands into the Swedish polity would mean allowing them representation in the *Riksdag* and possibly on the Council; why would the nobility wish to dilute its power? Moreover, Swedish administrators and generals had assembled tremendous *latifundia* in the subject lands. Integration of these lands as ordinary Swedish provinces would diminish the nobility's political, economic, and social control in what they saw as their private principalities. For these reasons, Axel Oxenstierna, among many others, argued against territorial assimilation, and the policy stuck. As a consequence, the Swedish administrative presence was minimal throughout much of the empire, particularly within Pomerania and Bremen-Verden. Life in Pomerania, for example, continued on much as it did before 1631, except that now the king of Sweden was also duke of Pomerania. Swedish rule did not make Pomerania Swedish, but it did make the king of Sweden a German prince.[5]

In commercial terms there was slightly more solidarity in the empire. By 1660, all of the major port-towns of the Baltic, save Copenhagen, Königsberg, and Danzig, belonged to Sweden. Potentially, this was a commercial gold mine for Stockholm. The Brömsebro treaty had granted free passage to all Swedish shipping, whether it came from Sweden and Finland or from the provincial ports. Axel Oxenstierna hoped that the loosening of Danish control over the Sound would result in freer and consequently more active shipping to and from the Baltic, with the Swedish-held ports acting as entrepôts for the vast agricultural wealth of the Baltic hinterland. Such traffic, if not overly regulated, could provide a tremendous income for the crown in the form of tolls and customs duties. In practice, however, neither a uniform system of tolls nor real freedom of trade was ever established in the empire. The provincial ports all enjoyed different privileges and freedoms, some regions (as in Livonia) being heavily regulated by Stockholm while others (like Ingria) were not. The exigencies of war could also wreak havoc on Baltic commerce, as the central government found it necessary from time to time to restrict exports of grain and other goods of strategic value. Nor did trade within the empire really thrive during the century, at least not until Sweden became truly dependent on grain from the provinces during the 1680s and 1690s. The provinces may well have prospered somewhat under Swedish rule and protection, but Sweden did not prosper from its empire. Despite the shorter distances involved – or perhaps because of the shorter distances – Sweden did not gain noticeably from the commerce of its Baltic dominions, nor were the provinces themselves dependent upon the motherland. An empire it might be, yet it did not compare – in wealth or cohesiveness – with the overseas empires of England, Spain, or the Netherlands.

This, perhaps, was the central fact that shaped the brief history of the Swedish empire: it cost far more to maintain than it returned in profits. Whether actively at war or protecting its borders in times of peace, Sweden could not support its own mechanisms of governance and security. While the war in Denmark had been self-sustaining up to a point, the Polish War of the late 1650s had demonstrated the inefficacy of the *bellum se ipsum alit* concept. That war had been financed largely on credit, credit extended because the financiers involved anticipated generous returns on their investments, based on Sweden's stellar performance in the Thirty Years' War. Sweden's native manpower, mobilized through *utskrivning*, was not up to the task of defending anything outside the borders of Sweden itself. Indirect taxes and commercial duties were inadequate to cover the needs of a growing bureaucracy. Already during the reign of Karl X Gustav the central government found itself unable to pay the salaries of much of its bureaucracy. The 1650 *Riksdag*, moreover, illustrated the social dangers inherent in sustaining conscription and indirect taxation at wartime levels for prolonged periods.[6]

The problem of financing the empire would be the greatest one that the rulers of Sweden would face, and everything depended on its resolution. With the income provided by direct and indirect taxes, and the manpower mobilized through conscription, stretched to their practical limits, the Swedish government had three options, all of them potentially painful. As suggested by the lower orders at the 1650 *Riksdag*, the nobility could make the ultimate sacrifice and permanently abandon their tax-exempt status. A full-fledged *reduktion* – not carried out in half-measures as was done in 1655 – could also ease the financial burden on the central government just enough, and mollify the grievances of the lower orders as well. The first solution was distasteful to the entire noble estate, and the second repugnant at least to the two upper classes of the nobility, those who had benefitted most from the massive land donations of previous decades. The third solution did not pose any threat to the established social order: finding a source of subsidies abroad, as Gustav Adolf and Oxenstierna had done with France in the 1630s. If maintaining an army on a wartime footing could be tailored to meet the ends of a great and wealthier power – like France or Spain – then perhaps there was hope for the Swedish empire after all. But it was a dangerous road to travel. Hiring out the entire nation to the highest bidder made it more likely that Sweden would become involved in unnecessary wars, and could reduce the proud Baltic superpower to international subservience, a doer of the bidding of others rather than an independent power in its own right.

Aristocratic Reaction: The Regency of Karl XI

The nobility had loyally backed Karl Gustav during his wars against Poland, Muscovy, and Denmark. Unlike their Danish counterparts, they did not incline towards pacifism and isolationism. War, after all, had brought them their wealth and influence, and they were bound to the monarch through their positions in the administration and the officer corps. Until the summer of 1658, they did not so much as question their king's foreign policy decisions. Loyalty to the crown, however, did not mean complete abandonment of self-interest; continuation of the Danish War after Roskilde, and emergency fiscal measures like the *reduktion*, were emphatically not in their collective self-interest. It is possible to speculate that had Karl X Gustav lived past 1660 Sweden could have experienced something like the clash between crown and noble interests that resulted in the 1660 royalist coup in Denmark. If so, the death of the king after the January 1660 *Riksdag* spared Sweden such a confrontation. With their warlike king gone, the nobility did not hesitate to demonstrate its sense of self-preservation in the regency government that followed.

Karl Gustav had made preparations for a regency while on his death-bed early in 1660, and these constitute a departure from what had become established constitutional practice in Sweden. Karl X Gustav's 'Testament' was the first such document to be produced since Gustav Vasa's testament of 1560. The purpose of Karl Gustav's testament, however, was much different from that of his forebear. Gustav Vasa had sought to preserve the efficient administration of a newborn and fragile monarchy, and to protect Sweden from the mutual jealousies of his offspring. Karl Gustav's testament, on the other hand, attempted to set up a system by which the interests of the royal house would be protected against noble attempts to curb the royal prerogative. A comparison with Gustav II Adolf's proposed regency government reveals the innovative and royalist nature of the later testament. Gustav Adolf had outlined a regency from which the royal family, except for Christina herself, was completely excluded. The key positions were held by Chancellor

Oxenstierna and the leading officers of state from the Council. Karl Gustav, on the other hand, proposed a regency that was predominately royal or at least royalist. Karl XI's minority regency would consist of the dowager-queen Hedwig Eleonora – undoubtedly better suited to political responsibility than Maria Eleonora had been – and the five leading officers of state. Several of these offices, however, were vacant, so the dying king made three last-minute appointments: his brother, Duke Adolf Johan, became Marshal; his brother-in-law and Christina's former favorite, Magnus Gabriel De la Gardie, became Chancellor; and the leading proponent of the *reduktion*, Herman Fleming, was made Treasurer.

This arrangement would not stand. The aristocratic Council would not sit idly by and watch its rights and privileges be eroded further. Meeting after the king's death, the Council proposed to exclude both Adolf Johan and Herman Fleming from the regency government. These alterations were given the estates' stamp of approval when the *Riksdag* met twice later that same year. The Council had reasserted itself; 1660 marks the 'emancipation of the Council' from royal control. The victory of the aristocratic reaction, however, was incomplete. As the price of its collaboration in overturning the king's last command, the *Riksdag* had put forward its own demands in the *Additament* to the 1634 Form of Government, approved in November 1660. The *Additament* reiterated that, in the future, all regency governments were to be conducted in accordance with the 1634 Form, and with the dowager queen and the five great officers in nominal charge of day-to-day administration. But the *Riksdag* itself would hold a position of great constitutional importance. It reserved the final right of approval of individuals appointed to the Regency; it required that it be convened at least once every three years, and at that point it would receive a detailed report about the Regency's actions in the intervening period; finally, the *Riksdag* stipulated that all major policy decisions made by the Regency would require the 'knowledge and approval' of – not just 'consultation with' – the assembled *Riksdag*. The *Riksdag* had taken upon itself a role not dissimilar to that of an English Parliament.[7] The *Additament*, however, should not be mistaken for a furtive movement towards parliamentary rule, for these conditions were not permanent; they were to end as soon as the king reached his majority and could assume the mantle of governance for himself. The demands of the *Riksdag* were aimed at redressing constitutional inequities that had arisen under Karl X Gustav. Its claim to legislative monopoly, for example, stemmed from Karl Gustav's reliance upon 'secret committees' and provincial meetings of the estates. But in the main, the conditions set forth in the *Additament* were meant to curb the power of the great magnates. The *Riksdag*, in other words, was to protect the interests of the crown from those of the nobility until such a time as the king could do so himself. It had not given up its traditional partnership with the monarchy.

One further clause in the *Additament* deserves special attention. At the November 1660 *Riksdag*, the lower orders gave vent to a telltale expression of anti-aristocratic feeling. The most important offices within the bureaucracy had long been dominated by men of high birth, and were usually reserved for the foremost families of the realm: the nobles of the first and second 'classes' as defined by the ordinance of 1626. The remaining estates understandably chafed at this, including the lesser nobility of the third class. In the *Additament*, this formidable alliance of peasants, burghers, and lesser nobles placed strict limits on the number of political offices that could be held by a single family, and insisted that in the future all administrative appointments and promotions be based on merit, not on birth. If the events of 1660 mark the emancipation of the nobility from the royal prerogative, they also mark the subjection of noble rule to a measure of the popular will.[8]

The regency of 1660–72 would not result in any violent constitutional upheaval. Quite the contrary; it functioned quite smoothly overall, much like the earlier regency of 1632–44. De la Gardie's Regency kept its word pledged in 1660, above all in the regular summoning of the *Riksdag*, which met in 1664, 1668, and finally in 1672. The similarities between the two regency governments, however, are largely superficial. Much more complex problems, at least in terms of foreign policy, confronted the 1632 Regency, and the national shock occasioned by Gustav Adolf's death should not be underestimated. Although riddled by faction, the 1632 Regency had performed well, not least because of the dedicated and brilliant administration of Axel Oxenstierna. Moreover, Oxenstierna and his fellow regents made an avowed and honest attempt to govern the empire in the way in which Gustav Adolf had done. The 1660 Regency was not quite so beset by faction, but neither did it have a figure of Oxenstierna's calibre presiding over it. The dominant figure of the 1660 Regency was Magnus De la Gardie, who like Oxenstierna held the position of chancellor. De la Gardie was bright, eloquent, and a competent administrator. While not unusually venal or corrupt by seventeenth-century standards, De la Gardie was also self-serving; in this regard, at least, the Regency would bear his personal stamp. And De la Gardie emphatically did *not* want to see Sweden continue along the same path it had embarked upon under his late sovereign.[9]

De la Gardie's character and abilities revealed themselves in the debates over the resolution of the government's fiscal crisis. The *reduktion* was, after 1660, a dead letter. Herman Fleming was not in a position to set it in motion, and the Council had no interest in pursuing a policy that would entail great personal loss to its members. Still, something had to be done to bring the crown's vast expenditures and minimal revenues into balance. At the time of Karl Gustav's death, government expenditures came to approximately 10.5 million *riksdaler* annually, but revenues amounted to a paltry 4 million *riksdaler*.[10] Gustav Bonde, Fleming's successor as treasurer, thought he had found the answer, and in 1661 he put it to paper. The treasurer outlined the place of each estate within the political economy of Sweden: the nobility should be able to count on regularly paid salaries for their administrative duties, yet still have lands to supplement their income; the clergy should take care not to overfill their ranks, which would lead to the impoverishment of parish priests. The state should encourage commerce and industry, since healthy commerce brought wealth to the burghers and to the state in the form of duties and tolls. The peasantry would continue to shoulder its share of the burden through direct taxation, but they should not be over-taxed, 'since it is better to milk the cow than hit it on the head'.[11] In view of these considerations, Bonde called for a balanced budget, to be achieved through moderate and equitable sacrifice combined with administrative belt-tightening.

Though neither specific nor controversial, Bonde's memorandum was at least a call for overall fiscal responsibility. It met the wholehearted approval of the Council, which drew up a balanced budget the following year. De la Gardie failed to apply Bonde's principles, however, and within a couple of years the regency government found itself still unable to pay salaries on a regular basis. The Council launched an investigation of De la Gardie's administration, finding it riddled with questionable expenditures and inaccurate bookkeeping, and in their scathing 'Blue Book' report of 1668 they demanded further expense cuts and the complete implementation of the 1655 *reduktion*. De la Gardie, who could be a successful demagogue if circumstances warranted it, somehow managed to keep the *Riksdag* from approving the Blue Book.

Thus the fiscal dilemma of Karl Gustav's reign remained unsolved nearly a decade after his demise. The most compelling solutions to the budget gap required that the landed aristocracy voluntarily give up some of their wealth and prestige. The Swedish nobility, to be sure, was unusually ready to make sacrifices for the good of the state, but this was too much to expect of them. The Council, moreover, did not have the clout to enforce something as damaging to noble interests as the *reduktion*, not with De la Gardie in control.[12]

There was another option, and that is what De la Gardie sought: to heal Sweden's fiscal illness with an injection of cash from a foreign ally. Though such a policy was fraught with danger, it was an easy solution, and there were several prospects as potential patrons. Westphalia might have ended the open hostilities in the Germanies, but it had not brought peace to Europe. The Habsburg–Bourbon conflict lived on, even after France and Spain made peace at the Pyrenees in 1659, owing to the ambitions of the young Louis XIV of France. When Louis XIV launched his attack against the Spanish Netherlands in the so-called War of Devolution (1667–68), the Council found the opportunity for which its treasurer had been looking. The war presented something of a dilemma to Sweden. During the Thirty Years' War, France had proven to be a valuable if difficult ally, and the Habsburgs – in Spain or in Austria – Sweden's foes. Moreover, thanks to the tireless diplomatic efforts of Oliver Cromwell and his son Richard, Anglo-Swedish relations were friendly; the end of the Protectorate in England, and the subsequent Restoration of the monarchy under Charles II, did not cool that relationship. The Dutch Republic, on the other hand, was locked in a series of naval wars with England, and had become one of Sweden's most dangerous enemies. The Dutch had given their military support to Denmark after Roskilde, and were directly responsible for the failure of the New Sweden and Cabo Corso colonies. Diplomatic sympathies in the regency Council were divided. De la Gardie favored the traditional alliance with France, but the bulk of the Council – led by Sten Bielke – were more interested in promoting ties with England. In January 1668, the Council brought Sweden into the so-called 'Triple Alliance' with the recently reconciled England and the Netherlands, with the ostensible purpose of halting French expansionism. The most attractive feature of this partnership was the financial reward it entailed, for Spain agreed to pay Sweden some 480,000 *riksdaler* in annual subsidies to sustain the anti-French coalition.[13]

The arrangement was not to De la Gardie's liking, and he bore enough influence in the Regency to negate it. England's defection from the Triple Alliance in 1670, reflecting Charles II's lukewarm friendliness towards France, undoubtedly helped the treasurer achieve this end. De la Gardie argued instead that Sweden should seek to maintain something like a middle position between France and her allies on the one hand, and the growing anti-French coalition on the other. This would be preferable to a commitment to immediate intervention on the side of one party or the other. Such a precarious position could be achieved, he insisted, by maintaining a large Swedish army in Pomerania, to be funded by the highest bidder. A powerful Swedish presence in northern Germany could at the very least ensure the non-involvement of the German princes in a renewed French War. This offered the tempting prospect of keeping a large force in arms, paid by external sources, but without the troublesome expenses that came from actual participation in active campaigning. De la Gardie prevailed, and his policy bore immediate fruit. Louis XIV offered the Swedes some 400,000 *riksdaler* in annual subsidies to keep an army in Pomerania. The Franco-Swedish subsidy treaty was signed in 1672. Perhaps De la Gardie and the Council envisioned a relationship with France similar to that created by the Bärwalde treaty in 1631, allowing Sweden to pursue its own objectives while in French pay. If so, they were sadly mistaken. France under Louis XIV and his ministers was not the same as it had been under Richelieu's able but hardly omnipotent direction. What the members of the Council failed to see in 1672 was that they had sold Sweden to France. Instead of solving Sweden's fiscal crisis, they had compounded it, and the result would bring Sweden once more to the brink of disaster.[14]

The Early Reign of Karl XI: Constitutional Debates and War

The year 1672 was important not only because of Sweden's renewal of its diplomatic ties with France; it was also the year in which the 1660 Regency ended. The young king, Karl XI, was 17, the age at which Swedish monarchs traditionally reached majority. The imminent expiry of the regency was the cause for factionalism in the *Riksdag* and trepidation within the ranks of the Council. Not the least cause for worry was the character of Karl himself. Shy, taciturn, and uncomfortable in the social life of the court, Karl XI had little in common with his illustrious predecessors. He was not especially well educated, nor did he have the same love of learning as most of the Vasa monarchs or even his father; he was a poor reader, spoke only Swedish and German, and may have been dyslexic. Karl X Gustav had had little direct influence on the boy's upbringing, since the prince was not even 5 years old when his absentee father died in 1660. Nonetheless, Karl XI did inherit his father's love for outdoor activities and the soldier's life. He eschewed the delights of the

comfortable life at court, instead spending much of his time riding and
hunting – according to foreign observers Karl was kinglike in bearing
only when on horseback – and orchestrating grandiose military exer-
cises which were notoriously realistic and even bloody. Although reportedly possessed of a hot temper that found its outlet in infrequent but
frightening fits of violent anger, ordinarily the new king was stoical and
ascetic.[15]

Such qualities would prove to be an asset later in the king's political
career, but in 1672 they added to the constitutional confusion that
prevailed in Stockholm. The political debates of 1672 were not the result
of a simple bifurcation between the royalists and the champions of noble
interests, but in the end that is how the internal conflict played out. The
coronation presented the nobility with the chance to secure the gains
they had made collectively after 1660. The Danish royalist 'revolution' of
that year undoubtedly added to the nobility's concern for their status
and privileges; it certainly helped to earn the loyalty of the formerly
Danish aristocracy of the Scanian provinces. But in 1672 the Swedish
nobility was too sharply divided over a number of issues to present
anything like a common front prior to Karl XI's coronation. All of these
issues focused on one topic central to the 1672 *Riksdag*: the formulation
of the king's coronation oath. A committee from the noble estate ham-
mered together an unusually restrictive oath, which among other things
stipulated that the king should be required to consult with the Council
and the Colleges before making administrative appointments. The nobility
of the third class, soon joined by the clergy, burghers, and peasants,
objected to this and other clauses as an encroachment on the traditional
prerogative authority granted to the king by God. The 1672 *Riksdag*
revealed a similar social fissure on related issues. The nobles of the third
class wanted to include a clause in the coronation oath providing that all
appointments and promotions within the administration be based solely
upon merit; the peasants and the other commoners demanded the annul-
ment of a 1671 decree, promulgated by the Council, that gave landowning nobles extensive powers to discipline those peasants holding tenancies
on noble land. When the regents asked the *Riksdag* for a grant of taxation
to meet current government needs, the lesser nobles and their commoner
allies pointedly refused; they would not agree to further taxation until
the limited *reduktion* called for in 1655 was carried out. The lesser nobility
and the commoner estates were displaying not only their anti-aristocratic
feelings, but also their interest in forming a partnership with the new
king to attack aristocratic interests.[16]

Significantly, the king's closest companions – the younger aristocrats and soldiers with whom he rode and hunted – subscribed to this platform as well, and undoubtedly had no small influence over Karl. This was not just a simple conflict, however, between lesser or younger nobles and the wealthier and more established aristocrats of the Council. The Council, too, was weak and divided over these issues that pressed so directly on the privileges of their estate. Some members – like Johan Gyllenstierna, De la Gardie's nemesis throughout the regency period – were avowedly royalist. Others, notably Chancellor De la Gardie himself, vacillated on these divisive political issues. De la Gardie might have acted as spokesman for the landed aristocracy during the regency, but he did not want to be seen as the leader of the aristocratic opposition to strong royal power; most likely he hoped to be able to continue in a position of high influence after Karl XI's coronation. For this reason, he refused to give his support to the 'innovations' in the coronation oath that sought to limit the royal prerogative.[17]

The confrontational position of the commoners and the lesser nobles, combined with the factionalism within the upper ranks of the nobility, amounted to a constitutional victory for Karl XI. The coronation oath, approved in November 1672 by all houses of the *Riksdag*, differed little from those of Gustav Adolf and Karl Gustav, with no additional restrictions placed upon kingly authority. This did not signal a radical change in governance; De la Gardie continued on as chancellor after the end of the Regency, and though the king continued to associate with young nobles who disliked De la Gardie this did not bring on any administrative shake-up. Moreover, all of the empire's energies were soon absorbed by immersion in yet another foreign war.

The hope behind the 1672 subsidy agreement with France was that Sweden would be paid to maintain an army – something it had to do anyway for the sake of its own security – without actually having to make a commitment to engage it in hostilities. To be sure, there were other, more legitimate, reasons behind the decision to ally with France. Sweden faced the prospect of diplomatic isolation without such an alliance, given the unremitting hostility of Denmark and Brandenburg. Frederik III of Denmark had been busily cultivating anti-Swedish feelings in northern Europe through a series of alliances in the 1660s. Louis XIV's shocking decision to invade the Netherlands in April 1672 destroyed Sweden's last hope of peaceful (if strained) coexistence with its neighbors. The new king of Denmark, Christian V (1670–99), joined with Brandenburg, several north German princes, and the emperor in a defensive alliance in the autumn of 1672, and in the following spring accepted Dutch military and naval subsidies for the war against France. De la Gardie, still acting as the architect of Swedish foreign policy, tried his best to remain aloof from the conflict without breaking his agreement with Louis XIV. For a brief while, it worked – Swedish emissaries even helped to broker a truce between France and Brandenburg in 1673 – but as the conflict over the Netherlands widened, Sweden could no longer remain neutral. In the spring and summer of 1674, the Holy Roman Empire, including Brandenburg, and Denmark were at war with France on the side of the Dutch. Louis XIV needed Sweden's support, promising more than a doubling of the 1672 subsidy if the Swedes augmented their military presence on the Continent and deployed it as France directed. Reluctantly, and with justifiable dread, the Council did Louis' bidding. The promise of foreign gold was simply too compelling, and the need for it inescapable.

The resulting conflict is usually called the Scanian War (1674–79), and that is misleading, for it was actually a war on several fronts against two enemies. In purely operational terms, the contest was not an unmitigated disaster for Sweden, but it was without doubt the most humiliating and unrewarding series of campaigns in which Sweden had been involved since the Livonian War at the beginning of the century. Late in 1674, an expeditionary force led by the aging Karl Gustav Wrangel set out from its bases in Pomerania into Brandenburg itself. The 'Great Elector', Friedrich Wilhelm, had taken measures to ensure that the invaders would not be able to find sufficient sustenance within his lands; Wrangel's army, small, unpaid, and starving, was dealt a crushing blow by Friedrich Wilhelm at Fehrbellin in June 1675. Sweden's defeat encouraged her other enemies. By the end of that summer, Denmark too had joined the fray, sending forces south to help the Great Elector in Lower Saxony. Complicating the situation was Sweden's loss of naval superiority in the Baltic. Denmark had enlarged and improved its fleet substantially since 1660, and had the advantage of superior leadership under Admiral Niels Juel; Dutch support, under the renowned Cornelis Tromp, made it an unstoppable force. The Swedish fleet suffered defeat after defeat in 1675–77. The explosion of the Swedish flagship *Kronan* in the battle off Öland (June 1676), and the bloodier fiasco at Køge Bugt (July 1677), marked the end of the days in which Swedish kings could shift their forces around the Baltic Sea unopposed. Unable to sustain its forces in Pomerania and elsewhere in Germany by sea, Sweden lost its German provinces one by one to the Danish and Brandenburger armies. By the end of 1678, the last Swedish possession in Baltic Germany, the port of

Greifswald, was no longer in Swedish hands. 'It had taken Sweden twenty years to acquire their German lands,' Robert Frost has noted; 'they were lost in under three.'[18]

The loss of naval superiority nearly cost Sweden its recent territorial acquisitions closer to home as well. Encouraged by his victories at sea, Christian V launched a war of revenge and reconquest in the Scandinavian peninsula in June 1676. The Danes sent an expeditionary force to Skåne while dispatching another into Bohuslän from Norway, with the intent of achieving a juncture of the two armies at Göteborg. Both armies made rapid progress. In Skåne and Blekinge, the local populations – still Danish in their loyalties – greeted the invaders as liberators; large numbers of Scanian peasants, fighting a guerrilla war, made logistical support for the defending armies difficult for the administration in Stockholm. As Karl XI moved his court to Ljungby to better direct the war effort, the Danish armies moved effortlessly through Swedish territory. Of all the major Swedish fortifications in Skåne, only Malmö held out. But the Swedish military had not entirely lost the martial abilities that lay behind its once-fearsome reputation. At Halmstad (August 1676), the Swedes brought the invasion from Norway to a halt; at Lund (December 1676), Karl XI personally led his troops to victory in a brilliant and bloody reversal. After such hopeful beginnings, Christian V's bid to reclaim Denmark's lost territories had failed. By 1678, Sweden was once again in full control of its disputed provinces to the west and south.

Despite his victory at Lund, a triumph that would give Karl XI the reputation of a great military leader cast in the same mold as his father and Gustav Adolf, the king of Sweden had presided over the rapid diminution of his realm. The German territories and command of the Baltic were lost. Were it not for French support, the Scanian War would have constituted Sweden's greatest imperial disaster of the century. Sweden's enemies were not of one mind, and as they wrangled over the spoils of war Louis XIV's diplomats were hard at work, compelling them individually to make favorable peace settlements with Karl XI. In separate peace treaties signed at St Germain (June 1679), Fontainebleau (August 1679), and Lund (September 1679), the French pressed Brandenburg and Denmark to disgorge nearly all of their gains made at Sweden's expense. Christian V retained absolutely nothing; Friedrich Wilhelm held onto a small portion of Pomerania as his trophy. All of Sweden's former lands in Germany were returned, including the vital port-towns of Wismar, Greifswald, Stralsund, and Stettin, as well as Bremen and Verden.[19]

The conclusion of the Scanian War was a lucky escape for Sweden. Perhaps Scandinavian and Prussian historians have made too much out of Sweden's close scrape; perhaps, as Robert Frost has observed, 'the outcome was not the result of French diplomatic pressure alone'.[20] The Swedish military did indeed demonstrate its potency at Halmstad and at Lund, but at most these victories prevented Denmark from taking back what it had lost in 1645 and 1660. Only French intimidation of Sweden's divided enemies kept Sweden from forfeiting its German possessions. Indeed, the manner in which Louis XIV went about these treaties, made without Swedish participation or consent, was taken by Karl XI as an act of condescension, an insult that the young Swedish king would not soon forgive. And, it should be remembered, that Sweden maintained significant armies at all owed largely to French cash subsidies. Regardless of the victory at Lund, the only real moment of triumph in an otherwise dismal war, Sweden *deserved* to lose the Scanian War: not in any ethical sense, but simply because the *status quo ante bellum* condition in which the empire ended the war cannot be attributed to Swedish valor or cunning. Sweden had not survived intact on its own merits. The significance of this lesson was not lost on Karl XI. More important, it was not lost on the lesser nobility and the commoner estates when the *Riksdag* convened at Stockholm in October 1680.[21]

Chapter 8: The Swedish 'Absolutist' State, 1679–97

Until relatively recently, historians rarely debated the utility of the terms 'absolutism' or 'absolute monarchy' when discussing the European state of the later seventeenth and eighteenth centuries. There was little need to define what was meant by 'absolutism', since it was readily apparent. One recognized absolutism when one saw it: Louis XIV's France was an absolutist state, while England after the Glorious Revolution most definitely was not. Over the past two or three decades, however, historians of early modern Europe have begun to retreat from this self-assured if vague position. Some, like Nicholas Henshall, do not see a fundamental constitutional difference between the princely autocracies of the later sixteenth century and the 'absolute monarchies' of the next century.[1] Others have avoided the debate altogether, focusing instead on alternative concepts in their attempts to explain the growth of central authority in most of the European polities between 1600 and 1750. In Scandinavia, for example, scholars have revived Otto Hintze's concept of the 'power state' (*Machtstaat*), based around the argument that the development of strong and intrusive central government was based on the need to mobilize national resources to support the needs of a military establishment engaged in prolonged warfare. Scandinavian economic historians have emphasized changes in fiscal administration, perceiving in the seventeenth-century Nordic lands a deliberate shift from a central authority whose income derived primarily from crown lands (the 'domain state') to one whose main revenues came mostly from regular taxation (the 'tax state').

Both of these latter two ways of looking at political, social, and economic change in the seventeenth century are easily applied to the Swedish

123

empire. Whatever the motives behind the formulation of foreign policy in *stormaktstid* Sweden, it is clear that most political change emanated from the need to mobilize resources efficiently in order to pursue foreign and security policies. The drift 'from domain state to tax state' probably more accurately applies to Denmark than to Sweden, for in the issue of the *reduktion* – first implemented on a broad scale after 1682 – the political economy of Sweden appears to have stepped backwards towards increasing reliance on the revenues generated by crown lands. Regardless of the popularity of these new methodologies, which emphasize institutional history over the actions and personalities of powerful individuals like the monarchs themselves, Scandinavianists do not question the assertion that something that we can indeed call 'absolutism' was firmly in place in the two Nordic kingdoms in the latter half of the century. In fact, its appearance can be dated precisely to the year – 1660 in Denmark, 1680 in Sweden; it is impossible to assign so definite a date to the establishment of absolute monarchy in those states that have conventionally become the 'models' of absolute monarchy, namely France and Brandenburg-Prussia.

The Imposition of Absolutism

The establishment of royal supremacy in the Scandinavian kingdoms happened by means of a process that was different overall from that which occurred in more familiar 'absolutist' states like the France of Louis XIV; and though there are some striking similarities between Danish and Swedish absolutism, even within Scandinavia the process was hardly the same. Both in Sweden and in Denmark, the rise of royal supremacy came about as the result of military defeat or near-defeat: in the 'Karl Gustav Wars' for Denmark, in the Scanian War for Sweden. In both kingdoms, the establishment of absolutism did not bring about an upward swing in the state's military and diplomatic fortunes. Denmark would never again wield much clout in international affairs after 1660, and Sweden was clearly on the defensive after 1660 as well. In short, absolutism marked the point at which the Scandinavian states retreated *from* great-power status. In Sweden as in Denmark, absolutism had a distinctly popular and anti-aristocratic character. In each case, the monarch was able to assert his authority because the lower orders and the lesser nobility supported it after military disasters discredited the conciliar aristocracy. These social elements perceived strong monarchy, not representative institutions, as the best safeguard against the diminution of their social and economic status by the aristocracy. In Sweden, therefore, the peasantry and its allies looked to the king and not to the *Riksdag* as the guarantor of their traditional liberties as free men. Absolutism required that aristocratic power be crushed, but a close partnership between prince and plebs was necessary for this to be achieved.

In these regards, Swedish and Danish absolutism appear to have followed the same path. But there was a distinct difference between the events that played out in Copenhagen in 1660 and those which took place in Stockholm between 1680 and 1682. The 'royalist revolution' of 1660 in Denmark was truly a revolution, albeit a bloodless one. It had to be revolutionary, simply because the Danish aristocracy had gained almost complete control over the central authority between 1647 and 1660; discredited by its poor performance during the wars with Sweden in the late 1650s, its grip over that authority had weakened just enough by 1660 to allow Frederik III and his supporters amongst the lesser nobility and the burghers to destroy the power of the Council for good. The transformation entailed a thorough restructuring of the administrative system, the emasculation of the Council of State and its transformation into a mere body of advisers, and a written constitution: the *Lex Regia* of 1665, which set out in detail the extent of the royal prerogative.[2] None of these features characterize Sweden's transition to strong royal government, and hence the transition was far less abrupt than it had been in Denmark. The 1634 Form of Government stood largely unchanged; the basic institutions of governance – the Council and the *Riksdag* – remained; and Karl XI and his protagonists did not feel compelled to compose an absolutist *credo*. The Swedish aristocracy was, in self-perception as well as in fact, a service class without the same kind of pretentions to constitutional supremacy that characterized their Danish cousins. The shift in power within the Swedish polity required no formal justification or written constitution, for it was not a violation of Swedish constitutional traditions. It hearkened back to Sweden's ancient code, the Land Law of Magnus Eriksson, which assigned primacy in the making of policy to the king. This was something that had always been respected, even by the great magnates during the 1632 and 1660 regency governments. In 1680, Karl XI was simply asserting that present conditions required that he exercise his traditional prerogative to its fullest.

Karl XI was well suited to carry out this transformation. Though unimaginative and poorly read, Karl was possessed of a deep and abiding personal piety. He truly believed that God had entrusted the welfare of

Sweden and its inhabitants to his care, and that it was his duty to work together with all the constituent elements of Swedish society to promote that welfare. In him there was no trace of the populist appeal of his father and his Vasa predecessors – he had no gift for oratory and preferred not to appear in public – but his performance at the battle of Lund in 1676, deep in the thick of the fighting, earned him a heroic reputation. To the commoner estates, Karl XI was the sole bright spot in an otherwise unpleasant war. Moreover, the king preferred to rule by himself, although he did rely heavily upon noble supporters within the Council. Johan Gyllenstierna and Hans Wachtmeister were particularly valuable in manipulating the noble estate, although neither served as a chief minister or as a royal favorite. The king's decisions were his alone; no one governed in his name.

Even before the end of the Scanian War, it was clear that there were changes afoot in Swedish constitutional practice. In his new court at Ljungby, the king sat in frequent and close consultation with his generals and a few trusted advisers, notably Johan Gyllenstierna. Gyllenstierna, Magnus Gabriel De la Gardie's most outspoken critic on the Council, was utterly dedicated to the service of the king. Gyllenstierna and Karl did not develop the kind of paternal partnership that Gustav Adolf and Oxenstierna had enjoyed – the two were not close personally – but they nonetheless made an effective team until Gyllenstierna's death in 1680. The move to Ljungby distanced the king from the Council, both physically and politically, and he consulted less and less with it in the closing phases of the war. The king signed the Lund treaty with Denmark without even notifying the Council of his intentions. And when Karl, with Gyllenstierna's enthusiastic support, consummated the treaty with Denmark early in 1680 by marrying Ulrika Eleonora, sister of Christian V, he as much as admitted that the exclusion had not occurred by accident. The Council, understandably befuddled by this apparently radical change in foreign policy, sent their written opinions on the match to the king. Karl, however, replied only briefly and haughtily: 'We do not remember having . . . committed the matter to you to discuss.'[3] The Council apologized for their affrontery. Even though they were well within their rights to expect the king to consult with them on an issue of such grave national importance, they did not wish to risk incurring the king's displeasure.

The reaction of the conciliar aristocracy to the news of the Danish marriage alliance helps to illustrate precisely how Karl XI was able to reduce the great magnates to near political impotence over the next few years. The Council, and the upper nobility as a whole, manifested no

desire to initiate a constitutional clash with the king and accepted his
dictates with little more than truculent acquiescence. That this attitude
might endanger the interests of the nobility was also evident before
the Scanian War ended. Reacting to the disastrous campaigns of 1675,
the commoner estates in the *Riksdag* had focused their anger on the
nobility, calling for the execution of the 1655 *reduktion* and an investigation
of fiscal improprieties during the regency. Johan Gyllenstierna, who
agreed with both measures – his enemy De la Gardie would be the chief
target of any such investigation – managed to sway the king in this direction as well. When Karl, at the request of the Council, summoned the
Riksdag to meet in 1678, the lower orders intensified their demands.
This time, however, they did not face an undivided and defensive nobility:
the royalist clique in the *Riddarhus*, ably managed by Gyllenstierna's
allies, split the noble camp. Nobles of the third class, mostly civil servants
who had not benefitted from the alienation of crown lands and whose
salaries had gone unpaid for years, joined the chorus demanding fiscal
reform at the expense of the great magnates. The old power elite stood
alone in its defense of noble privilege.[4]

The showdown would come at the first peacetime *Riksdag* to be held
after Karl XI's formal accession, in the autumn of 1680. It should have
been evident that, no matter how the king's propositions to the *Riksdag*
were formulated, the debate would quickly turn to the key issues of the
previous two meetings of the Diet: the *reduktion* and the creation of a
tribunal, the so-called Great Commission (*Stora Kommission*), to investigate
the Regency's accounts. Inexplicably, the Council did not attempt to
influence the *Riksdag*'s agenda. Karl XI's propositions to the *Riksdag*
were brilliantly drafted, so self-evident that they were almost incontro-
vertible: How should Sweden look after its national security? How
should the land and naval forces be reformed? And, finally, how would
Sweden marshal its resources to provide for the civil administration and
the military? The obvious answer to all of these propositions, at least
from the lower three estates, was through the Great Commission and the
reduktion. The fiscal benefits of the *reduktion* for the state were obvious; the
Great Commission, it was hoped, would also help to solve the long-
standing budget crisis by exacting penalties and repayment of misallo-
cated funds by the guilty parties within the now-defunct Regency. The
support of the lower orders for both of these issues was guaranteed. The
trick would be in securing the assent of the *Riddarhus* and the Council.
Victory in the first owed almost entirely to the managerial skills of Hans
Wachtmeister, the Admiral of the Realm and a man close to the king.

Wachtmeister succeeded in securing noble support for a tribunal, in part by making the naïve promise that the financial rewards for the state would be so substantial that further taxation would be almost unnecessary. Getting the *Riddarhus* to approve an unlimited *reduktion* was another matter altogether. A full-fledged *reduktion* would potentially entail the return of *all* crown lands alienated at any point since the rule of Gustav Vasa. Under this scheme, even many of the lesser nobles stood to lose, since the monarchy had given away smaller, less lucrative parcels to nobles of the third class. Wachtmeister proposed, however, that the nobility submit to the *reduktion* without any reservations, yet beg the king's mercy in sparing the smaller land grants. In this way, Wachtmeister, acting for the silent king, turned the *Riddarhus* proceedings into a chaos, turning the nobles of the third class and many of the second class against the great magnates of the first. With the *Riksdag*'s approval, accepted by the king, the Council could do little except gripe about the unprecedented attack on noble privilege. It is important to note that the 1680 *reduktion* was not in reality a full *reduktion*. Lands given to the titled nobility would be given back to the crown, as would all other donations of land made after 1632, with the exception of lands valued at less than 600 *riksdaler* in annual income. The nobility also stipulated that this *reduktion* was permanent and final; it could not be amended or extended, and was not open to further discussion.

Even as the *Riksdag* concluded its business in December 1680, Karl XI was not finished with his assertions of authority. The Great Commission, its members drawn from all four estates, launched itself into the task of handing down indictments of those held responsible for the fiscal irresponsibility of the Regency. When the Council objected to its indictment as a body, Karl turned once again to the *Riksdag* to reinforce his authority. In its 'Declaration' of 12 December 1680, the *Riksdag* ruled that the king was wholly sovereign, answerable only to God; the Council was not a separate estate, and not a mediator between king and subjects, for a sovereign king had no need for such mediation. The Great Commission began to deliver individual indictments in the spring of 1681, and the results were not likely to please the Council. All in all, about sixty individuals – members of the Regency, administrators in the Colleges, councillors, or their heirs – were held collectively responsible for around 12 million *riksdaler* in lost revenues. The Council protested – they could not be held responsible for the improprieties of the Regency – but Karl manipulated them into subservience all the same. Most of the accused within the Council's ranks submitted humbly to their fates, throwing themselves to the king's mercy. Those who did not submit retired from the Council, and were forced to pay their share of the settlement in full. Even more humiliating to the Council was Karl's insistence that they give their formal opinion on the *Riksdag*'s December 1680 declaration. Faced with no other options than either to accept the Declaration or to incur the king's displeasure, the Council opted for the former, subduing of their own accord those members who wanted to object to the implied limitation of their powers.[5]

The king and his agents carried the process even further at the next *Riksdag*, held in the autumn of 1682. The 1682 *Riksdag* was a masterpiece of royal manipulation: the crown solicited the participation of important supporters within the lower orders, the agenda was prepared in advance through a secret committee; and during the meetings of the *Riddarhus* in particular the king called for sensitive issues to be discussed in the open, with voting carried out by name rather than by number or simple acclamation. Once again, Karl XI made extensive use of hand-picked 'floor managers' to steer the course of the debates and to make known the king's will. Through these means, Karl succeeded in browbeating the nobility into accepting the permanent abolition of conscription – a process that gave the nobles considerable social control over their peasants as well as some political leverage with the king – in favor of a recruitment system that enhanced royal control. The issue of the *reduktion* came up again as well, despite the 1680 declaration that the matter was closed to further amendment or discussion. With the eager support of the lower orders, the *reduktion* was expanded to include crown properties alienated before 1632, and with no lower limit set on the extent of the donated properties. There was vehement debate, of course, but in the end the nobility as a body gave in. 'Most of them seem to have accepted a survival strategy of seeking royal protection to preserve their preeminence in society, rather than to assert their legal rights.'[6] What is most remarkable about the actions of the *Riddarhus* during the 1680 and 1682 *Riksdagar* was not just their acquiescence to royal policies that damaged or destroyed their economic and political interests, but also the tone of their political discourse. The responses of the nobility to royal propositions in 1680 and 1682 revealed a frightened willingness to accept the unquestioned authority of the king in principle, often expressed in the most humble terms. When one nobleman, Anders Lilliehöök, questioned the ability of the king to enforce the *reduktion* without the participation of the *Riksdag*, all of the estates took it upon themselves to denounce their erring member and to grovel before Karl. And when, in 1682, Karl drew up his own Testament for the governance of the realm after his death, all three classes in the *Riddarhus* made voluntary and abject apologies for the way in which the Council and the *Riksdag* had cast aside the testament of the king's father in 1660. The nobility, and especially the Council, had been reduced to subservience, a process to which they showed little resistance and in which they participated willingly. And Karl XI, for his part, reacted sharply to anything that he saw as an infringement of his divine right in action or in principle. 'You do not have the smallest share in my power,' he informed the Council, 'you are my Council, which I can consult or not at my will.' Indeed, the king announced in 1682 that the Council would henceforth be known as the 'King's Council' and not the Council of State.[7]

The Absolute Monarchy at Work

The *Riksdagar* of 1680 and 1682 did not transform Sweden into an autocracy at all levels. Karl XI and his supporters had liberated the monarchy from any vestige of aristocratic or popular control, but they had done so without formal constitutional innovations. The Land Law still stood; the king had simply placed greater emphasis on the principle that it was the king who had the final right to make decisions in state policy. The basic institutions of Swedish government remained intact, including the collegial administration and the *Riksdag* itself. Karl summoned the Diet regularly throughout his reign; it would convene again in 1686, 1689, 1693, and finally in 1697. Provincial diets remained important in local governance, and royal officials found that they still had to maintain good relations with local representatives of the peasantry and the burghers if they wished the king's commands to be executed smoothly. And the *Riksdag* continued to allow peasants to air their grievances directly to the king. For his part, Karl – neither vain nor power-hungry – did not try to keep the estates uninformed of his *arcana imperii*.

Still, between 1680 and 1682 the king had established his primacy in governance. Whatever leverage the nobility had once exerted over the sovereign power of the king had by now been shunted aside. Henceforth the king would make all major decisions in foreign policy, and reserved the right to make all appointments to civil and military office, on his own. The *Riksdag* might exist, but it was not the same institution it had been under the Vasa rulers. The 1682 *Riksdag* set the pattern for the remainder of the reign: the king and his core of advisers carefully prepared the agenda, and debates in all estates were strictly limited to the royal propositions. The king's inner circle skillfully played the commoner estates off of the *Riddarhus* on more sensitive issues. The *Riksdag* scarcely seemed to notice as its powers and privileges were whittled down, while representatives from all the estates competed to lavish fulsome praise on their pious monarch. This is not to say that the *Riksdag* was a mere 'rubber-stamp' institution; there was debate, quite acerbic at times, but the issues they debated were trivial. When the 1686 *Riksdag* debated a grant of extraordinary taxation requested by the king, for example, the estates were simply asked to consider the *means* of taxation and the *method* of its apportionment, not whether or not the grant should be made. Even in the *Riddarhus* there was no attempt to assert the nobility's traditional right of exemption. The king wanted the grant, and that could not be questioned. Karl would make it clear when the course or tone of a debate displeased him, and the estates would take good care to alter their discourse so as not to offend their sovereign. No one dared speak out against the king, his wishes, or what he could or could not do. Even this was made into law: the *Kassationsakt*, approved by the *Riksdag* of 1689, prohibited anyone from questioning the king's actions or intentions.[8]

The vigorous assertion of the royal prerogative was a means to an end, and that end was the overhaul of the machinery of the Swedish state. No one of any importance within the government debated the necessity of reform; that was made apparent by the near-disasters of 1675–79. Karl's political programme consisted of four main policy goals: first, the reform of state finances and the augmentation of revenues; second, the reform of the army and navy so that the two institutions could provide real security to the realm without reliance upon foreign subsidies or a never-ending policy of conquest for material support; third, the standardization of administrative practice within the Swedish–Finnish core and in the subject provinces; and fourth, a foreign policy that did not involve Sweden in unnecessary wars, without sacrificing Sweden's interests in the Baltic. All of Karl XI's policies, including his emasculation of the nobility, evolved from these imperatives.

The reform of the state fisc was obviously the most pressing issue. The Great Commission of 1680–82 had made an impressive start, but the reparations it exacted from those indicted for fiscal irresponsibility during the Regency would not be resolved until the end of the decade, and even so it was hardly a long-term solution. It brought only limited financial relief: of the 12 million *riksdaler* that had originally been assessed against the guilty parties, only some 4.66 million was actually collected. This was less than 40 percent of the hoped-for sum and the equivalent of only about a single year's revenues. The centerpiece of fiscal reform would instead be the *reduktion*. The 1682 *reduktion* was completely unrestricted, since the *Riksdag* had ruled that crown land was the personal property of the king, and the king alone had the right to distribute it or recall it at will. Assiduous record-keeping by the central bureaucracy since the mid-sixteenth century made tracking down all alienations of crown land a simple task, but reclaiming these lands was not easy. It was a convoluted process, made worse by the fact that many properties had changed hands since their alienation. The bureaucracy charged with the task was cumbersome; three separate bodies – the College of the *Reduktion* (1655), the *Reduktion* Commission (1680), and the *Reduktion* Deputation (1687) – were responsible for its prosecution, and the king himself displayed an irritating tendency to change his mind on specific rulings and then to apply these revisions to cases that had already been settled. The result was a climate of frightening insecurity, as noble families who had already suffered greatly on account of the *reduktion* could never be fully certain that the king was done with them yet. Karl could show mercy, but on the whole the *reduktion* was universally applied with few or no exceptions. Even the king's uncle, Duke Adolf Johann, was not exempt. Noble families who petitioned the king about imminent impoverishment could get a more favorable settlement, while those who objected or resisted incurred the king's manifest displeasure. The *reduktion* had great value as a constitutional weapon. It was the final blow to the political power of the great magnates.[9]

In terms of patterns of landownership, the effects were dramatic. The *reduktion* restored to the crown roughly the extent of the properties it had owned at the beginning of the century: after the reign of Gustav Adolf and before the *reduktion*, about one-third of peasant tenancies in Sweden and Finland were owned by the crown, and two-thirds by the nobility; by century's end, the crown's holdings had doubled at the nobility's expense. In the conquered provinces, where virtually all noble landholdings were the results of donations from the crown, the change was even more drastic. It has been estimated, for example, that by 1700 the *reduktion* in Estonia had brought close to 100 percent of all farms into the king's hands. In Livonia, the proportion of land owned by the crown grew from 1.25 percent in 1680 to 72.3 percent at the end of the reign. Unfortunately, the *reduktion* was so complicated a process that making any definitive statements about its benefits for the state finances would be impossible, but by restoring a large quantity of rental income to the crown it unquestionably aided the ailing state fisc. During the *Riksdag* of 1686, a crown spokesman could proudly report that bureaucratic and military salaries were once again being paid in full for the first time in many years. The *reduktion* added about 4 million *riksdaler* to the state's annual income; the national debt, which stood at nearly 50 million *riksdaler* in 1681, was slashed to 10 million by 1697.[10]

Another radical change occurred within the organization of the armed forces. The *utskrivning* system, practiced since the days of Gustav Vasa, had proven inefficient by the 1670s. Moreover, the system had been resented by all but the nobility, particularly when (as was usually done in wartime) the number of recruits was calculated by capitation and not by groups of farmsteads. To the nobility, *utskrivning* was an important tool for disciplining their peasant tenants, and the partial exemption of their tenants from conscription was at least an acknowledgment of noble privilege; to the peasants, conscription was an arbitrary, burdensome, and unfairly distributed imposition. At the 1682 *Riksdag*, the commoner estates had expressed their preference for the system that had been applied to Dalarna and other frontier provinces since the days of Gustav Adolf: individual contracts with the crown, by the terms of which the province pledged to provide a set number of recruits in return for the abolition of conscription. Over the vocal objections of the nobility, Karl XI went along with the recommendations of the peasant estate. *Utskrivning*, as it had been practiced for the past century, was abolished. All of the provinces would now provide troops by contract, a system called *knektehåll*. Each province was obligated to provide a single provincial infantry regiment of 1200 men and officers, plus a varying number of cavalrymen. Individual infantrymen would be recruited and supported by grouped pairs of farms, each pair called a 'file' (*rota*), while cavalrymen – who were more expensive to maintain – would be lodged and fed by wealthier crown peasants, a system called *rusthåll*. The peasants who kept soldiers, whether infantry or cavalry, were not liable for service themselves and were exempt from taxes, something that could prove to be quite profitable. Officers and NCOs would receive remuneration through the provision of farms, held tax- and rent-free, for their personal use. These farms were designated for the support of the armed forces; in other words, specific sources of income were permanently earmarked for specific military expenditures, a key feature that earned the overarching system its name: the *indelningsverk*. It owed a great deal to the practice of *indelning* (appropriation), by which Gustav Adolf had created his cavalry regiments, only it was now universally applied throughout the kingdom for the upkeep of the entire army.

The *indelningsverk* was a substantial improvement over the earlier forms of mobilizing native troops for service. Because it put the burden of the recruitment and upkeep of soldiers on the individual provinces, it returned a measure of local authority back to the countryside; because all peasants, including those holding tenancies on noble lands, were equally liable, it was seen as being more equitable by the peasants themselves. The provinces were not required to draw their recruits from within their own borders, and so it was possible to obtain recruits from the less prosperous regions in the north. In military terms, the *indelningsverk* provided a permanent army of considerable size: 23 infantry regiments (ca. 30,000 men) and 11 cavalry regiments (11,000 men) were in place at the end of the reign in 1697.[11]

Even a native army of that size was not enough to fill all of Sweden's security needs. It was intended for wartime use, not for garrisoning the overseas provinces in peacetime, nor did it provide for a navy. But the fiscal successes of Karl XI and his administration, through the *reduktion* and otherwise, made improvements in these other areas possible. Sweden could now afford to keep about 25,000 mercenaries in garrisons spread throughout the empire. The fleet, however, was the chief beneficiary of Sweden's newfound solvency. Under the able direction of Hans Wachtmeister, the navy moved its administrative and logistical headquarters from Stockholm to Trossön in the conquered province of Blekinge, where a new naval base called Karlskrona was established in 1685. The manpower of the fleet, collected both by conscription in coastal regions and by recruitment, was billetted on local populations in Blekinge much as the native land forces were. Wachtmeister consistently overspent his limited budget, and was frequently at odds with his tightfisted sovereign, but he succeeded in creating the best battle fleet in the Baltic. By the close of the century, Sweden had a fleet of 49 warships totalling 53,000 tons displacement, giving Sweden a substantial naval edge over Denmark. The move to Karlskrona brought the fleet closer to its likely theater of operations, namely Denmark and the Sound. It also had unforeseen domestic advantages as well. Blekinge was still firmly pro-Danish in popular sentiment three decades after its conquest by Karl X Gustav; the introduction of native Swedish sailors and especially craftsmen in large numbers speeded the process by which Blekinge was assimilated into the Swedish realm.[12]

This latter goal – the full integration of the conquered provinces into a truly Swedish empire – was part of a more challenging task: the creation of a state that was homogeneous in administrative practice and in law. In his attempts to enforce uniform administrative practices and legal codes for the entire empire, Karl XI was far more ambitious than any of his more learned predecessors had been. A new Church Ordinance, promulgated by the king and acknowledged by the *Riksdag* of 1686, established uniform religious practice and liturgy for the entire kingdom. The medieval Land Law, the legal basis for the king's assertion of constitutional supremacy in the early 1680s, was also ripe for revision. Karl created a Law Commission in 1687 with the express purpose of modernizing the language of the Law and making it the standard for the entire empire. Politically active Swedes tended to regard the Land Law, which had been available in print since 1608, as sacrosanct and therefore untouchable; the tremendous difficulties involved in altering it meant that the work of creating a modern national legal code would not be consummated until 1734. In bringing the subject provinces into line with Swedish legal and administrative practice, however, Karl was far more successful. The German lands, like Bremen-Verden and Pomerania, escaped this policy of centralization, but not so the eastern Baltic provinces and the Scanian territories. In Livonia and Estonia, Karl XI simply bypassed the traditional authority of the provincial diets, asserting that the jurisdiction of the crown and of the *Riksdag* superceded these. In 1688, the king went so far as to proclaim that his license to carry through the *reduktion* in the eastern provinces applied not only to lands alienated by earlier Swedish kings, but even to lands given away by territorial lords *before* Sweden took control over these areas. The old German nobility in Livonia and Estonia found its economic and political position significantly diminished.

There was a necessary cultural component to this policy of standardization and incorporation as well, though it was not evenly applied to the entire empire. The Swedish tongue was introduced as the common administrative language in most of the non-German provinces. In 1690, the king forced the Swedish church ordinance of 1686 upon Livonia, and required that all those who desired positions within the local administration study for at least two years at the new university at Dorpat, an institution whose faculty was thoroughly Swedish. In the Scanian provinces, Karl's governors – first Johan Gyllenstierna, then his successor Rutger von Ascheberg and the bishop of Lund, Canutus Hahn – compelled the local estates to accept Swedish law, and then introduced by force the Swedish language into Scanian culture. Parish priests now had to preach in Swedish and observe the Swedish liturgy; catechisms and devotional literature would be printed in Swedish. The effort paid off. When Danish forces invaded the region in 1676, they were greeted by their erstwhile countrymen as liberators; when a Danish army did the same in 1709, it found that the ties between the Scanians and Denmark had been all but forgotten.[13]

Armed Neutrality

The success of Karl XI's reforms ultimately meant that Sweden was in far better condition by the mid-1680s to conduct an aggressive foreign policy than it had been in 1655 or in 1675. Certainly Karl appears, through his personal behavior, to have been destined to lead Sweden once again into battle. He showed a strong predilection for all things military, and cultivated the memory of his father as a great warrior. His love for battle was demonstrated effectively at Lund in 1676, and throughout his reign he continued to work towards the improvement of the tactical proficiency of his army. And yet Sweden enjoyed peace and prosperity during the last seventeen years of the reign. It was not, however, an easy peace. Most of Sweden's enemies from the Scanian War were still antagonists a decade after the war's conclusion, and they had not lost their thirst for revenge. Indeed Sweden gained even more enemies – primarily France – in the last years of the regime. But while Sweden's military strength grew in size and proficiency, something that doubtlessly discouraged any overt attack, her enemies remained divided and unprepared, still licking their wounds from the last war. Nonetheless, Karl XI and his ministers should get at least some of the credit for keeping Sweden at peace. The economic and fiscal reforms of the 1680s made it possible for Sweden to sustain a powerful army and navy without enlisting foreign subsidies or engaging in wars of conquest, and Karl XI's diplomacy ensured that Sweden would have powerful allies as well as vengeful rivals.

Sweden's security concerns in 1680 were the same as they had been a decade before. Of the major Western powers, only England demonstrated any obvious goodwill towards Sweden; even the French had shown, in the Scanian War, that they could not be trusted. Karl XI, aided first by Johan Gyllenstierna and, later, by Chancery President Bengt Oxenstierna, dealt with the intimidating array of hostile forces creatively and, on the whole, successfully. At Gyllenstierna's urging, Karl XI first attempted to make a lasting peace with Denmark, still seen as Sweden's most dangerous foe. The result was the marriage alliance between Karl XI and the Danish princess Ulrika Eleonora, which Gyllenstierna hoped would usher in a period of cooperation between the two kingdoms. Together, Gyllenstierna felt, Denmark and Sweden could defend the Baltic with ease, and a friendly Denmark would allow Sweden to focus its attentions elsewhere in the region. The relationship did not work in practice. The enmity between the two Nordic kingdoms was too raw and deep, and neither Karl nor Christian V could bring themselves to trust the other.[14]

In his relationships with the Western powers, Karl XI was somewhat more successful. Although there were many in the Council who favored a continuation of the traditional alliance with France, the king himself distrusted France and held a deep personal dislike for Louis XIV. Among other things, Karl's patrimonial territory of Pfalz-Zweibrücken had fallen victim to Louis' infamous *reunions*. More important, this distrust was shared by Bengt Oxenstierna, the king's most influential foreign policy adviser. Oxenstierna, recognizing that Sweden needed a strong patron-state outside of the Baltic, preferred alignment with the anti-French coalition that centered around the Netherlands, the emperor, and England. The realignment began with a commercial agreement with the Dutch, the so-called 'Guarantee Treaty' of 1681. It was a dearly bought partnership, since the treaty offered Dutch merchants virtual freedom of trade in Swedish harbors, but the benefits of the reconciliation exceeded the costs. The 'Glorious Revolution' of 1688–89, which united England and the Netherlands under a common sovereign, meant that Sweden could count on substantial naval assistance in the event of a war with France or Denmark.

This alliance proved its worth in short order. In 1682, Christian V of Denmark concluded an alliance with Louis XIV; Denmark promised to support future French expansionism in western Germany in return for French recognition of Danish ambitions in Lower Saxony, in particular Holstein-Gottorp. As a Swedish client-state, Holstein-Gottorp diverted Danish attentions to the south, and hence was an important component of Swedish security policy *vis-à-vis* Denmark. When Christian V sent Danish troops to seize the duchy in 1684, Karl XI threatened war, and only the appearance of a French fleet in the Baltic restrained the Swedes from taking further action. Two years later, however, the Danish king's ambitions exceeded his abilities. Just as his grandfather and great-grandfather before him had done, Christian V attempted to force the city of Hamburg into the Danish orbit. Hamburg put up a fierce defense, and Denmark's act of overt aggression aroused the ire of the emperor and many northern German princes, including the 'Great Elector' Friedrich Wilhelm and the duke of Braunschweig-Lüneburg. When an international conference at Altona failed to resolve the Holstein issue, Karl XI concluded an offensive alliance with the duke of Braunschweig-Lüneburg, and prepared for an assault on Danish forces in Lower Saxony. With Sweden threatening war, and under extreme diplomatic pressure from England, the Netherlands, and much of the empire, Christian V backed down. The Altona settlement of 1689 forced the Danish king not only to desist in his efforts to take Hamburg, but also to restore ducal Holstein to the Gottorp dukes. Near the end of his reign, Karl XI bolstered his commitment to Holstein-Gottorp by arranging the marriage of his daughter, Hedvig Sofia, to Duke Friedrich IV. Sweden thus maintained its southern counter to Danish power.

Although Bengt Oxenstierna seems to have envisioned an activist foreign policy that would have involved Sweden intimately in the power struggles of western Europe, Sweden remained aloof from the events leading up to the War of the League of Augsburg (1688–97). This owed in part to Karl XI's naïve if admirable reluctance to insert himself into conflicts that had no direct bearing on Swedish security. Unusual among seventeenth-century monarchs, Karl was adamantly opposed to sacrificing the lives of his subjects in irrelevant wars. Sweden was formally tied, if loosely, to the array of nations that opposed French expansionism in the empire, but Karl – supported by Oxenstierna's opponents like Niels Bielke – endeavored to keep Sweden neutral in fact if not on paper. Sweden did provide military contingents of moderate size to the Dutch and their allies, but throughout the war Karl's diplomats continued to conduct sporadic negotiations with the French. The king was not passionately attached to either side; only the endless struggle between Denmark and Holstein-Gottorp held any interest for him.

By the time of Karl's death in April 1697, the king had achieved the very limited foreign policy goals he had sought since the end of the Scanian War. Holstein-Gottorp remained independent of Denmark, and provided a measure of security against Danish attack; and Sweden was able to withhold itself from the wars of Louis XIV without earning the overt hostility of either side. Sweden still held onto its reputation as a great power of the first rank, as demonstrated by the king's largely ceremonial role as mediator in the peace negotiations at Rijswick that brought the War of the League of Augsburg to an end just before his death. That reputation, seen in retrospect, was increasingly illusory. Sweden's security problems were not solved; Christian V of Denmark, piqued by Swedish involvement in the Holstein-Gottorp question, was bent on revenge, and shortly before the end of Karl XI's reign, changes in the political leadership of Russia and Poland – states that had been quiet during the 1680s and early 1690s – would threaten Sweden from the east.[15]

Absolutism and Swedish Society

Karl XI had effected a 'quiet revolution' of sorts in Swedish government, one which had profound implications for all levels of society in the kingdom. That is not to argue, however, that in the areas that exhibited the greatest degree of change – like the relationship between crown and subject, or the authority of the king as opposed to that of the nobility – Sweden was embarking on a new and uncharted course. Indeed, it could be postulated that the reign of Karl XI marked no more than the culmination of existing social trends within Sweden and the real integration of Sweden into the social and cultural norms of European life.

The most obvious and dramatic social changes occurred within the noble estate. The rift between the great magnates and the lesser nobility had completely destroyed whatever solidarity the nobility had enjoyed as a class in the earlier decades of the century. The Great Commission and the *reduktion* had weakened the nobility, especially the higher levels of the aristocracy, in terms both economic and constitutional. The *Riksdagar* of 1680 and 1682 had shown that the nobility was neither willing nor able to close its ranks in defense of its privileges. The *reduktion* had disrupted noble life, and for several magnate families the consequences were truly disastrous. Foreign observers wrote of great and distinguished noble families, their fortunes reduced to nothing, carting their last few material possessions to sell at market. By the end of the seventeenth century, a mere one-third of the Swedish nobility could lay claim to anything more than a couple of farmsteads. This loss of land, and the loss of noble control over conscription, also meant that the nobility did not have the same degree of control over the peasantry as it had once had. In Livonia, where the effects of the *reduktion* had been particularly severe, the local nobility did not acquiesce peacefully to change; the land reforms occasioned bitterness, even hatred, towards Stockholm, something that would prove to be more than a trivial problem after Karl XI's death.[16]

The demands of war and of government had also transformed the character of the nobility. Since the 'great compromise' of 1611–12, the noble estate had demanded a near monopoly on offices in order to safeguard its position and privileges. While monarchs from Gustav II Adolf to Karl XI honored this claim, the social composition of the nobility nevertheless changed gradually throughout most of the century. The *reduktion* had robbed the nobility of its post-1632 position as the foremost landowners in the realm. No longer able to rely on the incomes generated by their land-holdings, the nobles found themselves increasingly dependent on the salaries they earned through careers in the military or the central administration. Thanks to the fiscal reforms of the 1680s, these salaries were now paid regularly, and therefore were at least a viable means of support. The power of the monarch to ennoble foreigners or commoners, frequently exercised from the reign of Gustav Adolf onwards, also watered down the proportion of older landowning families within the nobility as it increased the overall numbers of individuals within the estate. In 1600, there were just over four hundred adult males claiming noble status; by 1650, there were about twice that number, half of them from families that had been recently elevated to noble status; by the end of the century, there were approximately 800 adult males in the nobility, but at least 80 percent came from 'new' families. To be sure, Christina and Karl X Gustav had ennobled prominent foreigners in a deliberate attempt to lessen the influence of the Oxenstierna clan and other established magnates, but the swelling of the noble ranks was a necessary response to the desperate need for noblemen to fill the manpower demands of a growing bureaucracy, and to compensate for the grim 'over-mortality' that the nobility suffered during Sweden's many wars.[17] Either way, the end result was the same: in Sweden, the nobility had undergone a transformation from a small elite of independent landowners into a larger class of civil and military 'servants of the state'.

The transformation of the Swedish nobility also embraced a change in the culture and *mentalité* of the entire order. The steady influx of foreigners into the nobility gave it an increasingly cosmopolitan outlook, not just within the nobility of the third class but within the upper ranks as well. The elevation of individuals like Hans Christoffer von Königsmarck – ennobled Germans who could not speak a word of Swedish – into membership on the Council meant that even that august body, the bastion of aristocratic self-interest, must have conducted much of its business in the German language.[18] The research of Peter Englund has shown that the ennoblement of foreigners and commoners altered the cultural ethos of the noble estate as well. During its 'golden age' between 1611 and 1680, noble culture had been overwhelmingly anti-mercantile and elitist, emphasizing the value of lineage over practical ability, and embracing current European norms of ostentatious display and conspicuous consumption. By century's end, however, the Swedish nobility had cast aside its earlier contempt for business-like pursuits, cultivating closer ties with the burgher class. Contemporary writings demonstrate a greater noble respect for thrift over luxury, and even suggest that the nobility had embraced the idea of a meritocracy in state service. In short, there was no 'feudalization' of the new nobility in Sweden as there was in France. The new nobility did not adopt the traditions and worldview of the old; rather, the noble estate as a whole was deeply influenced by the mentality of its newest additions.[19]

The peasantry had always held a more prominent and respectable place within Swedish political society than most of its counterparts on the Continent. They were, after all, 'free men' by the traditions of the Land Law, even if they held tenancies on noble land. Their willing support of the crown during the *riksdagar* of the 1680s and 1690s, however, tangibly enhanced their prominence. Under Karl XI, leaders of the peasant estate became political figures of some prestige; Per Ohlsson, spokesman for the peasantry at the *Riksdag*, even posed for a state portrait in 1686. Just as the aristocracy suffered from the economic policies of Karl XI, the lot of the peasantry improved. The new system was simultaneously less flexible and less burdensome. Under Gustav Adolf, Christina, and Karl Gustav, the crown – always anxious to maintain the goodwill of the peasants – had been extraordinarily accommodating to peasant grievances; individual families who claimed impoverishment could frequently expect that local crown officials would listen to their petitions for reduced taxation or conscription. Nonetheless, the overall burden of taxation and conscription was very high, especially during wartime.[20] After 1680, however, this situation was reversed. The crown was less willing to grant petitions based on impoverishment, but the number of such petitions dropped sharply, suggesting that under Karl's leadership the assessment of taxes had become more efficient and realistic, and hence less burdensome to individual peasants. The introduction of the *indelningsverk*, with its attendant tax-exemptions, was also in accordance with the desires of the peasantry as an estate. And though life would always be difficult for those who farmed in such severe northern climes, demographic trends tended to protect rather than to worsen the economic lot of the peasantry. Thanks in large part to a relatively high mortality rate, individual farmsteads were not being divided and subdivided from generation to generation; farms did not decrease significantly in size, and there was no large subclass of landless peasants. Nor did the nobility, whose control over the peasants had weakened since the early days of the century, attempt to carry out any kind of con-solidation of smaller tenancies into larger farms.

All classes of Swedish society had been thoroughly 'militarized' by the last quarter of the seventeenth century. The nobility's collective *raison d'être* was service to the state as military officers or civil administrators, and their recompense was primarily in the form of salaries paid by the crown. Since the days of the early Vasas, the officer corps had enjoyed considerable corporate power; by the reign of Gustav Adolf, they consti-tuted an unofficial, non-voting estate at the *Riksdag*. Under Karl XI, officership and noble status became closely tied together. Commoners dominated the lowest commissioned ranks, but as a rule they rose no further. The upper ranks, at least above captain, were reserved for the nobility, and Karl XI made sure that native noblemen, not foreigners, filled these appointments. More than any of his predecessors, Karl relied on army officers as his foremost advisers; the 'Table of Ranks' he introduced for use at court gave pride of place to officers above civilian administrators.[21] The peasantry, too, was organized by the monarchy in such a way as to provide as large an army and navy as the kingdom could possibly afford, only now their participation was consensual rather than coerced. Released from the iron grip of *utskrivning,* with the promise of tax benefits accruing from participation in the new system, the peasantry took part willingly. In the parish of Fellingsbro, for example, nearly one-third of all farmsteads supported a cavalryman through the *rusthåll* by 1684, and the number would rise even higher by the century's end.[22] The clergy also continued their previous roles as tax-assessors and census-takers. The monarchy had bent social organization to meet the needs of the state at war.

In its administrative structure, in its creation of a large and efficient national army under state control, and in the operational proficiency of its war machine, Sweden was a remarkably 'modern' state by European standards at the end of the seventeenth century. It is easy to see why Peter the Great saw its administration as worthy of emulation, and why the English ambassador Bulstrode Whitelocke praised Swedish efficiency and thrift, in contrast to Robert Molesworth's more famous indictment of Danish absolutism.[23] Yet in terms of expressions of high culture, Sweden remained stagnant and almost infertile. The crown had created an admirable system of regional universities, but these schools – even the primary university at Uppsala – were intended to meet the needs of the state and of the church rather than to promote learning for learning's sake; they produced professional administrators and clergymen. Under Christina, and again under Karl XI, the royal court glittered with spectacle and elaborate ceremony. Nevertheless, the integration of Sweden into the elite culture of the Baroque stopped at the confines of the court. There were, to be sure, native painters and musicians, but foreigners by and large provided portraiture and entertainments for the court. Sweden was better-known for the fortification skills of the military architect Erik Dahlberg than it was for palaces or churches fashioned by native hands.

Nor were there any significant changes in Swedish religious life during the Caroline era. Karl XI was a deeply religious man, whose literary tastes did not extend far beyond the Bible, but he was no theologian. Both he and his episcopacy were content to maintain the same Lutheran orthodoxy that had characterized the state church since the days of Gustav Adolf. Only in the standardization of the liturgy throughout the empire with the church ordinance of 1686, and in the clergy's stricter enforcement of social discipline, was there any noticeable change from the religious policies of earlier sovereigns. Under Karl's direction, the church exercised a firmer hand in the punishment of infractions of public morals, though the king characteristically reserved for himself the sole authority to commute or mitigate the sentences of his courts. The greater aggressiveness of the Caroline church in maintaining social discipline is perhaps best witnessed in the 'witchcraze' that afflicted southern Sweden starting in 1693.[24]

Sweden may have lacked the trimmings of a sophisticated Baroque state, but when Karl XI died in April 1697 he left his kingdom more secure and stable than it had been at any point in its history heretofore. The national debt had been cut drastically, so that it was no longer necessary to rely on foreign subsidies; an efficient administration ensured that Sweden could finally muster its meagre resources as effectively as the limitations of the time would permit. Its army and navy were clearly superior to those of any of the Baltic powers and contrasted favorably with those of much larger states, like France. Sweden was by no means wealthy, but it had achieved a measure of commercial prosperity. The bitter divisions between the orders of Swedish society, which had manifested themselves so ominously in the *riksdagar* of 1650 and 1680, had largely been subdued. The peasantry perhaps felt the heavy hand of intrusive government more than did most of their peers elsewhere on the Continent, but the crushing weight of extraordinary taxes and arbitrary conscription had been lifted from their shoulders for the most part after the early 1680s. The nobility had less cause for elation. The post-1680 reforms had constituted a stinging defeat for noble privilege. There is considerable evidence to suggest that the nobility felt little love for their strange and introverted king, and still less for his closest associates. But on the whole they had accepted their forced transformation into a service nobility with loyalty and grace. Sweden was a stronger power in 1697 than it had been when Gustav Adolf's tiny expeditionary force landed at Peenemünde in 1630.

Great-power status, however, is relative, not absolute. The European world was a much different place in 1697 than it had been at the time of Breitenfeld. In 1631, there were few states that could match Sweden's military might. This was no longer the case at the close of the century. Sweden, for all its progress, was not equal to the power of Louis XIV's France; the Netherlands and England each outstripped Sweden in wealth, productivity, and naval strength. Most troubling was the renewed threat that loomed in the East. In Poland, the Saxon elector August II ('the Strong') was elected to the throne in 1697, and the new Russian tsar Peter I (1696–1725) was already beginning to revamp Russia's administrative and military systems. Both August and Peter cast covetous eyes on Livonia, Estonia, and rich port towns like Riga. Although Karl was his brother-in-law, Christian V of Denmark still ached for revenge for the humiliations of the 1680s, a passion that he would pass down to his son, Frederik IV (1699–1730). Karl XI's death and the succession of his 15-year-old son, Karl XII, would give the three ambitious monarchs to the east the perfect opportunity to attempt the dismemberment of their hated foe.

Chapter 9: Epilogue

The Violent Death of an Empire

Karl XII was a worthy successor to his taciturn but capable father. Though only 15 at the time of Karl XI's passing in 1697, he was declared of age almost immediately, and hence Sweden avoided a potentially disruptive regency government. The young king was well educated, brighter than his father, but shared Karl XI's love and aptitude for all things military.

It was well that he did, for Sweden was in greater danger of attack in the late 1690s than it had been at any point in its history heretofore. Between 1698 and 1700, Sweden's foremost enemies – the king of Denmark, the Russian tsar, and the elector of Saxony – concluded a series of defensive and offensive alliances, ranging them in a formal coalition against Sweden. In 1700 they attacked: Frederik IV's army marched into Holstein-Gottorp, Augustus' Polish-Saxon forces moved into Livonia and took Dünamünde, and Peter the Great's troops attacked Ingria. Though the major Western powers were not unconcerned, their diplomatic and military attentions were focused elsewhere, on the imminent struggle over the Spanish succession. It was nothing short of catastrophe for Sweden, a confirmation of a century-long fear of encirclement. The conflict, known to historians as the Great Northern War (1700–21), should have ended quickly, for the odds opposing Sweden were overwhelming. Karl XII, however, demonstrated the full significance of his father's military and fiscal reforms. In July 1700, a Swedish fleet landed an army on Sjælland, besieging Copenhagen and forcing Frederik IV to sue for peace the following month. As Augustus' offensive in Livonia ground to an uncertain halt and his troops settled down for the winter, Karl led his army fresh from victory over Denmark to Estonia. There Karl XII utterly destroyed a far larger Russian army at Narva (November 1700), effectively knocking Peter out of the war for nearly two years. In the meantime, Karl turned on Augustus. Between 1701 and 1706, Karl's seemingly invincible army invaded Kurland, Lithuania, Poland, and Saxony. Swedish successes enabled Karl to unseat Augustus as king of Poland, substituting in his place Karl's chosen candidate, Stanisław Leszczyński.

The scope and pace of the Swedish victories over Denmark and Poland were breathtaking, far exceeding even those of Karl's grand-father, and earning him a place amongst the great generals of the eighteenth century. But despite Karl's skill as a commander, and despite the professionalism of his armies, it was an achievement that could not be sustained. The events of 1707–18 belied the fragile economic and demographic basis of Sweden's power. Peter the Great resumed the offensive, gradually, in 1702. Karl's forces could not move east against the Russians until 1707. As Peter's armies retreated into Russia, Karl launched an invasion of Russian territory late in 1708. Cut off from their supply line, and decimated by disease in the terrible winter of 1708–09, the Swedish forces endured tremendous losses; in June 1709, Peter's revived and much-improved army smashed them at Poltava. The survivors of the shattered Swedish army went into captivity in Russia, while Karl and a small entourage fled into exile in the Ottoman Empire.

While the defeated king tried in vain to convince his uncomfortable Turkish hosts to mount a full-fledged assault on Russia during his four-year exile, in Sweden the civil government proved surprisingly capable of minding its affairs in Karl's absence. Though there was some faction-alism at court over the future line of the royal succession, on the whole the central administration remained loyal to its king and functioned quite well, given the circumstances. But there was little that it could do to stave off the dismemberment of the empire. Encouraged by Poltava, the anti-Swedish coalition counterattacked immediately. A Danish army invaded the Scanian provinces; Peter the Great seized Sweden's eastern possessions and even invaded Finland. Augustus triumphantly returned to Poland and reclaimed his crown. The Danish invasion was halted, but not so the Russians. Karl himself returned in late 1714 to command Swedish troops attacking the Danes in Norway, but a musket-shot to the head ended his career and his life during an assault on the fortifications at Fredriksten in November 1718. By this time, other powerful enemies had joined in the fray by declaring war on Sweden: the new kingdom of

Prussia in 1715, George I of Britain in 1717. Only internal dissension amongst the members of the anti-Swedish coalition saved Sweden from complete partition. Sweden, however, would not be so lucky in 1720–21 as it had been in 1660. By the terms of the treaties of Stockholm (February 1720), Frederiksborg (June 1720), and Nystad (August 1721), Sweden managed to retain the Scanian lands and Finland, but lost virtually everything else: Bremen-Verden, most of Pomerania, Estonia, Livonia, Ingria, Kexholm, and most of Karelia. The once-proud ruler of the Baltic lay stripped of nearly all of its non-Scandinavian possessions.[1]

Analysis of Decline

The Swedish empire died with its enigmatic king at Fredriksten in 1718. The peace settlements only served to confirm this, to the world and perhaps to the Swedes themselves. Of Sweden's overseas possessions, only part of Pomerania remained, and that was a holding of dubious worth. Sweden would reappear from time to time to play a minor role in the conflicts that absorbed the attentions of the greater European powers during the eighteenth century, as for example during the Seven Years' War of 1756–63. But with the disasters of 1709–18, Sweden would once again and henceforth act as, and be considered as, a peripheral power of minor stature. All the sentimental yearnings of its statesmen in the century following Poltava could not bring back to Sweden the power and prestige it had enjoyed between Breitenfeld and the death of Karl X Gustav.

Why did the Swedish empire disintegrate when it did? That question has not attracted anywhere near so much scholarly attention as have the equally valid questions about the reasons and conditions behind the creation of the empire. Perhaps it is because the latter seem to be much more difficult than the former, and that the reasons for Sweden's rise to greatness are more complex and less clear-cut than the conditions that brought about its fall. It is relatively easy to find both a circumstance and a person to blame for the fall: overextension was the circumstance, and Karl XII was the person. By 1660, and probably earlier, Sweden had overextended its logical boundaries, and had conquered more than it could possibly defend. And while the empire seems to have regained its strength and to have achieved a certain balance under Karl XI's paternal but heavy hand, in little more than a decade Karl XII, in pursuit of impossible goals, destroyed all that his father had managed to accomplish since the Scanian War. The loss of empire was inevitable; Karl XII's ambitions only served to hasten the process.

The last of these two causal statements is easily dispensed with. Karl XII was indeed the monarch who presided over Sweden's fall from 'greatness'; it was he who led a well-trained Swedish army to disaster at Poltava. Yet Karl XII no more deserves the approbrium of historians than do his less tragic predecessors, including Karl IX, Gustav Adolf, and Karl Gustav. Like these men, he responded to a formidable array of threats that compromised his kingdom's security; also like them, his response took the form of a preemptive strike. The initial results of that strike were stunning. Even his invasion of Russia in 1708–09, the act that sealed his – and his country's – doom, was perhaps not so ridiculous or ill-advised as it appears from the vantage point of our time. Karl XII, of course, could not have *subjugated* the empire of the tsars, but he could at least have dealt the Russians a terrible blow, thereby neutralizing them temporarily, as he had done in 1700 and as Johann III and Karl IX had several generations earlier. We *know* that Petrine Russia was not the same entity as the chaotic, oftentimes dysfunctional Muscovite state of Boris Godunov and the 'Time of Troubles', but to discern that in 1708 would have required unimaginable foresight. Moreover, the coalition facing Karl XII in 1700, by bringing all of Sweden's Baltic enemies together in an unprecedented configuration, was something that previously had existed only in Axel Oxenstierna's worst nightmares. Karl XII confronted a threat whose magnitude exceeded anything that a Swedish sovereign had ever had to contemplate. It would be equally productive to blame Karl XI for failing to prepare adequately to meet an attack from the east, or to condemn Erik XIV for getting Sweden involved in Livonia in the first place. The recklessness of Karl XII's Russian adventure was no greater in degree than that of Gustav Adolf's German War or Karl Gustav's entire foreign policy.

But was the decline of the Swedish empire, then, inevitable? Though many scholars have unwittingly embraced the concept of inevitability, as a group historians find the idea, especially when applied to political development, difficult to swallow, smacking as it does of 'fate' and the metaphysical. Yet Scandinavian historians have displayed a tendency to see things in precisely these terms. To Danish historians, the very idea that tiny Denmark could ever have played a significant role in European affairs oftentimes seems ludicrous, and hence over the past century they have consistently played down Denmark's career as a major power in the late sixteenth and early seventeenth centuries. The role of Sweden

EPILOGUE

as a great and influential state is far more difficult to sidestep as a historical issue; Swedish scholars, instead, often view the *stormaktstid* as an almost inexplicable aberration. A recent Swedish-language survey of early modern Swedish history is in fact subtitled *Great-Power Dreams and Small-State Realities*. Such an approach is, however, counterproductive. It reflects a kind of historical teleology, implying that some states are fated to become great powers while others are not, and that somehow the current (or at least twentieth-century) condition of states reflects their stature in the sixteenth and seventeenth centuries. Britain, France, and Germany were *fated* to become great powers; the Scandinavian kingdoms most assuredly were not. Sweden had no business aspiring to greatness, and hence its fall was only a matter of time. Not only is this perception presentist in nature, but it also disregards a fundamental truism of human society: all power is fleeting.

It may be more productive to explain the fall of the Swedish empire in less fatalistic and more concrete terms. It could be, and has been, argued that the empire declined because it no longer served its intended purpose. This, too, is a specious argument, because the empire *never* fulfilled its hoped-for function, whether that was to provide commercial wealth to an impoverished kingdom or to provide security by demolishing perceived territorial encirclement. The search for security was indeed one of the most important, and probably *the* most important, motivation behind the expansion of Swedish sovereignty in the Baltic region, but it was never achieved *in toto*. Denmark was crippled, but not crushed, in 1660; Poland, a mere shadow of its former self at the end of the seventeenth century, still presented a very real threat to Karl XII. Russia was just coming into its own at the end of the *stormaktstid*. Sweden's successes in Germany after 1631 may have served to intimidate its enemies, but only for a while, and with every addition to its empire Sweden only made more enemies and further embittered the ones it already had.

Michael Roberts has suggested a different and compelling explanation for the fall of the Swedish empire. It did not decline because it had outlived its purpose. Its very existence in 1700 did not pose a threat to a perceived 'balance of power', and hence was not bound to provoke attack and partition. Sweden may still have been poor, but not enough – in Roberts' estimation – to have compromised the survival of the empire. Nor can its decline be traced to a degenerate nobility. The aristocracy, it is true, did become accustomed to luxury and ostentation after the Thirty Years' War, but it did not become effete or indolent; it did not lose its almost neo-stoic sense of duty to the state. Instead, it was the loss of the valuable eastern Baltic lands – 'those provinces which were still discharging a vital political function' – that brought the Swedish *imperium* crashing down during the reign of Karl XII.[2]

An interesting argument, to be sure, but one which puts – like the purely economic explanations of Sweden's rise to greatness – the proverbial cart before the horse. Sweden had risen to great-power status, and hence had gained its empire, because a unique conjuncture of political conditions in the mid-seventeenth century allowed it to do so, and because its geopolitical insecurity in the Baltic world forced its sovereigns and leading statesmen to create it. The conditions that had *permitted* the creation of the empire were gone by the end of the century, but the threats that *compelled* its formation were not. One threat in particular, namely Russia, was in fact far greater than it had ever been. Perhaps Sweden was not actually 'poor' in 1700, and largely thanks to Karl XI and his ministers the kingdom had achieved a comfortable prosperity. It was still not up to the task of maintaining and protecting provinces that lay outside the Scandinavian peninsula. Karl XI had created a self-sustaining army that could protect Sweden, and even maintain respectable garrisons in the German lands of the empire, but it could not hold out in the east indefinitely. The strategic balance was in favor of Russia. It all comes down to a question of resources: Sweden did not have the resources to sustain its empire, and the empire did not provide Sweden with the resources to do so.

Indeed, the empire was a drain on those resources. Sweden's holdings in Germany were perhaps the worst in this regard. Sweden's foothold in the Holy Roman Empire, intended initially to safeguard the Baltic against incursion by an aggressive Habsburg state, had become a diplomatic and economic liability shortly after Westphalia. It gave the Swedish monarchs a voice in imperial politics, but at the same time diverted men and cash that could have been more profitably employed elsewhere. Swedish membership in three different imperial 'circles' involved Sweden, needlessly, in the interminable and petty disputes of the German *Reichsfürsten*, and – worse still – in French intrigues in the empire during the ministry of Mazarin and the reign of Louis XIV. Serving as a guarantor of the Westphalian peace was a thankless and expensive task. Most important, involvement in German politics did not win the Swedes any friends in central Europe; in fact, just the opposite. More often than not, even Sweden's former allies in the Germanies resented the presence of a meddlesome and powerful foreigner in their affairs. Possession of Pomerania was an insult to Brandenburg, and the enmity of Brandenburg necessitated the presence of large numbers of Swedish troops in the province.

In short, the evidence demonstrates that the simplest explanation is the most likely: Sweden lost its empire because its upkeep was well beyond the financial or manpower capabilities of the Swedish state itself. At its height, the empire survived and expanded because of the audacity and skill of its warrior-kings and of its military and naval forces. It existed *because* it expanded, but the kingdom could not forever keep up the frenetic pace of expansionism that peaked with the wars of Karl X Gustav. Its position, in the Baltic world as well as in central Europe, precluded long-term adherence to the watchful neutrality of Karl XI's last two decades. Sweden's Baltic rivals, and the rest of Europe, would not leave it alone. In 1700, therefore, it could expand or die, and further expansion was simply impossible.

We should address another parallel question: What brought about Sweden's decline as a European power of the first rank? At first glance, this might appear to be the same thing as asking why Sweden's 'imperial experience' failed. The two issues are certainly intertwined intimately, but they are not identical. When Sweden acquired Estonia, or at least when Gustav Adolf took Riga in 1621, Sweden was an imperial state, but not yet a 'great power' in the estimation of the rest of Europe. That would not come until the victory at Breitenfeld in 1631. For the next three decades, Sweden would be the dominant military power of northern Europe, eclipsing Denmark, England, the United Netherlands, and the larger German principalities, even rivalling France. That it could do so was a reflection of the primary Vasa achievement, the establishment of administrative mechanisms for maintaining the state at war. Sweden was distressingly poor in comparison with, say, France or England, yet it was far more efficient than either in exploiting and mobilizing what it had. Sweden's enemies and allies in the Thirty Years' War were either torn by faction or obsessed with their own problems, constitutional and confessional; after the compromise of 1612, Sweden was not. Yet this, too – just like the diplomatic conditions that allowed Sweden to create a Baltic empire – would pass. The gap between Sweden and its competitors, except Denmark, narrowed visibly during the last half of the century. France and England at least partially surmounted the internal conditions that hampered their potential as states of overwhelming influence, and the Dutch developed a fleet that superceded the collective naval strength of both Scandinavian kingdoms. With the wars of mid-century, both the Torstensson War and the conflicts initiated by

Karl X Gustav, the maritime powers of northwestern Europe displayed a greater willingness to flex their muscles in curbing Swedish power. The Karl Gustav wars were the last expressions of Sweden's great-power status. When the Regency that followed Karl Gustav's death in 1660 tried – naïvely – to bankroll Sweden's military forces with foreign subsidies without making a commitment to alliance, it showed plainly the hollowness of Sweden's once-feared might. Sweden could remain neutral, though not for long, or it could make itself a client state to a larger and wealthier power. It could no longer, however, exert a decisive influence on European international politics on its own merits. After 1660, Sweden still possessed its empire, and commanded respect outside of the Baltic, but it was already slipping into the ranks of the secondary powers.

Sweden's career as a great power and as an empire was transitory, and may have been doomed from the beginning, but it was by no means a pointless or fruitless exercise. It permanently changed the balance of power in the Baltic, contributing directly to Denmark's demise and indirectly to Poland's. No state was more important in securing the defeat of the Austrian Habsburgs and their allies during the Thirty Years' War. The compulsion to be prepared constantly for war drove all of the administrative and constitutional innovations of Sweden's monarchs and ministers from Gustav Vasa to Karl XI, leading to the establishment of absolute monarchy and the creation of an administrative system that would serve as a model for several of its contemporaries. Moreover, and perhaps most important, the seventeenth century brought Sweden into the European mainstream. The kingdom's horizons – economic, cultural, social, and political – were no longer tightly circumscribed by the shores of the Baltic Sea.

Notes

Chapter 1: The Sixteenth-Century Inheritance

1. Jan Glete, *War and the State in Early Modern Europe. Spain, the Dutch Republic, and Sweden as Fiscal-Military States, 1500–1660* (London, 2002), p. 179.
2. Sven-Erik Åström, 'The Swedish Economy and Sweden's Role as a Great Power 1632–1697', in *Sweden's Age of Greatness 1632–1718*, ed. Michael Roberts (New York, 1973), p. 67; Eli F. Heckscher, *An Economic History of Sweden*, trans. Göran Ohlin (Cambridge, Massachusetts, 1963), pp. 70–72, 84–109.
3. Heckscher; Åström, 'The Swedish Economy', pp. 58–101.
4. On Sweden's noble economy, see Jan Samuelson, *Aristokrat eller förädlad bonde? Det svenska frälsets ekonomi, politik og sociala förbindelser under tiden 1523–1611* (Lund, 1993), pp. 45–60, 70–75, 255–64; Olle Ferm, *De högadliga godsen i Sverige vid 1500-talets mitt. Geografisk uppbyggnad, räntestruktur, godsdrift och hushållning* (Stockholm, 1990), pp. 32–42. On the rusttjänst, see Sven A. Nilsson, *Krona och frälse i Sverige 1523–94* (Lund, 1947), pp. 18–85.
5. On the role of towns in Swedish domestic and international commerce, see: Åke Sandström, *Plöjande borgare och handlande bönder. Mötet mellan den europeiska urbana ekonomin och vasatidens Sverige* (Stockholm, 1996).
6. Lars-Olof Larsson, *Bönder och gårdar i stormaktspolitikens skugga. Studier kring hemmansklyvning, godsbildning och mantalssättning i Sverige 1625–1750* (Växjö, 1983); Sören Klingnéus, *Bönder blir vapensmeder. Protoindustriell tillverkning i Närke under 1600-och 1700-talen* (Uppsala, 1997), especially pp. 120–85; Sven A. Nilsson, 'Landbor och skattebönder. En studie av

extraskattens fördelning under 1500-och 1600-talen', in *Historieforsk-ning på nya vägar. Studier tillägnade Sten Carlsson 14.12.1977* (Lund, 1977), pp. 143–68; Janken Myrdal, *Jordbruket under feodalismen 1000–1700* (Stockholm, 1999); Eino Jutikkala, *Bonden, adelsmannen, kronan. Godspolitik och jordegendomsförhållanden i Norden 1550–1750* (Lund, 1979).

7. Michael Roberts, *Swedish Imperial Experience 1560–1718* (Cambridge, 1979), p. 43. On the rural economy, see Johan Söderberg and Janken Myrdal, *The Agrarian Economy of Sixteenth-Century Sweden* (Stockholm, 2002), especially pp. 91–110.

8. On the dissolution of the Kalmar Union and early 'national' sentiment in the Nordic kingdoms, see Harald Gustafsson, *Gamla riken, nya stater. Statsbildning, politisk kultur och identiteter under Kalmarunionens upplösningsskede* (Stockholm, 2000). Also Michael Roberts, *The Early Vasas. A History of Sweden 1523–1611* (Cambridge, 1968), pp. 1–45; Mikael Venge, *Christian 2.s fald* (Odense, 1972); Lauritz Weibull, *Stockholms blodbad* (Stockholm, 1965), pp. 120–83.

9. Nilsson, *Krona och frälse*, pp. 90–107.

10. Herman Schück, 'Riksdagens framväxt: tiden intill 1611', in *Riksdagen genom tiderna*, ed. Herman Schück, Göran Rystad *et al.* (Stockholm, 1985), pp. 7–44.

11. Nilsson, *Krona och frälse*, pp. 132–41.

12. The definitive biography of Erik remains Ingvar Andersson, *Erik XIV* (Stockholm, 1948). On the king's disputes with his brothers, see Frede P. Jensen, *Bidrag til Frederik II's og Erik XIV's historie* (Copenhagen, 1978), pp. 83–125.

13. Lennart Hedberg, *Företagarfursten och framväxten av den starka staten. Hertig Karls resursexploatering i Närke 1581–1602* (Örebro, 1995); Nilsson, *Krona och frälse*, pp. 142–347. On Johan's Catholicism, see Gustaf Ivarsson, *Johan III och klosterväsendet* (Lund, 1970); Magnus Nyman, *Förlorarnas historia. Katolskt liv i Sverige från Gustav Vasa till drottning Kristina* (Uppsala, 1997), pp. 135–76; Oskar Garstein, *Rome and the Counter-Reformation in Scandinavia*, vol. 1: *1539–1583* (Oslo, 1963), pp. 72–260; Vello Helk, *Laurentius Nicolai Norvegus S.J.* (Copenhagen, 1966), pp. 25–201.

14. There is still no satisfactory recent biography of Johan III in Swedish or English; one must rely on the brief but compelling account of his reign in Roberts, *Early Vasas*, pp. 242–326.

15. David Norrman, *Sigismund Vasa och hans regering i Polen* (Stockholm, 1978).

16. Heikki Ylikangas, *Klubbekriget. Det blodiga bondekriget i Finland 1596–1597* (Stockholm, 1999).

17. Åke Hermansson, *Karl IX och ständerna. Tronfrågan och författnings-utvecklingen i Sverige 1598–1611* (Uppsala, 1962); Sven A. Nilsson, *Kampen om de adliga privilegierna 1526–1594* (Lund, 1952), pp. 100–31; Roberts, *Early Vasas*, pp. 327–461.

18. Ingun Montgomery, *Värjostånd och lärostånd. Religion och politik i meningsutbytet mellan kungamakt och prästerskap i Sverige 1593–1608* (Uppsala, 1972). There is a convenient English summary in Montgomery, 'The institutionalisation of Lutheranism in Sweden and Finland', in *The Scandinavian Reformation*, ed. Ole Peter Grell (Cambridge, 1995), pp. 144–78.

19. On the debate over the motivating forces behind Sweden's 'imperial' career, see Roberts, *Swedish Imperial Experience*, pp. 1–42; Klaus-Richard Böhme, 'Building a Baltic Empire. Aspects of Swedish Expansionism, 1560–1660', in *In Quest of Trade and Security. The Baltic in Power Politics 1500–1990*, ed. Göran Rystad (2 vols, Lund, 1994–95), vol. 1, pp. 182–3; Sverker Oredsson, *Gustav Adolf, Sverige och Trettioåriga kriget. Historieskrivning och kult* (Lund, 1992).

20. Artur Attman, *Swedish Aspirations and the Russian Market during the 17th Century* (Göteborg, 1985); Jan Peters, *Die alten Schweden* (Berlin, 1986); Jan Lindegren, *Utskrivning och utsugning. Produktion och reproduktion i Bygdeå 1620–1640* (Uppsala, 1980); idem, *Maktstatens resurser. Danmark och Sverige under 1600-talet* (Uppsala, 2001); idem, '"Med glädje och utan suckan" eller samhällskontrollen i ett lokal-perspektiv', in *Kustbygd och centralmakt 1560–1721. Studier i centrum-periferi under svensk stormaktstid*, ed. Nils Erik Villstrand (Helsingfors, 1987), pp. 203–29; S. Troebst, 'Debating the mercantile background to early modern Swedish empire-building: Michael Roberts versus Artur Attman', *European History Quarterly*, 24 (1994), 485–509.

21. Aksel Christensen, *Dutch Trade to the Baltic around 1600* (Copenhagen, 1941).

22. Frede P. Jensen, *Danmarks konflikt med Sverige 1563–1570* (Copenhagen, 1982); Jason Lavery, *Germany's Northern Challenge. The Holy Roman Empire and the Scandinavian Struggle for the Baltic, 1563–1576* (Leiden, 2002); Sven Ulric Palme, *Sverige och Danmark 1596–1611* (Uppsala, 1942).

23. By far the best account of the conflicts between Sweden, Russia, Poland, and Denmark is Robert I. Frost's phenomenally clear analysis: *The Northern Wars 1558–1721* (London, 2000). See also Kari Tarkiainen,

'*Vår Gamble Arffiende Ryssen*'. *Synen på Ryssland i Sverige 1595–1621* (Stockholm, 1974).

24. Karl Hildebrand, *Johan III och Europas katolska makter* (Uppsala, 1898).
25. Nilsson, *Kampen om de adliga privilegierna*; idem, *Krona och frälse*.
26. At Stettin, the Danish and Swedish negotiators agreed that, in the future, all conflicts between their kingdoms would first be mediated by means of 'border-meetings' (*gränsemöte*), in which members of both Councils would attempt to resolve the conflict before allowing their sovereigns to declare war.
27. Bernt Douhan, *Arbete, kapital och migration. Valloninvandringen till Sverige under 1600-talet* (Uppsala, 1985), pp. 22–28; Klingnéus, *Bönder blir våpensmeder*; Hedberg, *Företagarfursten*.
28. Ylikangas, *Klubbekriget*.
29. Nils Erik Villstrand, *Anpassning eller protest. Lokalsamhället inför utskrivningarna av fotfolk till den svenska krigsmakten 1620–1679* (Åbo, 1992), pp. 39–48; Sven A. Nilsson, *På väg mot militärstaten. Krigsbefälets etabliring i den äldre vasatidens Sverige* (Uppsala, 1989).
30. Jan W. Wijn, 'Johann der Mittlere von Nassau-Siegen', *Klassiker der Kriegskunst*, ed. Werner Hahlweg (Darmstadt, 1960), pp. 119–33; On the growth of 'professionalism' in the officer corps, see Gunnar Artéus, *Till militärstatens förhistoria. Krig, professionalisering och social förändring under Vasasönernas regering* (Stockholm, 1986); Sven A. Nilsson, *De stora krigens tid. Om Sverige som militärstat och bondesamhälle* (Uppsala, 1990), pp. 107–16; idem, *På väg mot militärstaten*.

Chapter 2: The Reign of Gustav II Adolf

1. The best brief biography of Gustav Adolf is the more recent one by Michael Roberts: *Gustavus Adolphus* (2nd edition, London, 1992). See also idem, *Gustavus Adolphus. A History of Sweden 1611–1632* (2 vols, London, 1953–58); Nils Ahnlund, *Gustav Adolf den Store* (2nd edition, Stockholm, 1932); Johannes Paul, *Gustaf Adolf* (3 vols, Leipzig, 1927–32); Günter Barudio, *Gustav Adolf–der Große. Eine politische Biographie* (Frankfurt am Main, 1982).
2. Nils Runeby, *Monarchia Mixta. Maktfördelningsdebatt i Sverige under den tidigare stormaktstiden* (Stockholm, 1962), pp. 45–78; Carl Arvid Hessler, 'Gustav II Adolfs konungaförsäkran', *Scandia*, 5 (1932), 167–204.
3. Tor Berg, *Johan Skytte. Hans ungdom och verksamhet under Karl IX:s regering* (Stockholm, 1920).

4. A biography of Oxenstierna, especially one covering his early years in office, is sorely needed. One must rely on a number of older works: Nils Ahnlund, *Axel Oxenstierna intill Gustav Adolfs död* (Stockholm, 1940); Wilhelm Tham, *Axel Oxenstierna, hand ungdom och verksamhet intill år 1612* (Stockholm, 1935). On Oxenstierna's patronage activities within the central administration, see Svante Norrhem, *Uppkomlingarna. Kanslitjänstemännen i 1600-talets Sverige och Europa* (Stockholm, 1993).

5. This was a sensitive issue of long standing. The 'Three Crowns' represented the old Kalmar Union of Denmark, Norway, and Sweden; disagreement over this symbolism, which hinted at Danish pretensions to sovereignty over Sweden, had also contributed to the outbreak of the Seven Years' War in 1563.

6. On the Kalmar War and the Peace of Knäröd, see Axel Liljefalk Larsen, *Kalmarkrigen* (Copenhagen, 1889); Leo Tandrup, *Mod triumf eller tragedie* (2 vols, Aarhus, 1979), vol. 1, pp. 59–223.

7. The recent researches of the 'power-state project' (*maktstatsprojekt*) focus in particular on institutional development within the central administrations of the Scandinavian kingdoms. See ed. E. Ladewig Petersen, *Magtstaten i Norden i 1600 tallet og dens sociale konsekvenser (Rapporter til den XIX nordiske historikerkongres, bd. I)* (Odense, 1984); ed. Leon Jespersen, *A Revolution from Above? The Power State of 16th and 17th Century Scandinavia* (Odense, 2000).

8. Böhme, 'Building a Baltic Empire', p. 201.

9. Roberts, *Gustavus Adolphus* (1992), pp. 75–81; Jespersen, 'Constitutional and administrative situation', pp. 108–17; Norrhem, *Uppkomlingarna*, pp. 51–57.

10. David Gaunt, *Utbildning till statens tjänst. En kollektivebiografi av stormaktstidens hovrättsauskultanter* (Uppsala, 1975), pp. 1–38.

11. Göran Rystad, 'Med råds råd eller efter konungens godtycke? Makten över ämbetstilsättningarna som politisk stridsfråga under 1600-talet', *Scandia*, 29 (1963), 157–249; Ulf Sjödell, *Riksråd och kungliga råd. Rådskarriären 1602–1718* (Västerås, 1975); idem, *Infödda svenska män av riddarskapet och adeln. Kring ett tema i Sveriges inre historia under 1500-och 1600-talen* (Lund, 1976), pp. 33–44.

12. Michael Roberts, ed., 'Charles X and his Council: "dualism" or co-operation?', in *From Oxenstierna to Charles XII. Four Studies* (Cambridge, 1991), pp. 90–92.

13. Göran Rystad, 'Stormaktstidens riksdag (1611–1718)', in Schück, *Riksdagen genom tiderna*, pp. 60–66.

14. Leon Jespersen, 'The Constitutional and Administrative Situation',
    in *Revolution from Above*, ed. Jespersen, pp. 139–42; Bill Widén,
    'Bönedagsplakaten och opinionsbildningen under Gustav II Adolfs
    tid', *Kyrkohistorisk Årsskrift* (1987), 17–22; Sverker Arnoldsson,
    'Krigspropagandan i Sverige före Trettioåriga Kriget', *Göteborgs
    Högskolas årsskrift*, 47 (1941).
15. Nilsson, *De stora krigens tid*, pp. 150–77; Jan Glete, *War and the State*,
    pp. 204–06; Villstrand, 'Adaptation or Protestation', pp. 268–72.
16. The literature on the Swedish tactical reforms is truly immense, and
    the debate over the significance of these reforms has become quite
    acerbic at times. Michael Roberts' view of Gustav Adolf as a key
    figure in the 'military revolution' of the seventeenth century is best
    expounded in two of his essays: 'Gustav Adolf and the Art of War',
    and 'The Military Revolution, 1560–1660', both included in *Essays in
    Swedish History*, ed. Michael Roberts (Minneapolis, 1967), pp. 56–81,
    195–225. On the debate in general, see Geoffrey Parker, *The Military
    Revolution* (2nd edition, Cambridge, 1996), pp. 6–44; ed. C. Rogers,
    *The Military Revolution Debate. Readings on the Military Transformation
    of Early Modern Europe* (Boulder, CO, 1995); Frost, *Northern Wars*,
    pp. 102–06.
17. Jan Glete, *Navies and Nations. Warships, Navies and State Building in
    Europe and America, 1500–1860* (2 vols, Stockholm, 1993), vol. 1,
    pp. 133–39; Roberts, *Gustavus Adolphus* (1953–58), vol. 2, pp. 272–304.
18. Artéus, *Till militärstatens förhistoria*, pp. 27–82.

Chapter 3: Sweden on the World Stage: The Foreign Policy of Gustav II Adolf

1. See the thorough discussion in Oredsson, *Gustav Adolf, Sverige och
   Trettioåriga kriget*.
2. Erik Ringmar, *Identity, Interest and Action. A Cultural Explanation of
   Sweden's Intervention in the Thirty Years War* (Cambridge, 1996). See
   also Lockhart's review of Ringmar's book in *The International History
   Review*, 20 (1998), 162–64.
3. Tandrup, *Mod triumf*, vol. 1, pp. 225–344.
4. Tarkiainen, *'Vår Gamble Arffiende Ryssen'*; Roberts, *Gustavus Adolphus*
   (1953–58), vol. 1, pp. 72–91.
5. Helk, *Norvegus*, pp. 331–92; Oskar Garstein, *Rome and the Counter-
   Reformation in Scandinavia*, vol. 2: *1583–1622* (Oslo, 1980), pp. 251–406;

idem, *Rome and the Counter-Reformation in Scandinavia*, vol. 4: *The Age of Gustavus Adolphus and Queen Christina* (Leiden, 1992), pp. 184–309.

6. Axel Norberg, *Polen i svensk politik 1617–26* (Stockholm, 1974).

7. Tandrup, *Mod triumf*, vol. 1, pp. 345–510.

8. Tandrup, *Mod triumf*, vol. 2.

9. On the Danish–Swedish rivalry over Protestant leadership, see Paul Douglas Lockhart, *Denmark in the Thirty Years' War: King Christian IV and the Decline of the Oldenburg State* (Susquehanna, PA, 1996); idem, 'Religion and Princely Liberties: Denmark's intervention in the Thirty Years War', *The International History Review*, 17 (1995), 1–22.

10. Norberg, *Polen i svensk politik*; Frost, *Northern Wars*, pp. 102–09.

11. Arnoldsson, 'Krigspropagandan'; Pärtel Piirimäe, 'Just war in theory and practice: the legitimation of Swedish intervention in the Thirty Years War', *The Historical Journal*, 45 (2002), pp. 499–523.

12. Knud J.V. Jespersen, 'Kongemødet i Ulfsbäck præstegård februar 1629', *Historie*, 14 (1982), 420–39; E.K.H. Wilmanns, *Der Lübecker Friede* (Bonn, 1904).

13. Michael Roberts, 'The Political Objectives of Gustav Adolf in Germany, 1630–32', in *Essays in Swedish History*, ed. Michael Roberts (Minneapolis, 1967), pp. 82–110.

14. On the political 'fallout' of the Restitution, see Robert Bireley, *Religion and Politics in the Age of the Counterreformation* (Chapel Hill, NC, 1981).

15. Roberts, *Gustavus Adolphus* (1953–58), vol. 2, pp. 426–538; Silvia Serena Tschopp, *Heilsgeschichte Deutungsmuster in der Publizistik des Dreißigjährigen Krieges. Pro- und antischwedische Propaganda in Deutschland 1628 bis 1635* (Frankfurt am Main, 1991).

16. Roberts, *Gustavus Adolphus*, p. 160.

17. Roberts, *Gustavus Adolphus* (1953–58), vol. 2, pp. 538–773.

Chapter 4: The Interregnum and Queen Christina, 1632–54

1. Michael Roberts, 'Oxenstierna in Germany, 1633–36', in *From Oxenstierna to Charles XII*, pp. 8–20.

2. Jespersen, *Constitutional and Administrative Situation*, p. 68.

3. Ibid., p. 69.

4. Ibid., p. 69.

5. Roberts, *Oxenstierna*, pp. 16–18.

6. Claes Peterson, *Peter the Great's Administrative and Judicial Reforms: Swedish Antecedents and the Process of Reception* (Lund, 1979); Jespersen, 'Constitutional and Administrative Situation', p. 75.

7. This figure is taken from the aggregate state budget for 1633, in which the overall state income was probably a bit higher than it was during the 1640s. Of the 3.26 million *riksdaler* in revenues that year, 400,000 (almost 13 percent) came from French subsidies, and 614,000 (nearly 19 percent) came from the Prussian shipping tolls, which would expire in 1635. Åström, 'The Swedish Economy', pp. 82–3.

8. Lars Ekholm, *Svensk krigsfinansiering 1630–31* (Uppsala, 1974).

9. For Oxenstierna's actions in Germany and the motivations behind his policies, see Roberts, *Oxenstierna*; Sigmund Wilhelm Goetze, *Die Politik des schwedischen Reichskanzlers Axel Oxenstierna gegenüber Kaiser und Reich* (Kiel, 1971); Pekka Suvanto, *Die deutsche Politik Oxenstiernas und Wallenstein* (Helsinki, 1979); Geoffrey Parker, *The Thirty Years' War* (2nd edition, London, 1997), pp. 119–29, 140–45.

10. This was not a new claim. Duke Frederik of Denmark had been elected as administrator of both bishoprics, as well as several others, during the early 1620s. See Lockhart, *Denmark in the Thirty Years' War*, pp. 92–95.

11. Lockhart, *Denmark*, pp. 240–45; B.F. Porshnev, *Muscovy and Sweden in the Thirty Years' War 1630–1635* (Cambridge, 1995); Frost, *Northern Wars*, pp. 142–47.

12. In addition to the sources on Oxenstierna cited in note 9, see Sune Lundgren, *Johan Adler Salvius. Problem kring freden, krigsekonomien och maktkampen* (Lund, 1945); Sverker Arnoldsson, *Svensk-fransk krigs- och fredspolitik i Tyskland 1634–36* (Göteborg, 1937).

13. Klaus-Richard Böhme, 'Lennart Torstensson und Helmut Wrangel in Schleswig-Holstein und Jütland 1643–1645', *Zeitschrift der Gesellschaft für schleswig-holsteinische Geschichte*, 90 (1965), 41–49; Lockhart, *Denmark*, pp. 259–65; J.A. Fridericia, *Danmarks ydre politiske Historie i Tiden fra Freden i Prag til Freden i Brömsebro* (Copenhagen, 1881), pp. 345–524.

14. Göran Rystad, 'Dominium maris Baltici – dröm och verklighet. Sveriges freder 1645–61', in *Mare nostrum. Om Westfaliska freden och Östersjön som ett svensk maktcentrum*, ed. Kerstin Abukhanfusa (Stockholm, 1999), pp. 97–100.

15. Clas Odhner, *Die Politik Schwedens im Westphälischen Friedenscongress und die Gründung der schwedischen Herrschaft in Deutschland* (Hannover, 1973).

16. Despite Christina's fame, there is at the moment no recent scholarly treatment of her life and reign. One must be satisfied with two older biographies: Georgina Masson, *Queen Christina* (New York, 1968), which is sound though informal, or the thin and somewhat dated work by Curt Weibull, *Drottning Christina* (4th edition, Stockholm, 1931).

17. Nils Ahnlund, 'Königin Christine von Schweden und Reichskanzler Axel Oxenstierna', *Historisches Jahrbuch*, 74 (1955), 282–93.

18. Masson, *Queen Christina*, p. 82.

19. Eva Österberg, 'Bönder och centralmakt i det tidigmoderna Sverige. Konflikt – kompromiss – politisk kultur', *Scandia*, 55 (1989), 73–95; Anders Olsson, *Borgmästare, bastioner och tullbommar. Göteborg och Halmstad under statligt inflytande 1630–1660* (Lund, 1995), pp. 128–30; Arne Jansson, *Bördor och bärkraft. Borgare och kronotjänare i Stockholm 1644–1672* (Stockholm, 1991), pp. 140–54.

20. Ingvar Andersson, *Sveriges historia* (5th edition, Stockholm, 1960), p. 215.

21. Anthony F. Upton, *Charles XI and Swedish Absolutism* (Cambridge, 1998), pp. 8–10; Olsson, *Borgmästare*, pp. 157–60.

22. Andersson, *Sveriges historia*, p. 216.

23. That Christina could devote such energy to enhancing cultural life at court reflects her style of rulership. The earlier Vasas, including her father, had kept a quasi-peripatetic court that frequently moved away from Stockholm; Christina, on the other hand, was the first Swedish monarch to keep the court permanently ensconced at the capital. Fabian Persson, *Servants of Fortune. The Swedish Court between 1598 and 1721* (Lund, 1999), pp. 40–48.

24. Garstein, *Rome and the Counter-Reformation*, vol. 4, pp. 525–764; Sven Ingemar Olofsson, *Drottning Christinas tronavsägelse och trosförändring* (Uppsala, 1953).

Chapter 5: The Swedish 'Power State': Society, Culture, and the Burden of War

1. On Swedish war finance, see Lars Ekholm, 'Kontributioner och krediter. Svensk krigsfinansiering 1630–1631', and Roland Norlund, 'Krig genom ombud. De svenska krigsfinanserna och Heilbronnförbundet 1633', in *Det kontinentala krigets ekonomi*, ed. Landberg *et al.* pp. 143–270 and 271–451.

2. Roberts, *Gustavus Adolphus*, p. 111.
3. Böhme, 'Building a Baltic Empire', p. 186.
4. Behre, Larsson, and Österberg, *Stormaktsdröm*, pp. 94, 131; Nilsson, *De stora krigens tid*, pp. 31–55, 91–97, 150–77; Sandström, *Plöjande borgare*, pp. 129–36; Jansson, *Bördor*, pp. 110–38.
5. Sven-Erik Åström, *From cloth to iron. The Anglo-Baltic trade in the late seventeenth century* (Helsingfors, 1963); idem, 'Swedish Economy', p. 66.
6. Åke Sandström, *Mellan Torneå och Amsterdam. En undersökning av Stockholms rolle som förmelare av varor i regional-och utrikeshandel 1600–1650* (Stockholm, 1990); idem, *Plöjande borgare*; Robert Sandberg, *I slottets skugga. Stockholm och kronan 1599–1620* (Stockholm, 1991), pp. 265–379; idem, 'Anima regni: Stockholm under den svenska stormaktstidens början', in *Kustbygd och centralmakt. Studier i centrum-periferi under svensk stormaktstid*, ed. Nils Erik Villstrand (Helsingfors, 1987), pp. 115–38; Jansson, *Bördor*, pp. 21–32; Einar Wendt, *Det svenska licentväsendet i Preussen, 1627–1635* (Uppsala, 1933).
7. Glete, *War and the State*, pp. 206–10.
8. Lars Ekholm, *Svensk krigsfinansiering 1630–1631* (Uppsala, 1974); Sven Lundkvist, 'Svensk krigsfinansiering 1630–1635', *Historisk Tidskrift* 86 (1966), 377–421; Nilsson, *De stora krigens tid*, pp. 150–96.
9. Åström, *Swedish Economy*, p. 85.
10. Åström, *Swedish Economy*, p. 85.
11. Fredric Bedoire, *Guldålder. Slott och politik i 1600-talets Sverige* (Stockholm, 2001), pp. 29–144; Arne Losman, 'Skokloster – Europe and the World in a Swedish Castle', and Margareta Revera, 'The Making of a Civilized Nation. Nation-Building, Aristocratic Culture and Social Change', in *The Age of New Sweden* (Stockholm, 1988), pp. 85–101, 103–31.
12. Behre, Larsson, and Österberg, *Stormaktsdröm*, p. 126.
13. Sjödell, *Riksråd och kungliga råd*, pp. 8–13; idem, *Infödda svenska män*, pp. 37–57. On the ennoblement of foreign officers, see Mary Elizabeth Ailes, *Military Migration and State Formation. The British Military Community in Seventeenth-Century Sweden* (Lincoln, NE, 2002).
14. Olsson, *Borgmästare*, pp. 80–127; Jansson, *Bördor*, pp. 139–54.
15. Nils Erik Villstrand, 'Adaptation or Protest? Local community facing the conscription of infantry for the Swedish armed forces, 1620–1679', in *Revolution from Above*, ed. Jespersen, p. 264.
16. Behre, Larsson, and Österberg, *Stormaktsdröm*, p. 128.
17. Kurt Ågren, *Adelns bönder och kronans. Skatter och besvär i Uppland 1650–1680* (Stockholm, 1964).

18. Lundkvist, 'Svensk krigsfinansiering', p. 385; Roberts, *Gustavus Adolphus*, p. 123.

19. Villstrand, 'Adaptation or Protest', pp. 264–76. This essay is a distillation of Villstrand's larger work on conscription in two Finnish districts: *Anpassning eller protest. Lokalsamhället inför utskrivningarna av fotfolk till den svenska krigsmakten 1620–1629* (Åbo, 1992).

20. Lindegren, *Utskrivning och utsugning*, pp. 144–77; Villstrand, 'Adaptation or Protest', pp. 273–75. On the historiographical debate regarding Lindegren's research on Bygdeå, see Frost, *Northern Wars*, pp. 205–08.

21. Villstrand, *Adaptation or Protest*, pp. 291–92.

22. Lars-Olof Larsson, 'Lokalsamhälle och centralmakt i Sverige under 1500-och 1600-talen', in *Kustbygd och centralmakt*, pp. 187–202; Eva Österberg, 'Local political culture versus the state. Patterns of interaction in pre-industrial Sweden', in *Mentalities and other realities. Essays in Medieval and Early Modern Scandinavian History* (Lund, 1991), pp. 176–91.

23. Behre, Larsson, and Österberg, *Stormaktsdröm*, pp. 143–44; Roberts, *Gustavus Adolphus*, pp. 85–86; Sven Lundström, *Gustav II Adolf och Uppsala Universitet* (Uppsala, 1982).

24. Lars Niléhn, *Peregrinatio academica. Det svenska samhället och de utrikes studieresorna under 1600-talet* (Lund, 1983); Arne Losman, *Carl Gustaf Wrangel och Europa. Studier i kulturförbindelser kring en 1600-talsmagnat* (Stockholm, 1980); Gaunt, *Utbildning*.

25. Stina Hansson, *Svenskans nytta, Sveriges ära. Litteratur och kulturpolitik under 1600-talet* (Göteborg, 1984); Bengt Ankarloo, 'Europe and the glory of Sweden: The emergence of a Swedish self-image in the early 17th century', in *Europe and Scandinavia*, ed. Rystad, pp. 237–44; Roberts, *Swedish Imperial Experience*, pp. 70–75; Kurt Johannesson, *The Renaissance of the Goths in Sixteenth-Century Sweden: Johannes and Olaus Magnus as Politicians and Historians*, trans. James Larson (Berkeley, 1991). On Sarmatianism, see Maria Bogucka, *The Lost World of the 'Sarmatians': Custom as the Regulator of Polish Social Life in Early Modern Times* (Warsaw, 1996).

26. Behre, Larsson, and Österberg, *Stormaktsdröm*, pp. 156–57.

27. Stellan Dahlgren, Allan Ellenius, Lars Gustafsson, and Gunnar Larsson, *Kultur och samhälle i stormaktstidens Sverige* (Stockholm, 1967); Gunnar Eriksson, 'Stiernhielm, Rudbeck och Östersjön', and Allan Ellenius, 'Stormaktstida konst och miljö i mentalitetshistoriskt perspektiv', in *Mare nostrum. Om Westfaliska freden och Östersjön som ett*

svenskt maktcentrum, ed. Kerstin Abukhanfusa (Stockholm, 1999), pp. 165–71 and 172–89; Persson, *Servants of Fortune*.
28. Bengt Ankarloo, *Trolldomsprocesserna i Sverige* (2nd edition, Stockholm, 1984).
29. Roberts, *Swedish Imperial Experience*, p. 64.

Chapter 6: Proto-absolutism or 'Military Monarchy'? The Brief Reign of Karl X Gustav, 1654–59

1. There is no recent biography of Karl X Gustav. One must make do with: Sven Ingemar Olofsson, *Carl X Gustaf: Hertigen-Tronföljaren* (Stockholm, 1961); and Sten Bonnesen, *Karl X Gustav* (Malmö, 1924–58). Anders Florén has written a brief sketch of the king: Anders Florén, Stellan Dahlgren, and Jan Lindegren, *Kungar och Krigare. Tre essäer om Karl X Gustav, Karl XI och Karl XII* (Stockholm, 1992), pp. 11–80.
2. Frost, *Northern Wars*, pp. 164–67.
3. On Dutch relations with Sweden after Brömsebro, see Yngve Lorents, *Efter Brömsebrofreden. Svenska och danska förbindelser med Frankrike och Holland, 1645–49* (Uppsala, 1916).
4. There is an extensive literature on Karl Gustav's campaigns and on the Swedish army of the period. Arne Stade, *Erik Dahlbergh och Carl X Gustafs krigshistoria* (Stockholm, 1967); Arne Stade, Lars Tersmeden, and Jonas Hedberg, *Carl X Gustafs armé* (Stockholm, 1979); Finn Askgaard, *Kampen om Östersjön på Carl X Gustafs tid: Ett bidrag till nordisk sjökrigshistoria* (Stockholm, 1974).
5. Frost, *Northern Wars*, pp. 166–83.
6. It was not the first dynastic connexion between Sweden and Gottorp. Karl IX's second wife, the mother of Gustav Adolf, was Christina of Holstein-Gottorp.
7. Arne Stade, *Carl X Gustaf och Danmark* (Stockholm, 1965).
8. Michael Roberts, 'Cromwell and the Baltic', in *Essays in Swedish History*, ed. Roberts, pp. 138–94.
9. Behre, Larsson, and Österberg, *Stormaktsdröm*, p. 100; Göran Rystad, 'Med råds råd'.
10. Hans Landberg, 'Kungamaktens emancipation. Statsreglering och militärorganisation under Karl X Gustav och Karl XI', *Scandia* 35 (1969); idem, *Statsfinans och kungamakt. Karl X Gustav inför polska kriget* (Stockholm, 1969).

11. Michael Roberts, 'Charles X and his Council: "dualism" or co-operation?', in Roberts, *From Oxenstierna to Charles XII*, pp. 55–99; Stellan Dahlgren, 'Charles X and the Constitution', in *Sweden's Age of Greatness*, ed. Roberts, pp. 174–202.

12. Roberts, 'Charles X and his Council', pp. 65–67; Villstrand, 'Adaptation or Protestation', p. 268; Nilsson, *De stora krigens tid*, pp. 178–95.

13. Roberts, 'Charles X and the Constitution', pp. 84–86; Åström, 'The Swedish Economy', pp. 87–88.

14. Stellan Dahlgren, *Karl X Gustav och reduktionen* (Stockholm, 1964). There is a convenient English-language summary of the debates in Roberts, 'Charles X and his Council', pp. 86–92.

Chapter 7: The Swedish Empire in Louis XIV's Europe, 1660–79

1. Carol E. Hoffecker, *New Sweden in America* (Newark, Delaware, 1995); Christopher Ward, *New Sweden on the Delaware* (Philadelphia, 1938); Amandus Johnson, *The Swedish Settlements on the Delaware* (2 vols, Philadelphia, 1911).

2. Glete, *War and the State*, p. 179.

3. Knud Fabricius, *Skaanes Overgang fra Danmark til Sverige. Studier over Nationalitetsskiftet i de skaanske Landskaber* (4 vols, Copenhagen, 1906–58); Jerker Rosén, *Hur Skåne blev svenskt* (Stockholm, 1943); Olsson, *Borgmästare*, pp. 63–66.

4. Böhme, 'Building a Baltic Empire', pp. 190–92; Birger Fahlborg, *Sveriges yttre politik, 1660–1664* (Stockholm, 1932).

5. Behre, Larsson, and Österberg, *Stormaktsdröm*, pp. 113–14; Helmut Backhaus, *Reichsterritorium und schwedische Provinz. Vorpommern unter Karls XI. Vormündern 1660–1672* (Göttingen, 1969); Klaus-Richard Böhme, 'Die Krone Schweden als Reichsstand 1648 bis 1720', in *In Europas Mitte. Deutschland und seine Nachbarn*, ed. Heinz Duchhardt (Bonn, 1988), pp. 33–39; Beate-Christine Fiedler, *Die Verwaltung der Herzogtümer Bremen und Verden in der Schwedenzeit 1652–1712* (Stade, 1987); Jonas Nordin, *Ett fattigt men fritt folk. Nationell och politisk själv-bild i Sverige från sen stormaktstid till slutet av frihetstiden* (Stockholm, 2000).

6. Hans Landberg, 'Krig på kredit. Svensk rustningsfinansiering våren 1655', in *Det kontinentala krigets ekonomi. Studier i krigsfinansiering*

under svensk stormaktstid (Uppsala, 1971), eds Hans Landberg, Lars Ekholm, Roland Nordlund, and Sven A. Nilsson, pp. 1–141.

7. Upton, *Charles XI*, pp. 12–13.

8. Ulf Sjödell, *Kungamakt och högaristokrati. En studie i Sveriges inre historia under Karl XI* (Lund, 1966), pp. 24–50; idem, *Infödda svenska män*, pp. 52–62; Runeby, *Monarchia mixta*, pp. 513–29.

9. Rudolf Fåhræus, *Magnus Gabriel De la Gardie* (Stockholm, 1936); Margareta Revera, *Gods och gård 1650–1680. Magnus Gabriel de la Gardies godsbildning och godsdrift i Västergötland* (Stockholm, 1975); Göran Rystad, 'Magnus Gabriel De la Gardie', in *Sweden's Age of Greatness*, ed. Roberts, pp. 203–36; Leif Åslund, *Magnus Gabriel De la Gardie och vältaligheten* (Uppsala, 1992).

10. Behre, Larsson, and Österberg, *Stormaktsdröm*, p. 101.

11. Upton, *Charles XI*, pp. 13–14.

12. Sjödell, *Infödda svenska män*, pp. 63–69; Åslund, *De la Gardie*, pp. 87–93, 98–116, 122–29.

13. Behre, Larsson, and Österberg, *Stormaktsdröm*, pp. 119–20; Upton, *Charles XI*, p. 14; Åslund, *De la Gardie*, pp. 94–98, 117–22.

14. Georg Landberg, *Den svenska utrikespolitikens historia*, vol. 1, Part 3 (Stockholm, 1952), pp. 160–72.

15. The most detailed and convincing portrait of the king to date is Göran Rystad, *Karl XI. En biografi* (Lund, 2001), especially pp. 358–67. Upton, *Charles XI*, is the only worthwhile account in English. Stellan Dahlgren provides a succinct account of the reign in *Kungar och Krigare*, eds Florén, Dahlgren, and Lindegren, pp. 83–148.

16. Upton, *Charles XI*, pp. 15–21.

17. On the constitutional issues of Karl XI's early personal rule and the 1672 *riksdag*, see Sjödell, *Kungamakt och högaristokrati*, pp. 51–106; Göran Rystad, *Johan Gyllenstierna, rådet och kungamakten. Studier i Sveriges inre politik 1660–1680* (Lund, 1955), pp. 3–115; Åslund, *De la Gardie*, pp. 135–48; Upton, *Charles XI*, pp. 14–24.

18. Frost, *Northern Wars*, p. 212.

19. On the conduct and conclusion of the Scanian War, see Finn Askgaard and Arne Stade, eds, *Kampen om Skåne* (Copenhagen, 1983); Frost, *Northern Wars*, pp. 208–16; Berndt Fredriksson, *Försvarets finansiering. Svensk krigsekonomi under skånska kriget* (Uppsala, 1975).

20. Frost, *Northern Wars*, p. 213.

21. Sjödell, *Kungamakt och högaristokrati*, pp. 107–282; Åslund, *De la Gardie*, pp. 149–53.

Chapter 8: The Swedish 'Absolutist' State, 1679–97

1. Nicholas Henshall, *The Myth of Absolutism. Change and Continuity in Early Modern European Monarchy* (London, 1992).
2. J. A. Fridericia, *Adelsvældens sidste Dage. Danmarks Historie fra Christian IV's Død til Enevældens Indførelse* (Copenhagen, 1894); C. O. Bøggild Andersen, *Statsomvæltningen i 1660* (Copenhagen, 1936); Leon Jespersen and Asger Svane-Knudsen, *Stænder og magstat. De politiske brydninger i 1648 og 1660* (Odense, 1989).
3. Upton, *Charles XI*, p. 29.
4. Rystad, *Johan Gyllenstierna*, pp. 162–237.
5. On the 1680 *Riksdag*, see Anthony Upton, 'The Riksdag of 1680 and the Establishment of Royal Absolutism in Sweden', *English Historical Review*, 102 (1987), 281–308; idem, *Charles XI*, pp. 25–43; Rystad, *Johan Gyllenstierna*, pp. 268–95; idem, *Karl XI*, pp. 165–80; Sjödell, *Kungamakt*, pp. 283–300.
6. Upton, *Charles XI*, p. 48.
7. On the 1682 *Riksdag*, see Upton, *Charles XI*, pp. 42–50; Rystad, 'Stormaktstidens riksdag', pp. 75–82.
8. Behre, Larsson, and Österberg, *Stormaktsdröm*, pp. 161–63; Upton, *Charles XI*, p. 125; Rystad, 'The King, the Nobility and the Growth of Bureaucracy', pp. 67–69; Sjödell, *Kungamakt*, pp. 306–43.
9. On the *reduktion*, see Upton, *Charles XI*, Chapter 4; Ola Lindqvist, *Jakob Gyllenborg och reduktionen* (Lund, 1956); Kurt Ågren, 'The *reduktion*', in *Sweden's Age of Greatness*, ed. Roberts, pp. 237–64; Sven A. Nilsson, *På väg mot reduktionen* (Stockholm, 1964); idem, *De stora krigens tid*, pp. 245–63; Rystad, *Karl XI*, pp. 181–203.
10. Böhme, 'Building a Baltic Empire', p. 213; Behre, Larsson, and Österberg, *Stormaktsdröm*, p. 167; Alexander Loit, *Kampen om feodalräntan. Reduktionen och domänpolitik i Estland 1655–1710* (Uppsala, 1975); Frost, *Northern Wars*, pp. 220, 229; Edgars Dunsdorfs, *Der grosse Schwedische Kataster i Livland 1681–1710* (Stockholm, 1950).
11. Frost, *Northern Wars*, pp. 220–23; Upton, *Charles XI*, pp. 71–89; Janne Backlund, *Rusthållarna i Fellingsbro 1684–1748. Indelningsverket och den sociala differentieringen av det svenska agrarsamhället* (Uppsala, 1993), pp. 15–38, 69–111. On the antecedents to *indelningsverket*, see Jussi T. Lappalainen, 'Forskningsproblem inom det äldre indelningsverket', in *Kustbygd och centralmakt*, pp. 57–66.
12. Upton, *Charles XI*, pp. 83–87; Glete, *Navies and Nations*, vol. 2, p. 608.

13. Nordin, *Ett fattigt men fritt folk*, pp. 49–96, 267–327; Rystad, *Karl XI*, pp. 307–44.

14. Georg Landberg, *Johan Gyllenstiernas nordiska förbundspolitik* (Uppsala, 1935).

15. The only recent studies of Karl XI's foreign policy are: Upton, *Charles XI*, Chapters 6 and 11; Rystad, *Karl XI*, pp. 266–79.

16. Peter Englund, *Det hotade huset. Adliga föreställningar om samhället under stormaktstiden* (Stockholm, 1989); Frost, *Northern Wars*, p. 229.

17. Ingvar Elmroth, *För kung och fosterland. Studier i den svenska adelns demografi och offentliga funktioner 1600–1900* (Lund, 1981), especially pp. 97–137.

18. Böhme, 'Building a Baltic Empire', p. 212.

19. Englund, *Det hotade huset*.

20. Berndt Fredriksson, 'Krig og bönder. Hur drabbades skåningarna av kriget 1675–79?', in *Bördor, bönder, börd i 1600-talets Sverige*, ed. Margareta Rivera and Rolf Torstendahl (Lund, 1979), pp. 163–213.

21. James Cavallie, *De höga officerarna. Studier in den svenska militära hierarki under 1600-talets senare del* (Stockholm, 1981); Björn Asker, *Officerarna och det svenska samhället 1650–1700* (Uppsala, 1983).

22. Backlund, *Rusthållarna i Fellingsbro*, pp. 39–68.

23. Gerald E. Aylmer, 'English Perceptions of Scandinavia in the Seventeenth Century', in *Europe and Scandinavia*, ed. Rystad, pp. 181–93.

24. Per Sörlin, *'Wicked Arts'. Witchcraft and Magic Trials in Southern Sweden, 1635–1754* (Leiden, 1998).

Chapter 9: Epilogue

1. There is a massive literature, especially in Swedish and German, on the reign of Karl XII and Sweden's role in the Great Northern War. The best available accounts in English are: Frost, *Northern Wars*, pp. 226–300; Ragnhild Hatton, *Charles XII* (London, 1968).

2. Roberts, *Swedish Imperial Experience*, pp. 151–52.

Further Reading

The following titles are perhaps the most useful among those available today in English. It should also be noted that, in recent years, most Swedish monographs are accompanied by an English-language summary, as are most articles in the journals *Historisk Tidskrift* and *Scandia*. The journal *Scandinavian Journal of History* generally publishes English-language translations of articles written by Scandinavian historians.

The Age of New Sweden (Stockholm, 1988). A brief collection of essays, written in English by Swedish historians, on Swedish society and culture at mid-century.

Ågren, Kurt. *Aristocrats, Farmers, Proletarians. Essays in Swedish Demographic History* (Stockholm, 1973).

Ahnlund, Nils. *Gustav Adolf the Great*, trans. Michael Roberts (Princeton, 1940).

Ailes, Mary Elizabeth. *Military Migration and State Formation. The British Military Community in Seventeenth-Century Sweden* (Lincoln, Nebraska, 2002).

Åström, Sven-Erik. *From Cloth to Iron. The Anglo-Baltic Trade in the Late Seventeenth Century* (Helsingfors, 1963).

Attman, Artur. *Swedish Aspirations and the Russian Market during the 17th Century* (Göteborg, 1985).

Böhme, Klaus-Richard. 'Building a Baltic Empire. Aspects of Swedish Expansionism, 1560–1660'. In *In Quest of Trade and Security*, ed. Rystad, vol. 1, pp. 177–220.

Frost, Robert I. *The Northern Wars. War, State and Society in Northeastern Europe, 1558–1721* (London, 2000). Unquestionably the best survey of conflict in the early modern Baltic.

Garstein, Oskar. *Rome and the Counter-Reformation in Scandinavia* (4 vols, Oslo and Leiden, 1963–92).

Glete, Jan. 'Bridge and Bulwark. The Swedish Navy and the Baltic, 1500–1809'. In *In Quest of Trade and Security*, ed. Rystad, vol. 1, pp. 9–60.

——. *War and the State in Early Modern Europe. Spain, the Dutch Republic and Sweden as Fiscal-Military States, 1500–1660* (London, 2002).

Hatton, Ragnhild. *Charles XII* (London, 1968).

Heckscher, Eli. *An Economic History of Sweden*, trans. Göran Ohlin (Cambridge, Massachusetts, 1963).

Jespersen, Knud J.V. 'Rivalry without Victory. Denmark, Sweden and the Struggle for the Baltic, 1500–1720'. In *In Quest of Trade and Security*, ed. Rystad, vol. 1, pp. 137–76.

Jespersen, Leon, ed., *A Revolution from Above? The Power State of 16th and 17th Century Scandinavia* (Odense, 2000). Three essays from participants in the 'power-state project'; Jespersen's essay on comparative Scandinavian constitutional and administrative structures, and that by Nils Erik Villstrand on the popular reaction to conscription in Finland, are especially pertinent.

Johannesson, Kurt. *The Renaissance of the Goths in Sixteenth-Century Sweden: Johannes and Olaus Magnus as Politicians and Historians*, trans. James Larson (Berkeley, 1991).

Kirby, David. *Northern Europe in the Early Modern Period. The Baltic World 1492–1772* (London, 1990).

Lindegren, Jan. 'The Swedish "Military State", 1560–1720'. *Scandinavian Journal of History*, 10 (1985), 305–36.

Masson, Georgina. *Queen Christina* (New York, 1968).

Metcalf, Michael, ed., *The Riksdag: A History of the Swedish Parliament* (Stockholm, 1987).

Monro, Robert. *Monro: His Expedition with the Worthy Scots Regiment Called Mac-Keys*, ed. William S. Brockington (Westport, Connecticut, 1999). Monro, a mercenary who served in both the Danish and Swedish armies during the Thirty Years' War, provides a fascinating glimpse into soldier life in the army of Gustav II Adolf.

Montgomery, Ingun. 'The institutionalisation of Lutheranism in Sweden and Finland'. In *The Scandinavian Reformation*, ed. Ole Peter Grell (Cambridge, 1995), pp. 144–78.

Oakley, Stewart P. *War and Peace in the Baltic 1560–1790* (London, 1992).

Österberg, Eva. *Mentalities and Other Realities. Essays in Medieval and Early Modern Scandinavian History* (Lund, 1991).

Persson, Fabian. *Servants of Fortune. The Swedish Court between 1598 and 1721* (Lund, 1999).

Porshnev, B. F. *Muscovy and Sweden in the Thirty Years' War 1630–1635*, trans. Brian Pearce (Cambridge, 1995).

Ringmar, Erik. *Identity, Interest and Action. A Cultural Explanation of Sweden's Intervention in the Thirty Years' War* (Cambridge, 1996).

Roberts, Michael. *The Early Vasas. A History of Sweden 1523–1611* (Cambridge, 1968).

——. *Essays in Swedish History* (London, 1967).

——. *From Oxenstierna to Charles XII: Four Studies* (Cambridge, 1991).

——. *Gustavus Adolphus. A History of Sweden 1611–1632* (2 vols, London, 1953–58).

——. *Gustavus Adolphus* (Longman's *Profiles in Power* series; London, 1992).

——. ed., *Sweden as a Great Power 1611–97: Government, Society, Foreign Policy* (London, 1968). A collection of important Swedish primary sources, translated and annotated by Roberts.

——. ed., *Sweden's Age of Greatness, 1632–1718* (London, 1973). An anthology of essays by notable Swedish historians.

——. *The Swedish Imperial Experience 1560–1718* (Cambridge, 1979).

Rystad, Göran, ed., *Europe and Scandinavia: Aspects of the Process of Integration in the 17th Century* (Lund, 1983).

Rystad, Göran; Böhme, Klaus-Richard, and Carlgren, Wilhelm M., eds, *In Quest of Trade and Security. The Baltic in Power Politics 1500–1990* (2 vols, Lund, 1994).

Söderberg, Johan, and Myrdal, Janken. *The Agrarian Economy of Sixteenth-Century Sweden* (Stockholm, 2002).

Upton, Anthony F. *Charles XI and Swedish Absolutism* (Cambridge, 1998).

——. 'The Riksdag of 1680 and the establishment of royal absolutism in Sweden', *English Historical Review*, 102 (1987), 281–308.

Index